The Ecology of Language Evolution

This major new work explores the development of creoles and other new languages, focusing on the conceptual and methodological issues they raise for genetic linguistics. Written by an internationally renowned linguist, the book discusses the nature and significance of internal and external factors – or "ecologies" – that bear on the evolution of a language. The book surveys a wide range of examples of changes in the structure, function and vitality of languages, and suggests that similar ecologies have played the same kinds of roles in all cases of language evolution. Drawing on major theories of language formation, macroecology and population genetics, Mufwene proposes a common approach to the development of creoles and other new languages. *The Ecology of Language Evolution* will be welcomed by students and researchers in creolistics, sociolinguistics, theoretical linguistics, and theories of evolution.

SALIKOKO S. MUFWENE is Professor and Chair in the Department of Linguistics, University of Chicago. He has written extensively on the development of creoles, genetic linguistics, and language endangerment. He is editor of *Africanisms in Afro-American Language Varieties* (1993), and co-editor of *Topics in African Linguistics* (with Lioba Moshi, 1993), and *African-American English: Structure, History, and Use* (with John R. Rickford, Guy Bailey, and John Baugh, 1998).

Cambridge Approaches to Language Contact

General editor
SALIKOKO S. MUFWENE
University of Chicago

Editorial board
Robert Chaudenson, *Université d'Aix-en-Provence*
Braj Kachru, *University of Illinois at Urbana*
Lesley Milroy, *University of Michigan*
Shana Poplack, *University of Ottawa*
Michael Silverstein, *University of Chicago*

Cambridge Approaches to Language Contact is an interdisciplinary series bringing together work on language contact from a diverse range of research areas. The series focuses on key topics in the study of contact between languages or dialects, including the development of pidgins and creoles, language evolution and change, world Englishes, code-switching and code-mixing, bilingualism and second language acquisition, borrowing, interference, and convergence phenomena.

Published titles
Salikoko Mufwene, *The Ecology of Language Evolution*

Further titles planned for the series
Michael Clyne, *The Dynamics of Language Contact*
Guy Bailey and Patricia Cukor-Avila, *The Development of African-American English*

The Ecology of Language Evolution

Salikoko S. Mufwene

University of Chicago

CAMBRIDGE
UNIVERSITY PRESS

PUBLISHED BY THE PRESS SYNDICATE OF THE UNIVERSITY OF CAMBRIDGE
The Pitt Building, Trumpington Street, Cambridge, United Kingdom

CAMBRIDGE UNIVERSITY PRESS
The Edinburgh Building, Cambridge CB2 2RU, UK
40 West 20th Street, New York, NY 10011–4211, USA
10 Stamford Road, Oakleigh, VIC 3166, Australia
Ruiz de Alarcón 13, 28014 Madrid, Spain
Dock House, The Waterfront, Cape Town 8001, South Africa

http://www.cambridge.org

First published 2001

Printed in the United Kingdom at the University Press, Cambridge

Typeface Monotype Times N.R. 10/12 pt.   *System* QuarkXPress™ [SE]

A catalogue record for this book is available from the British Library

Library of Congress Cataloguing in Publication data
Mufwene, Salikoko S.
The ecology of language evolution / Salikoko S. Mufwene.
    p.   cm. – (Cambridge approaches to language contact)
Includes bibliographical references and indexes.
ISBN 0 521 79138 3 (hardback) – ISBN 0 521 79475 7 (paperback)
1. Historical linguistics.   2. Creole dialects – History.   3. Language in contact.
4. Social ecology.   I. Title.   II. Series.
P140.M84   2001
417′.7–dc21   00–052925   CIP

ISBN 0 521 79138 3 hardback
ISBN 0 521 79475 7 paperback

To the memory of

Ntazyel,
Ekyey,
Osum,
Zaki,
Sevehna,
and
Tumunete

I am indebted to all of you
for courage and determination

For

Tazie
and
Embu

Together we work for a better world

Contents

Illustrations

Preface

This book presents some of my positions over the past decade regarding the development of creole vernaculars in relation to *language evolution* in general. The latter notion is used here to cover long-term changes observable in the structures and pragmatics of a language, as well as the not-so-unusual cases where a language speciates into daughter varieties identified at times as new dialects and at others as new languages. It also covers questions of language endangerment and death.

Together, these writings reflect the growth of my scholarship on, among other things, subjects conventionally identified as "creole genesis,"[1] second-language acquisition, and genetic linguistics. They are responses to some colleagues' invitations that I propose a cogent alternative to hypotheses which I have disputed. Those responses boil down to the position that creoles are epistemologically special only by an accident of the way we have been doing linguistics, not because they have developed by any evolutionary processes that have not occurred in the developments of other languages, nor because their geneses are embedded in sociohistorical ecologies that are drastically different in kind from those in which noncreole languages have evolved, nor even because they represent any global structural type of linguistic systems. They are as natural as noncreole languages. As a matter of fact, the better we understand them, the more we should be prompted to re-examine a number of things we thought we understood well about Language.

I have organized the essays chronologically, in the order in which they were written. I thought this the best way to capture progress in my thinking especially over the following topics: the development of creoles, the nature and significance of language-contact ecology in determining their structures, whether or not similar ecologies have not played the same kinds of roles in the changes as have traditionally concerned genetic linguists, whether it is true that creoles are not genetically related to their lexifiers, and whether we should continue to treat them as "children out of wedlock." Also, I try to answer the questions of what can we learn about language diversification, and what light can research on the development of creoles shed on the present heightened concern among linguists with language endangerment?

This selection also reveals that the enterprise I have embarked on is much more complex than the relevant literature has typically led us to believe. It seems necessary in diachronic linguistics to develop a research program of the same name as the title of this book, addressing the actuation question with the ecology of language evolution in focus. This amounts to paying attention not only to the socioeconomic and ethnographic environment in which a language has evolved (its *external ecology*) – such as the contact setting and power relations between groups of speakers – but also to the nature of the coexistence of the units and principles of a linguistic system before and/or during the change (its *internal ecology*). I argue that both external and internal ecologies play significant roles in determining the evolutionary trajectories of a language, which I analogize with a biological parasitic species.

Inspired by population genetics, I capitalize on variation within a species, or within a larger population consisting of several coexistent species. I show how ecology rolls the dice in the competitions and selections which determine not only which of the competing languages prevails but also which units and principles are selected into the prevailing variety. Basically the same processes that produced creole vernaculars have also yielded new noncreole varieties from the same lexifiers during the same period of time. From the same perspective we can also understand what causes a language to thrive at the expense of others and conversely what erodes the vitality of a language in a particular socioeconomic ecology. While the chapters of this book show that these questions are all interrelated, they also reveal that I am just scraping the tip of the iceberg and much more work remains to be done, including rethinking some working assumptions of genetic linguistics. I introduce the issues more specifically in chapter 1.

Typically I use creoles as the starting point of my discussions, simply because this is where I have done more research and can pretend to understand anything about language evolution. I am otherwise pursuing the expected dialogue between research on specific languages and that on Language, focusing here on the contribution that scholarship on creoles can make to understanding Language. In the case of this book, things are somewhat complicated by the fact that creoles have been grouped together and distinguished from other languages more because of similarities in the sociohistorical conditions of their development than for any other convincing reason.

Contrary to what has often been claimed by several creolists, creole vernaculars are not abrupt evolutions, nor are they by-products of breaks in the transmission of the languages from which they developed. A genetic connection is established between them most conspicuously by the fact that the overwhelming proportion of their vocabularies comes from these European languages, identified in this context as their *lexifiers*. The origins of creoles' grammars are a more complex matter, but one can hardly deny the contributions of their heterogeneous nonstandard lexifiers to these new systems, derived by blending inheritance. Neither did creoles emerge in settings where there was no target, though one can concede that, given the availability of diverse varieties (native and non-native) of the lexifier in the plantation colonies, such a target was definitely more diffused than in other cases of language transmission. Nor were these new vernaculars created by children; they would not be as complex as they are and they surely give no indication of being in an arrested developmental stage compared to non-creole languages. They are not the only cases of language restructuring – or system reorganization – prompted by contact, nor are the kinds of contact that motivated their developments different from those that should be invoked in, for instance, the speciation of Vulgar Latin into the Romance languages.

In the way I identify them in chapter 1, creole vernaculars are new language varieties which originated in the appropriation of nonstandard varieties of Western European languages by populations that were not (fully) of European descent in seventeenth-to-nineteenth century European (sub)-tropical colonies. Like any other vernacular that developed from a Western European language in the same (ex-)colonies, they have diverged structurally from the varieties spoken in Europe and from each other. Although it has typically been argued that some of the new vernaculars differ from their metropolitan counterparts and from one another – some to a greater extent than others – there is no operational yardstick for this assessment, starting with the fact that the lexifier was hardly the same from one setting to another. Mutual intelligibility is not reliable, especially since there are other colonial vernaculars spoken by descendants of Europeans that rate equally low on the mutual intelligibility scale but have not been identified as creoles, e.g., English in the Old Amish communities in North America. The main implicit criterion, which is embarrassing for linguistics but has not been discussed, is the ethnicity of their speakers. Most hypotheses proposed in creolistics to account for the development of creoles would have been better thought out, had it not been partly for this factor, as strong as my accusation may sound. The other reasons are given below and discussed in the following chapters.

I have been encouraged in the approach presented in this book by questions which research on the emergence of creoles has shown to be relevant to understanding language evolution but which appear to have been unduly overlooked in genetic linguistics, for instance: the role of ecology in language speciation. The essays included in this book reflect an effort to prevent creolistics from simply being a consumer subdiscipline which espouses gratuitously, without questions asked, some still-unjustified working assumptions and theoretical models accepted in other subdisciplines of linguistics. Like any of these, creolistics should contribute to understanding Language in part by highlighting those assumptions about this peculiarity of humans which are not supported by any creole data.

Five of the following chapters (2, 3, 4, 5, and 6) have been published as self-contained essays in different fora. Perhaps just a handful of creolists who share my research interests have read them all as covering inter-related topics. The purpose of this book is to make them more accessible and highlight the unifying threads that link them. They are complemented here with some recent, hitherto unpublished essays (chapters 1, 7, and 8) which continue the unfolding of my research program on language evolution and my effort to bridge topics on the development of creoles with issues in genetic linguistics and on language endangerment. Those who have read at least some of the previously published essays should know that these have been revised, sometimes extensively, to keep up with my current thinking on the subject matter. I have used this opportunity to clarify some earlier positions, to correct some mistakes that I recognize, or simply to restate things more accurately. I have also made every effort to make the book less repetitive, by crossreferencing the chapters and excising portions of the original essays that became redundant under the same cover.

The approach to language evolution presented here owes part of its present form to Bill Smith (Piedmont College) and Chuck Peters (University of Georgia). The first encouraged me to read literature on chaos theory (given my interest in nonrectilinear and nonunilinear evolutionary paths) and the second introduced me to ecology and population genetics. I have also benefited enormously from discussions with Bill Wimsatt (University of Chicago). Thanks to him, I gave up unsuccessful attempts to clone the linguistic species on the biological species (which one?) and developed my own notion of a linguistic species with its own kinds of peculiarities, especially feature transmission properties. Not all species evolve according to the same principles. It is thus as normal for linguistic species to reproduce themselves according to their own patterns of feature transmission and evolutionary principles as it is for bacterial species to differ in the same respects from animal species. It remains that all evolution presupposes variation within the relevant species, heredity (or generational continuity) of features, and differential reproduction, while being subject to various ecological factors. Chapters 1, 2, and 6 have benefited in clarity from the Ecology of Language Evolution course that I taught in

Spring 1999 and from the *Biological and Cultural Evolution* course that Bill, Jerry Sadock, and I taught in Autumn 1999. They have also benefited from generous comments from Robert Perlman (biologist, University of Chicago) and from Manuel O. Diaz (geneticist, Loyola University of Chicago).

My general thinking on several genetic linguistic issues owes a lot to discussions and friendship with several other colleagues, chiefly, the late Guy Hazaël-Massieux, Robert Chaudenson, Louis-Jean Calvet (all of the Université d'Aix-en-Provence), and Sali Tagliamonte (University of York). Sali also encouraged me the most consistently to bring the present essays together in the form of a book, as she thought it was time I started outlining the big picture that should be emerging from them. Eyamba Bokamba and Braj Kachru (University of Illinois at Urbana-Champaign) were especially helpful in inviting me to test my hypotheses against the development of indigenized Englishes. They offered me the right conference platforms where I was prompted to think of the big picture and situate problems of the development of creoles in those of language evolution in general, and thus to relate genetic creolistics to genetic linguistics.

Several of my discussions in chapter 1 owe part of their substance and clarity to questions from Michel DeGraff (Massachusetts Institute of Technology), Marlyse Baptista (University of Georgia), and Rakesh Bhatt (University of Illinois at Urbana), mostly from the point of view of theoretical linguistics. They reminded me that I address scholars of diverse persuasions and backgrounds in my essays and that I cannot take it for granted that other creolists, let alone other linguists and nonlinguists, share my working assumptions or know what I am talking about. I was served this message again by Bernd Heine (University of Cologne) and Richard C. Lewontin (Harvard), in their comments on the last draft of the same chapter. I hope that thanks to all of them my positions are presented more clearly and accessibly to readers of different backgrounds.

Among my students at the University of Chicago, off of whom I bounced several of my earlier "heresies" and who knew the right questions to ask, Chris Corcoran and Sheri Pargman deserve special mention. They read a few drafts of subsets of the present essays and pointed out unclarities and omissions, which I hope do not stand out any more, at least not as eyesores. Drew Clark, a first-year graduate student of mine, decided that reading the whole manuscript and checking its accessibility was a reasonable way of not getting bored during his 1999–2000 Christmas break. I could not have had a more dedicated style reader. I feel equally indebted to Citi Potts for carefully copy-editing the essays with a keen eye on their accessibility.

Jenny Sheppard helped me by producing electronically all my maps of Africa in this book and the illustrations of competition and selection included in the inset in chapter 1. She was very good in implementing carto-graphically ideas I expressed verbally. A month of residence as a Visiting Scientist at the Max Planck Institute in Leipzig in May 2000 enabled me to complete the preparation of this book. To all the above individuals and institutions, and to several colleagues whose names I cannot continue listing and who have assisted me one way or another, especially in challeng-ing me with alternative views, I feel very much indebted. I assume alone full responsibility for all the remaining shortcomings.

Last but not least, I am deeply indebted to Tazie and Pat for accommo-dating me with more time than I could have afforded to write these essays and revise them. Time has been more than a highly priced commodity during the last phase of this exercise, while chairing a prestigious linguistics department in a tragic and daunting transition, after the death of a dear colleague and former major professor, Jim McCawley, whose practice of linguistics was absolutely encyclopedic and very inspiring to me. My days too last twenty-four hours. I could not have accomplished this project without Tazie's and Pat's concessions in family time, even after I have cheated myself of indispensable sleep time.

I hope this end result does not let down most of you family, friends, col-leagues, and students who have supported me all along, as well as you inter-ested readers who are patient enough to explore the workings of my occasionally contentious mind.

Acknowledgments

Chapter 2 was first published as "The Founder Principle in Creole Genesis," in *Diachronica* (1996, 13: 83–134). Chapter 3 was first published as "The development of American Englishes: some questions from a creole genesis perspective," in *Focus on the USA*, ed. Edgar Schneider (1996, pp. 231–64). Chapter 5 was first published as "What Research on Creole Genesis Can Contribute to Historical Linguistics," in *Historical Linguistics*, ed. Monika Schmid et al., (1997, pp. 315–38). All of the above chapters are reprinted here in substantially revised versions with the permission of John Benjamins. Chapter 4 is a substantially revised version of an essay with the same title first published in *World Englishes 2000*, ed. Larry Smith and Michael L. Forman, College of Languages, Linguistics and Literature, University of Hawaii and the East–West Center (1997, pp. 182–203), reprinted with kind permission. Chapter 6 is a revised version of an essay with the same title first published in *Assessing Ethnolinguistic Vitality*, ed. Gloria Kindell and Paul Lewis, SIL International, Dallas, Texas (2000, pp. 39–64), reprinted with kind permission.

Tables and Maps

Chapter 2, table 1, from *The Atlantic Slave Trade* by Philip D. Curtin © 1969, reproduced with permission of the University of Wisconsin Press.

Chapter 2, tables 2, 3, and 4, from "Substrate influence in creole language formation: the case of serial verb constructions in Sranan" (MA thesis) by Bettina Migge, Ohio State University, 1993.

Chapter 2, table 5, excerpts regarding South Carolina from "Estimated southern population by race and region, 1685–1790," in "The changing population of the Colonial South: An overview by race and region, 1685–1790," published in *Powhatan's Mantle: Indians in the Colonial Southeast*, ed. Peter H. Wood, Gregory A. Waselkov and M. Thomas Hatley © 1989, reprinted with permission of the University of Nebraska Press.

Chapter 2, table 6 ("Africans arriving in South Carolina") from *Black*

Majority by Peter H. Wood © 1974, reprinted with permission of Alfred A. Knopf a Division of Random House Inc.

Chapter 7, "Map of Bantu dispersal" from *The Peopling of Africa* by James Newman © 1995, reprinted with permission of Yale University Press.

Chapter 7, "Map of labor migrations" from "Labor migration," by Caroline Wright, in the *Encyclopaedia of Africa South of the Sahara*, edited by J. Middleton © 1997 (originally published by Simon & Schuster), reprinted with permission of the Gale Group.

Chapter 7, two maps ("8000 BC" and "AD 1950") from *The Penguin Atlas of African History* by Colin McEvedy © 1980 (revised edition © 1995) reproduced with minor adaptations with permission of Penguin Books Ltd.

1 Introduction

This chapter is written primarily to clarify concepts such as "ecology," "evolution," and "language," which are central to the book. It also states some of my most important arguments, e.g., (1) creoles have developed by the same restructuring processes that mark the evolutions of noncreole languages; (2) contact is an important factor in all such developments; and (3) the external ecological factors that bear on restructuring also bear on aspects of language vitality, among which is language endangerment. I will go beyond the brief explanations given in the Preface but will not pre-empt the more elaborate discussions presented in, for instance, chapters 2 and 6. In the present chapter, I simply provide basic information that readers will find useful to understand the book.

1.1 Communal languages as ensembles of I-languages

To the lay person the term *language* means something like "way of speaking." Thus *English* originally meant "the way the English people speak" and *kiSwahili* "the way the waSwahili speak." In the case of *kiSwahili*, the Bantu noun class system makes it clear through the instrumental prefix *ki-*, which suggests a means used by *waSwahili* to communicate. Those more knowledgeable about communication extend the notion "language" beyond the spoken mode, applying it also to written and signed means.

Linguists have focused more on the abstract systems that generate utterances and written or signed strings of symbols identified as English, American Signed Language, or the like in lay speech. The systems consist of sets of units and principles, which are selected and applied differently from one language to another, despite many similarities. The units are identifiable in various interfacing modules: e.g., the phonological system (dealing with sounds), the morphological system (dealing with minimal meaningful combinations of sounds), and syntax (how words combine into sentences). Some principles are generally combinatoric, in the form of positive rules and negative constraints on how the units can combine together into larger units. Some others are distributive, specifying, for instance, how the phoneme /t/ in American English is pronounced differently in words such as

1

tea, state, and *water,* viz., aspirated before a stressed vowel, unaspirated after /s/ regardless of what follows, often with unreleased air at the end of a word, and as a flap between a stressed and an unstressed vowel.

Language change is generally about different aspects of linguistic systems. For the purposes of language **transmission** from one group of speakers to another,[1] any of these units and principles may be identified as a linguistic feature, roughly on the model of *gene* in biology. Let us bear in mind that the notion of linguistic species proposed below need not be analogous to that of biological species in all respects, not any more than there is an empirically validated unified notion of biological species in the first place.

Quite germane to some of my arguments about language evolution is Chomsky's (1986:19–24) distinction between internalized language (**I-language**) and externalized language (**E-language**). An I-language is basically an **idiolect**, an individual speaker's system of a language. It is to a language what an individual is to a species in population genetics. Among the questions I address are the following: How and when can features of individual idiolects be extrapolated as characteristic of a language as a **communal system**? Is knowledge of a language as a property of an individual speaker coextensive with knowledge of a language as a property of a population? What is the status of variation in the two cases and how does it bear on language evolution?

Chomsky defines an "E-language" as the set of sentences produced by a population speaking a particular language. This conception of a language is inadequate (McCawley 1976). Chomsky is correct in rejecting it as leading the linguist nowhere toward understanding how language works in the mind. It just provides data for analysis. Fortunately, few linguists have subscribed to this notion of a language. Most linguists have been Saussurean, both in treating languages as mental systems and in assuming them to be social institutions to which speakers are enculturated. Meanwhile they have failed to address the following question: What role do individual speakers play in language change? This question is central to language evolution and I return to it below.[2]

Idiolects and communal languages represent different levels of abstraction. The former are first-level abstractions from speech, the latter are extrapolations that can be characterized as ensembles of I-languages. Neil Smith (1999:138) denies the validity of "collective language." However, we cannot speak of language change or evolution, which is identified at the population level, without accepting the existence of a communal language.

To be sure, a communal language is an abstraction inferred by the observer. It is an extrapolation from I-languages whose speakers communicate successfully with each other most of the time. It is internalized to the extent that we can also project a collective mind that is an ensemble of individual minds in a population. Since this higher-level abstraction is what discussions of language change are based on, I capitalize on interidiolectal variation, among other properties of communal languages, and argue in chapter 6 that a language is a species. I will then use the competition-and-selection dynamics of the coexistence of I-languages to explain how a language evolves over time.

Two questions arise from this position:
(i) Is every feature that is true of a communal language qua species also necessarily true of I-languages? For instance, does the fact that the following sentences are acceptable in some nonstandard English dialects necessarily make them well formed in all English idiolects or even dialects?

(1)   *I ain't told you no such thing.*
        "I haven't told you such a thing" or "I didn't tell you such a thing."
(2)   *Let me tell you everything what Allison said at the party.*
        "Let me tell you everything that Allison said at the party."

(ii) When do changes that affect individual members amount to communal changes?

As noted above, the latter level of change is among the phenomena I identify as **language evolution**. This can also involve nonstructural changes, for instance, the acceptability of peculiarities of the sentences in (1–2) for a larger or smaller proportion of speakers in a community. This book says almost nothing about such nonstructural changes. However, much attention is devoted to **speciation**, when, for structural or ideological reasons, it is found more appropriate to no longer group together I-languages that used to form one communal language. Rather, they are classed into subgroups identified as separate languages or as dialects of the same language. This is precisely where the identification of creoles as separate languages fits, in contrast with the equally novel and contact-based varieties of European languages spoken by descendants of Europeans (e.g., American English and Québécois French) which have been identified as dialects of their lexifiers (chapters 4–5). I return to these questions in sections 1.3 and 1.4.

1.2   Pidgins, creoles, and koinés

Pidgins and koinés play a very negligible part in the next chapters. However, it is difficult to define creoles without mentioning them and it is almost impossible to make sense of some of the issues I raise in this book without also clarifying the conceptual distinction between creoles and koinés. There is a genetic relationship between these two, because the **lexifiers** of creoles, those varieties from which they have inherited most of their vocabularies, have often been correctly identified as colonial **koinés**. These are compromise varieties from among diverse dialects of the same language. Instead of selecting one single dialect as their lingua franca, speakers of the European lexifiers wound up developing a new colonial dialect which included their common features but only some of those that distinguished them from one another. Such selections did not necessarily originate from the same dialect, nor were they the same from one colony to another – a fact that accounts in part for regional variation. Why those particular selections were made and not others is a question that deserves as much attention as the selections that produced different creoles from the same lexifier (chapters 2 and 3). The inset text sheds some light on this question.

Restructuring into koinés, creoles and other varieties

These three diagrams illustrate dialect and language contact where creoles developed. They suggest that basically the same mechanisms were involved in the restructuring processes which produced creoles as in those which generated koinés. They show that the contact of the different metropolitan varieties brought over by the European colonists (represented in the upper tiers) produced the "feature pool" shown by the box in the middle tiers. The outputs (represented in the bottom tiers) are the local, colonial varieties as they developed in forms that differed from the metropolitan varieties. There is no particular input-to-output ratio of number of varieties. There may be fewer outputs than input varieties and vice versa, just as the number may be equal. What matters is that the structures of the output and input varieties are not identical.

The middle tiers represents the "arena" where features associated with the same or similar grammatical functions came to compete with each other. It is also the locus of "blending inheritance," in that features which are similar but

---

not necessarily identical came to reinforce each other, regardless of their sources, and produced modified variants of the originals in the emergent varieties. The outputs represent variation in the ways particular (combinations of) features were selected into the emergent varieties, according to principles that still must be articulated more explicitly as we get to understand language evolution more adequately. Markedness has been proposed to be among those principles, but the subject matter can also be approached with alternative constraint models, as long as they account for the specific choices made by speakers of particular varieties. The diagrams also suggest that there is little in the structures of the new vernaculars that has not been "recycled" from the lexifier and/or the other languages it came in contact with. What makes the new varieties restructured is not only the particular combinations of features selected, often from different sources, into the new language varieties but also the way in which the features themselves have been modified, "exapted," to fit into the new systems.

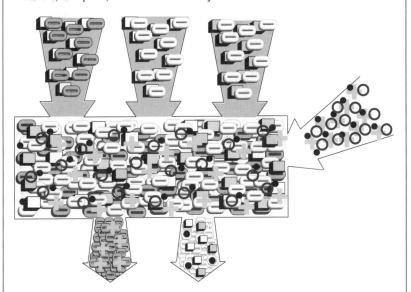

The first diagram represents what has been identified as *koinéization*. It diverges from the established position that koinés develop by leveling out differences among dialects of the same language or among genetically and typologically related languages, and by reducing the varieties in contact to their common denominator. This is not what has been observed in places where, for instance, English dialects in England have been in contact with each other. The outcomes show apparent replacive adoptions by some dialects of elements from other dialects, more like the results of competition and selection than any kind of common denominators of the dialects in contact. Simplification of morphosyntax in the development of the original *koiné* in the Hellenic world did not amount to a common denominator of

Greek dialects. After all cross-dialectal variation had been eliminated, it would have consisted of a skeletal basic system that probably would not have been helpful to the Greeks themselves, barring any concurrent drastic changes in their world view. The name left alone, *koinéization* is but the restructuring of a language into a new dialect out of the contact of its pre-existing dialects or, by extension, the development of a new language variety out of the contact of genetically and typologically related languages.

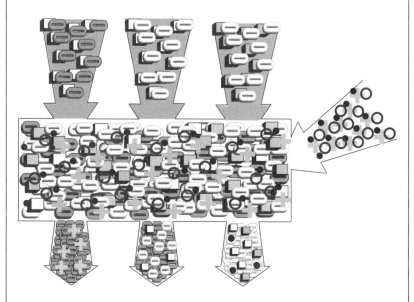

The other two diagrams illustrate what happened when those metropolitan dialects of a prevailing European language came in contact with other languages. Since linguistic features are abstractions that are in a way different from the forms that carry them, those other languages too made their contribution to the feature pool, increasing the complexity of the condition of competition. Thus they bore on the structures of the outcome varieties, making allowance for selection of features from outside the range provided by the metropolitan dialects of the lexifier. For instance, languages that allow copula-less adjectival predicates would make this syntactic option an alternative for the colonial varieties of the lexifier. In some cases they simply favored an option that was already available in some of the metropolitan varieties but was statistically too insignificant to produce the same output under different ecological conditions. The colonial varieties of European languages reflect this more complex level of feature competition. Thus aside from the social bias in the naming practice, the diachronic difference between koinés, creoles, and other new varieties lies not in the restructuring process but in the numbers and kinds of languages that came in contact, and sadly also in the ethnic identities of their typical speakers.

What I present below about pidgins and creoles is only a brief summary of what is discussed in substantial detail in Mühlhäusler (1986), Chaudenson (1992), and Mufwene (1997a). Pidgins have traditionally been characterized as reduced linguistic systems which are used for specific communicative functions, typically in trade between speakers of different, mutually unintelligible languages. They are second-language varieties that developed in settings where the speakers of the lexifier had only sporadic contacts with the populations they traded with. The adoption of the lexifier as a lingua franca by multilingual populations who had little exposure to fluent models accounts in part for its reduced and, to some linguists such as Bickerton (1981, 1984, 1999) and Holm (1988), seemingly chaotic structure.

Although part of colonial history has tied the development of pidgins with slavery, the connection is accidental. In trades between the Europeans and Native Americans, fur was the chief indigenous commodity. On the West coast of Africa, not only slaves but also food supplies (especially along the "Grain Coast"), ivory, and gold were traded. The common denominator is the *sporadic* pattern of the trade contacts and this is equally true of those varieties identified pejoratively by the French colonists or travelers as *baragouins* "gibberish, broken language" and more commonly by others as *jargon*, with almost the same meaning.

In many parts of the world, as in Nigeria, Cameroon, and Papua New Guinea, pidgins have increased their communicative functions and are also spoken both as mother tongues for large proportions of their populations and as major lingua francas. They are called **expanded pidgins**. The stabilization and complexification of their systems have to do less with nativization than with more regular usage and increased communicative functions.

Creoles have been defined as nativized pidgins. Aside from the arguments presented below against this position, it is useful to consider the following. If creoles had really been developed by children, they would be languages in arrested development stage (Mufwene 1999a). The alternative is that they would have acquired adult structures when the children became adults, which raises the question of why their parents would have been incapable of developing such structures during the pidgin stage. Would slavery have affected their language faculties so adversely?

The irony of deriving creoles from pidgins lies partly in the fact that the term *pidgin* (from the English word *business*, in the phrase *business English*) emerged only in 1807 (Baker and Mühlhäusler 1990), over one century since the term *creole* had been used in Romance languages for a vernacular. The date of 1825 reported by the *OED* for *creole* applies to English only. In the colonies where new vernaculars which developed from European languages were identified by laymen as *creoles* or *patois* the term *pidgin* is nowhere attested in reference to earlier stages of their developments. Besides, the first variety to have been identified as *pidgin English*

(< *business English*) developed in Canton in the late eighteenth century, long after most creoles had developed. Moreover, no creole has been identified in that part of the world.

These arguments are not intended to deny the plausible hypothesis that those who contributed the most to the restructuring of the European languages into the classic creoles (e.g., Jamaican, Guyanese, Gullah, Mauritian, Seychellois, and Papiamentu) must have gone through interlanguage stages. However, **interlanguages** are individual phenomena, restricted to the development of I-languages. They are based on no communal norm, especially in the settings where the creoles developed (chapter 2). In this respect, they are very much unlike the pidgins as communal systems.

The socioeconomic history of European colonization suggests a territorial division of labor between the places where creoles developed and those where pidgin and indigenized varieties of European languages did. The best known pidgins developed in European **trade colonies** of Africa and the Pacific (around trade forts and on trade routes), before they were appropriated politically and expanded into **exploitation colonies** in the second half of the nineteenth century.[3] They were based on the nonstandard vernaculars spoken by the European traders, to which their non-European counterparts were exposed during their occasional mercantile encounters. Although they have often evolved structurally and ethnographically to serve diverse and more complex communicative functions, originally they were indeed structurally reduced and served very basic and limited communicative functions. Note that in trade transactions nonverbal communication often compensates for shortcomings in the verbal mode (Calvet 1999).

During the exploitation colony period, when territories larger than the original trade colonies were under the administrative control of European nations, scholastic varieties of their languages were introduced through the scholastic medium, so that they could serve as lingua francas between the indigenous colonial auxiliaries and the colonizers. Owing to regional multilingualism, the colonial rankings of languages led the emerging local elite to appropriate these scholastic varieties as lingua francas for communication among themselves too. This process nurtured their **indigenization** into what is now identified with geographical names such as Nigerian, Indian, and East African Englishes.

In places like Nigeria and Cameroon, Pidgin English and the local indigenized English varieties have coexisted happily, with the pidgin almost identified as an indigenous language (vernacular for some but lingua franca for others) while the indigenized variety is associated with the intellectual elite. An important difference remains between, on the one hand, pidgins (including also West African "français tirailleur" and "le français populaire d'Abidjan") and, on the other, indigenized varieties of European languages (e.g., Indian English and African French), lying in the following fact: the former's lexifiers are nonstandard varieties, whereas the latter have developed from the scholastic English or French introduced through the school system, usually through teachers who were not native speakers. See, e.g., Kachru (1983), Gupta (1991), and Bamgbose et al. (1995) on the latter varieties.

Pidgins in the Americas developed out of similar trade contacts between Europeans and Native Americans, before the latter were absorbed by the expanding European settlements. However, creoles developed in **settlement colonies**, marked by contacts that were initially regular and intimate between the slaves and the European colonists. Most of these were indentured servants and a large proportion of them did not speak the European lexifier natively (chapter 2). Like pidgins, creoles too had nonstandard lexifiers.

The socioeconomic histories of the New World and Indian Ocean, on which our **heuristic prototypes** of creoles are based,[4] do not suggest that these vernaculars have any structural features which are not attested in pidgins (Mufwene 1991a; Baker 1995a), nor that creoles developed (necessarily) from pidgins (Alleyne 1971, 1980; Chaudenson 1979, 1992), nor that creoles developed by **nativization**, as acquisition of a community of native speakers, from any erstwhile pidgins (Mufwene 1999a, contra Bickerton 1999). In the New World, it is not obvious that European-lexifier jargons or pidgins spoken by Native Americans contributed more than some lexical entries to the creoles developed by the African slaves. From the founding stages of the colonies until the times when these new vernaculars developed, the Africans interacted regularly with speakers of the lexifiers, although these were not always native or fluent speakers (chapter 2).

Creole vernaculars, originally confined to plantations of the Atlantic and Indian Ocean island and coastal colonies, emerged in contact settings where the development of pidgins would be inconsistent with the received doctrine that they are reduced systems for limited and specialized communicative functions. Creole populations, those born in the settlement colonies from at least one nonindigenous parent,[5] preceded the emergence of creole vernaculars, in the homestead conditions in which non-Europeans were minorities and well integrated, though socially discriminated against. They had full access to European languages, albeit their colonial, koiné varieties, which they acquired through regular interactions with their native or fluent speakers, just like European indentured servants did (Tate 1965; Chaudenson 1979, 1989, 1992; Berlin 1998; Corne 1999). They did not speak the varieties identified later on as creoles.

It was indeed later approximations of their colonial vernaculars by slaves of the plantation period which produced creole vernaculars, through what Lass (1997:112) characterizes as "imperfect replication" and Deacon (1997:114) as "transmission error." This process was intensified this time by

the decreasing disproportion of native and fluent speakers (creole and seasoned slaves) relative to nonproficient speakers (the bozal slaves). As discussed in chapter 2, the **basilectalization** process that produced creoles was
gradual.[6] However, avoiding treating it as a regular case of language evolution, some creolists (e.g., Bickerton 1984; Thomason and Kaufman 1988)
have characterized the process as abrupt. Ironically, there is no evidence
that, for example, Gullah – the creole of coastal South Carolina and
Georgia in the USA – developed more rapidly than any other North
American English variety. Nor has it been proved that the evolution that
produced it was not as gradual as those that yielded other contemporary
English varieties, which developed between the seventeenth and nineteenth
centuries.[7]

The development of creoles has also been associated with a break in the
transmission of the lexifier (e.g., Polomé 1983). There is, however, hardly
any evidence of this, even in polities such as Suriname, where native and
large proportions of speakers of the lexifier left roughly fifteen years after
the colony was founded in the mid-seventeenth century. A break in the
transmission of the lexifier would have entailed no exposure to any form of
the language and therefore nothing to restructure. This is quite different
from the historical reality that the slaves who arrived during the plantation
period were exposed to varieties more and more different from the languages brought from Europe or spoken in earlier colonial periods.

As noted above, the earliest documentation of the term *pidgin* is reported
to be 1907 (Baker and Mühlhäusler 1990). This was over two hundred years
after the term *creole* had been in usage in reference to colonial language
varieties, in contradistinction from the metropolitan ways. Linguists have
posited in anachronistic order the dubious developmental link between
pidgins and creoles. No evidence other than that pidgins have more reduced
systems than creoles has been adduced.

In the absence of evidence of structural features peculiar to creoles
(Mufwene 1986a, 2000a), Chaudenson's (1992) characterization that
creoles are specific vernaculars which are defined by the time, place, and
conditions of their development seems correct. They emerged during the
European colonization of the rest of the world starting in the seventeenth
century, typically on island or coastal colonies between the tropics, in the
contact settings of plantations. In these places, the non-European labor
outnumbered even the European indentured servants, not only the native
speakers of the lexifier. The creoles developed during a period when the
populations were also racially segregated and grew more by importations of
new labor than by birth.

Consequently, I use the term *creole* in its sociohistorical sense to identify
primarily those varieties that have been identified as "creole" or "patois" by
nonlinguists. I use it also loosely for varieties such as Gullah, which linguists

have identified as creoles because they developed under conditions similar to varieties such as Louisiana, Haitian, and Mauritian Creoles. Although I claim in Mufwene (1997a) that creole vernaculars were originally associated with creole populations, Chaudenson (p.c., October 1999) has reminded me that in Martinique the classic creole populations are White, called *Beke*, and are not the ones primarily associated with Martinican Creole. In Louisiana, Creole is associated only with Black creole populations but not with the White ones; and in Mauritius the creole population is of Black African ancestry, while Creole is claimed by Mauritians of diverse ethnic groups to be their national language. The historical practice of identifying some new colonial vernaculars as creoles does not have the kind of logic that linguists have mistakenly invoked to justify it. Thus, I will resist applying the term *creole* to contact varieties which developed in continental Africa, because there were no European settlement colonies there, except in South Africa, where the identification of Afrikaans as a creole remains controversial. No creole populations in the historical sense developed in the rest of continental Africa, and European languages were not appropriated as vernaculars by the indigenous Africans.[8] Identifying varieties such as (Kikongo-)Kituba, Lingala, and Sango, which were lexified by indigenous African languages, as creoles just adds more confusion (Mufwene 1997a). Though they show some similarities in patterns of morphosyntactic restructuring, they also show some important structural differences from classic creoles (for instance in the domain of time reference).[9] As I argue in chapters 3, 4, and 5, the fact that more general explanations can be proposed for some structural evolutions attested both in classic creoles and in other languages is good reason not to assume a dubious structural process of "creolization."

1.3   Language evolution

As in biology, I use the term *evolution* without suggesting progress of any kind from a less satisfactory state to a more satisfactory one (e.g., Gould 1993:303), nor necessarily from a simpler to a more complex system or vice versa.[10] Evolution has no goal, certainly not to repair any putative deficiencies in a language. Linguistic change is inadvertent, a consequence of "imperfect replication" in the interactions of individual speakers as they adapt their communicative strategies to one another or to new needs. Such adaptations are similar to exaptations in biology or perhaps to kludges in computing. They can introduce generalizations or increase irregularities, just as they can introduce or obliterate useful distinctions (Keller 1994; Croft 2000).

Since linguistic change occurs even when no contact of languages is involved, it is evident that non-native speakers of a language are not the only ones that acquire it imperfectly. One must remember that idiolects of language are not identical. The mutual accommodations that speakers make to each other and their nonidentical creative innovations set in motion constant competition-and-selection processes that bring about changes of all kinds. Those changes that spread from some I-languages to become exclusive, dominant, minority, or latent patterns in the communal language are the focus of this book. They are like those microevolutionary processes that become significant at the macroevolutionary level when they justify positing speciation. For instance, in the history of the English language, we may consider as speciation the kinds of changes that started in adaptive manipulations of the colonial English systems by individual speakers and amounted to the development of recent varieties like Jamaican Patwa, Jamaican English, Gullah, African-American vernacular English (AAVE), Appalachian English, and why not New England's English or English in the Bronx? It is of course necessary to invoke ecology to account for such speciation, and I return to this topic below.

By *evolution*, I mean no more than the long-term changes undergone by a language (variety) over a period of time. They involve a succession of restructuring processes which produce more and more deviations from an earlier stage. **Restructuring** itself amounts to a reorganization of the mechanical system of a language and/or of the pragmatic principles regulating its use. The process is in fact similar to *genetic recombination* in biology, in which "the parental chromosomes are broken and reassembled" (Mayr 1997:188). An important difference is that language transmission is not necessarily on the parent-to-offspring model. As a matter of fact, language transmission is primarily horizontal. It is variably **polyploidic**, without a limit on the number of individuals or groups that can pass features on to a speaker's idiolect. Moreover, despite numerous recent useful invocations of apparent time in quantitative sociolinguistics to prove systemic change (e.g., Bailey and Maynor 1987, 1989),[11] the development of an idiolect does not really end until its speaker either dies or becomes linguistically disabled, even though most of the linguistic system is formed by puberty. Some linguistic features are acquired additively or replacively several times in a speaker's life, although in the vast majority of cases most of these changes bear no significant effect on the basic system developed by puberty. In this respect, a linguistic species is like a Lamarckian species (chapter 6).

Syntactic examples of **adaptations** which amount to system restructuring include uses of a word meaning "say" not only as a verb but also as a complementizer after verbs of saying and of perception, as in the following Gullah sentences (represented in eye dialect using deliberate distortions of standard English spellings to suggest a different pronunciation):

(3)   a. *Faye answer <u>say</u> Robert coming.* "Faye answered that Robert was/is coming."
      b. *Uh hear <u>say</u> Robert coming.* "I heard that Robert was/is coming."

In the present case, the adaptations amount to the new uses into which the verb *say* is put that are not attested in the lexifier. The verb *say* is commonly used in all English dialects to introduce reported speech quotatively or indirectly (followed by *that* or a null complementizer in the latter case). However, it is not used as a serial verb (3a), nor as a complementizer (3b). Moreover, whoever is tempted to infer that "say" has replaced the complementizer *that* in English creoles should remember that it is not used to introduce relative clauses or other complements in complex noun phrases (Mufwene 1989a). The relative clause in (4c) is illformed.

(4)   a. *This da young man come yah yesiday.*
         "This [is] the young man [that] came here yesterday."
      b. *This da young man <u>weh</u> come yah yesiday.*
         "This [is] the young man who came here yesterday."
      c. **This da young man <u>say</u> come yah yesiday.*
         "This [is] the young man that came here yesterday."

In this case, the subsystem of English complementizers has simply been reorganized to assign to *say* a subset of the contexts in which the English complementizer *that* would occur but certainly not all such contexts. For the purposes of this book, any change in the structural system of a language involves restructuring, including loss of some units or rules, addition of new ones, and certainly modifications in the direction of simplification, generalization, or complexification by the addition of conditions to the application of a rule.

A set of basic evolutionary questions that have retained much of my attention include the following: Are the restructuring processes that produced creole vernaculars different, in kind or in speed, from those that produced other new varieties of European languages during the same period in the colonies or even earlier in Europe (chapters 3, 4, and 5)? Is it plausible to assume that vernaculars such as Jamaican Patwa and Louisiana Creole developed faster than Jamaican English and Louisiana French varieties? Or is it more accurate to assume that they developed concurrently and that evolutionary speed has nothing to do with whether or not a new variety should, or should not, be called a creole? Is there any justification for the position that "classic creoles" developed abruptly, over one generation (Bickerton 1981, 1984, 1999), while languages such as French took centuries to evolve into what they are like today?

I argue in chapter 2 that creoles evolved gradually, just like the Romance languages, for instance. As a matter of fact, the speed of restructuring into a new system does not matter, since it depends largely on the ecology in which a language evolves. Besides, it is hard to argue that Jamaican Patwa or Gullah developed faster than Jamaican English or White American English varieties, respectively. Chapters 3, 4, and 5, deal with different aspects of this subject matter.

One can also ask whether there is a global restructuring process that can be called *creolization*, which changes a noncreole language wholesale into a creole. Such a hypothesis does not seem to account for crosscreole variation in domains such as time reference and number delimitation, where putatively "creole features" vary in some respects (Mufwene 1991a). For example, Papiamentu has an INDEFINITE PLURAL (a "noncreole" feature) but does not have an ANTERIOR marker. Likewise, Gullah has an indefinite article (a "noncreole" feature) – in the form of a schwa, as in (other) English dialects – whereas it is debatable whether Jamaican and Guyanese Creoles' *wan* is really an article or a regular quantifier.

There are several other interesting questions. For instance: Is contact so peculiar to creoles and other "mixed languages" as to make them evolutionarily unique compared to other languages? Are the language-level contacts that produced them different in kind from those which produced the Romance languages, for instance, or those occurring among idiolects? Are idiolect contacts not as much responsible for internally motivated change as for the externally motivated changes associated with the development of creoles? Recall that it is typically the small acts of individuals, or the effects of the ecology on them, which wind up having wide-ranging effects on the overall population. The dynamic of this has been identified as the "invisible/hidden hand."

As observed by Weinreich (1953), contact takes place in the mind of the speaker. Relevant to this book is also James Milroy's (1997:311) view that "linguistic change is speaker-based," which is also consistent with my position that communal languages are abstract extrapolations from idiolects. Moreover, it is dubious whether real co-ordinate bilingualism exists, in which linguistic systems are kept separate. Thus, how much sense does it make to speak of language contact as a separate phenomenon from the contact of idiolects? Speakers are central to bringing idiolects, dialects, and languages into contact while communicating with each other. Chapters 2 and 6 capitalize on this peculiarity to explain the means by which languages evolve.

It is now critical to explain the analogy between a communal language and a biological species as an ensemble of individuals. Although a detailed discussion is presented in chapter 6, the practical organization of this book calls for a sketchy and complementary introduction for chapters 2–5 at this stage.

1.4 Thinking of a language as a species

Traditionally, a language has been analogized to an organism.[12] This position has artificially prevented historical linguists from identifying the real causes of **internally motivated change** – what they consider to be "normal" or "regular" kinds of change, in opposition to **externally motivated change**, triggered by contact with another language. The causation actually lies in the competition and selection that arise from the communicative system(s) available to speakers, and in both the accommodations they make to each other and the adjustments that they make to new communicative needs in their speech acts. Language or dialect boundaries are osmotic, as evidenced by research on code-mixing. Thus speakers' mutual accommodations and adjustments to new communicative needs can draw materials from either the same linguistic system or separate ones.

This alternative perspective entails questioning the distinction between internally and externally motivated change. In fact this distinction becomes a moot question under the assumption that a language is a species. Contact among idiolects and the ensuing competition and selection in the means available to their speakers become the default causation for change. Thus what McMahon (1994:248) identifies as "the real **actuation question**" becomes more significant: "why [do] some of these innovations die out and others catch on, spreading through the community, or why [do] certain instances of variation become changes and others don't[?]" These well-justified questions apply better to a language conceived of as an ensemble of idiolects than to a language regarded as an organism without internal variation.

The same assumption that a language is an organism has also prevented genetic linguists from explaining adequately why linguistic speciation occurs in the first place. Geographical dispersal and/or separation alone do not explain why Proto-Indo-European or Proto-Bantu diverged into so many different languages, especially if the proto-language is assumed to have been homogeneous. Could random evolution alone, acting on an erstwhile unified and uniform proto-system, really have led to so much diversity without the intervention of ecology? Or, as suggested by Trubetzkoy (1939) about Proto-Indo-European, was the proto-language itself already heterogeneous and was subsequent speciation the consequence of dynamics of interaction within that internal diversity, with or without the contribution of ecology? Didn't language contact have any role to play in the speciation of Proto-Germanic or Proto-Bantu into the different Germanic or Bantu subfamilies and individual languages? Did speakers of the proto-languages disperse into uninhabited territories? These questions deserve more attention than they have received in genetic linguistics. Chapters 5 and 6 address them.

Chapter 7 focuses on the role that contact must have played in shaping the present linguistic landscape of Africa. It shows how successive waves of indigenous and nonindigenous colonization played a role in bringing populations and languages into contacts that produced language diversification. The focus here is on Bantu migrations into Pygmy and Khoisan territories in Southern Africa, on the Arab colonization of North Africa, and on the European trade contacts and subsequent domination of Africa especially since the seventeenth century.

The notion of organism is certainly inconsistent with the reality of idiolects and the fact that these vary among themselves, often minimally and perhaps insignificantly, but sometimes quite significantly. In this connection, it is also useful to remember that language and linguistic communities are typically discontinuous, more like **metapopulations** in ecology, which, according to Hanski (1996), consist of "**habitat patches**" connected by "**dispersing individuals.**" These observations underscore the significance of analogizing a language with a species. I submit that a language is a Lamarckian species, whose genetic makeup can change several times in its lifetime. It is also a **parasitic species**, whose life and vitality depend on (the acts and dispositions of) its **hosts**, i.e., its speakers, on the society they form, and on the culture in which they live.

A language is a species which happens to share with a parasitic species quite a number of the characteristics discussed in chapter 6, but also differs from it in several ways. For instance, within a population, linguistic features (roughly analogized with genes) are transmitted not only vertically (from older to younger speakers) and horizontally (among peers) but also bidirectionally: children do in turn influence their parents' linguistic behaviors, in some cases more so than their parents influence theirs. Moreover, change in the linguistic species can be replacive, substituting one peculiarity for another, for example, the vocalic chain shifts in northern American cities discussed in Labov (1994). But it can also be additive (e.g., the addition of the flap /D/ to the inventory of English alveolar stops in American English, as in the pronunciation of *matter*) and/or subtractive (e.g., loss of the interdental fricatives /θ, ð/, as in the words *thought* and *this* respectively, in some English dialects). Equally interesting about the linguistic species is the fact that even within idiolects (its individual members) competing features often coexist, a state of affairs that gives the speaker a choice (free or conditioned) in using them.

Another important difference is the intervention of will in linguistic behavior, such as conscious decisions to speak like, or differently from, some other specific speakers, for reasons of identity. Natural selection in the biological species is independent of will, definitely out of the control of individual members of a species, especially at the level of genes, even in human communities where mating patterns are often controlled by rigid social conventions. In language evolution, the interplay of conscious and unconscious choices in speech acts complicates the scenario of the general impact on a communal language of selections that individual speakers make.

However, such differences between the linguistic and parasitic species need not discourage the population genetics approach adopted in this book. In the first place, there are various kinds of biological species, and variation among them has not prevented the development of evolutionary theories, which remain sensitive to this fact. What we need is a common approach to similar structural and evolutionary patterns in both the biological and the linguistic species, while resorting to species-specific accounts of their respective peculiarities. As shown in chapter 6, there are indeed noteworthy similarities between the linguistic and the parasitic species which justify a population genetics approach to language evolution. For instance, the speed of language change is similar to that of evolution in the parasitic species, where generation is not an important factor, unlike in the animal species. Such differences in speed of change are correlated in part with differences in modes of feature/gene transmission and with the nature of the species.

The language-as-species trope also makes more obvious the fact that the idiolects that make up a language are similar on the Wittgensteinian family resemblance model. Speakers sometimes claim to speak the same language by invoking a common linguistic ancestor but not because they necessarily understand one another. Such a notion of a species is among the alternatives available in biology (O'Hara 1994). The often-invoked argument of mutual intelligibility really amounts to the potential that speakers of a language have to communicate with each other, just like members of a biological species have the potential to interbreed. Overall, in both biology and linguistics, the life of a species is conceived of as a function of the lives of its constituent members. A species is changed by the effects that the environment (one of the relevant meanings of *ecology*, see section 1.5) exerts directly on individual members, rather than on the species itself. As suggested in section 1.1, a language is an abstraction which linguists should not overly reify.

From an evolutionary standpoint, an important question about both the linguistic and the biological species follows from the above conclusion: how do selections made at the level of individuals sometimes wind up as selections at the level of the species, while numerous other selections are of no particular consequence to the species? When do linguistic choices made by individual speakers translate into changes in the communal language? When ecology is adequately factored in, these questions boil down to the problem of **multiple articulation of selection** in a population, with different selections applying concurrently at different levels within the population. On the one hand, there are selections made by individual speakers which assign each idiolect what in biological terms would be identified as its geno-type. Each idiolect has its idiosyncrasies, despite its overwhelming similar-ities with others in the same communal language. On the other hand, the community at large makes its own selections through the fact that the inno-vations or idiosyncrasies of some speakers, for instance the vocalization of /r/ in the word *floor* [flɔə], are copied by other speakers while others are not, for instance the alternative rhotic pronunciation [flɔr]. (Interestingly, those features that spread within a community need not originate in the same speakers.) The community-level selection is what produces macroevolu-tionary developments identified as changes in a communal language. However, so far the principles regulating both individual and group selec-tions are not fully understood. My invocation of an ecology-sensitive model of markedness in chapter 2 to account for feature selection hardly deals with this challenge for future research.

Clearly, individual speakers are critical unwitting agents of language evolution. This occurs through the day-to-day accommodations which speakers make to one another, the adjustments they make to new communi-cative needs, and the simple condition of imperfect replication during lan-guage transmission. Accommodation emphasizes the significance of idiolect contact within a population of speakers and the central role it plays in language change. While interacting with one other, speakers contribute features to a **pool** from which they make their selections that can affect the evolutionary trajectory of a language. The features they contribute can be from the same language or dialect, or from different ones. The selections they make are not necessarily constrained by the origins of the features, and each idiolect reorganizes its selections on the model of **blending inheritance** in biology. However, we must remember that, unlike in the animal species, this blending is **polyploidic**, subject to threshold effects. What becomes obvious here is that the extent to which a language is restructured is in part determined by structural differences between it and the other systems with which it has been in contact (chapter 2). This is obvious at the interidiolec-tal level. I submit that contact as an ecological factor is everywhere in our day-to-day interactions. It nurtures the invisible hand that executes change.

There is another fold of competition in a linguistic community, that among alternative means of communication. In many places around the world, speakers use more than one language and/or dialect. Usually they alternate between these codes. However, in some cases they are forced by their circumstances to use only, or mostly, one of the dialects or languages, developing passive, or no, knowledge of the other alternatives. The facts discussed in chapters 2, 3, and 6 show that the choices of language varieties and/or of the features that wind up being associated with such varieties are not necessarily exclusive.

Situations where speakers have a choice between two or more languages/

dialects also lead to mixing. Much of the literature that has proposed all sorts of names for different kinds of mixed systems (e.g., Thomason and Kaufman 1988; Arends et al. 1995) only shows that there are diverse ways and degrees of mixing linguistic systems. What is relevant to this book is that these different kinds and/or degrees of mixedness illustrate ways in which a language may speciate in ecologies where it has been in contact with at least one other language. A language or dialect may borrow heavily in vocabulary, another heavily in grammar, and another in both. Mixing of grammars can even take place in different ways, for instance, in the verb phrase but not in the noun phrase, or vice versa, as in Michif (Papen 1987; Bakker 1997) and Copper Island Aleut (Golovko and Vakhtin 1990). What the literature reveals is simply that there are probably no constraints other than those imposed by Universal Grammar on how materials from heterogeneous sources can be combined to form a new language variety. Schuchardt (1884) and Hjelmslev (1938) were right in arguing that every language is mixed to some extent.[13]

There is no clear measure of what extent of mixedness would make a language variety genetically not derivable from another. Political considerations notwithstanding, we cannot continue to privilege the prevalent origin of the vocabulary in some cases (the practice for accepted genetic connections in genetic linguistics) and ignore it in others (the case of creoles), nor to consider the correct grammatical contributions for some languages but the wrong ones for others. This embarrassing practice is obvious when one compares traditional genetic linguistics with studies of the development of creoles. We may as well start considering alternative ways of grouping and representing languages genetically that accommodate either multiple parentage or, simply, the influence of other languages on the evolution of a particular language (chapter 5).

From the point of view of speciation in genetic linguistics, there seems to be no reason for not considering creoles as offspring of their lexifiers (chapters 4 and 5), regardless of whether they are considered as separate languages or dialects of their lexifiers.[14] The structural differences between creoles and their noncreole kin which have misled linguists into attributing different genetic statuses to them do not amount to differences in the evolutionary processes that produced them. Yet the evolutionary processes are what account and should matter for language speciation. Structural differences between creoles and their noncreole kin amount to differences in outputs as determined by variation in the ecological conditions affecting the same language restructuring equation.

Such ecological variation, which includes differences in the kinds of systems which competed with each other during the restructuring of the lexifier, also accounts for structural variation from one creole to another. Like the growing evidence on code-mixing, creoles indicate that there is more osmosis in language than has usually been assumed in linguistics. In a lot of ethnographic settings, as made evident by the literature on code-mixing and nonlinguistic gestures,[15] speakers are more concerned with communicating, by any of the means available to them, than with language or dialect boundaries. Code-mixing or, more generally, language or dialect contact, is probably more central to normal language evolution than has been recognized in historical and genetic linguistics.

The competition-and-selection model also makes it possible for us to discuss fruitfully another aspect of language evolution, viz., whether or not a language thrives or is endangered by the competition of other languages in a particular population of speakers. In chapter 6, I survey the fates of some languages around the world, covering different periods over the past two millennia and highlighting various ecological factors that bear on their vitality. I show that the typically unconscious selections made at the ethnographic level for, or against, some languages are concurrent with choices that individual speakers made of linguistic features which contributed to language speciation. These selections did not consistently favor one and the same language. For instance, the development of the Romance languages reflects two facts: (i) Vulgar Latin prevailed over the Celtic languages of today's Romance countries, and (ii) in turn it was affected by Celtic substrate features and by later contacts with Frankish (a Germanic language variety) in France and with Arabic in Iberia (Posner 1996). Indeed Vulgar Latin won a **pyrrhic victory**, prevailing over its competitors but quite modified by them in the process.

An understanding of this evolution helps us realize that little of what is happening today to the Romance languages and to the languages with which they have been in contact outside Europe is unique to these recent situations. For instance, the fact that there are now restructured New World varieties of French, Portuguese, and Spanish which have vernacularized at the expense of Native American languages is reminiscent of the contact of Vulgar Latin and the Celtic languages in Europe. One can say that history is repeating itself.

Chapter 7 provides similar information about language speciation in Africa. It articulates further the difference between settlement and exploitation colonization in order to explain the differing evolutionary trajectories of Arabic and European colonial languages on this continent. The spread of Arabs in North Africa was on a settlement model similar to that of the European colonization of the New World, with the language of the settlers prevailing at the expense of those more indigenous to the area and yet speciating into new varieties. This is also similar to the linguistic consequences of Bantu dispersal south of the Sahara.

On the other hand, with the exception of the Afrikaners, the Europeans colonized Africa on the exploitation model. They imposed social segregation from the beginning and limited the exposure of the colonial languages to small fractions of the indigenous populations, relying mostly on the school system for their spread. The result has been the emergence of indigenized varieties which function as lingua francas only for very specific functions and are not endangering the indigenous African languages in any way.

A significant linguistic impact of the European colonization is the development of lingua francas such as Kituba, Lingala, Sango, and Shaba Swahili from labor migrations. They have made more compelling the role of contact in language speciation. We need not worry about whether they should be called pidgins, creoles, or otherwise. We should focus on the fact that population movement and language contact have typically underlain language evolution in Africa and elsewhere. Such language varieties and other, noncreole ones discussed in this book cast doubt on the position that the role of contact is negligible in "normal" language evolution.

It is hard to resist noting similarities between the developments of the creole and noncreole varieties, especially in the New World (chapter 6). In both cases, a European language has been appropriated as a vernacular (in part) by groups which spoke different languages and must have influenced its restructuring. Also, in both cases the contact and ensuing change took place in an **exogenous** colony, nonindigenous to both those whose language has prevailed over others and to those who shifted to it. The differences between the evolutions that produced the creole and noncreole vernaculars turn out to be especially ecological in the sense explained below. Much of the outcome was determined by the specific structural features of the European varieties to which the non-native speakers were exposed, by the patterns of interaction under which the latter shifted from their own vernaculars to the European languages, by the structural features of the non-European languages, and so on. We linguists must ask ourselves whether, by arguing without convincing demonstration that creoles have developed by their own unique processes, we have not contributed to disfranchising these new vernaculars.

1.5   What is the ecology of language?

Gould (1993) identifies ecology as the decisive factor that rolls the dice over the competition both among individuals within a species and among species that share the same habitat. It favors some individuals and/or species, giving them selective advantage over others. Otherwise, there are no individuals or species which out of context are more fit than others. This notion of ecology supports the layperson's identification of it with the environment. This is also the interpretation in linguistics since Voegelin, Voegelin, and Schutz (1967), in the few cases where "ecology" has been invoked to account for language evolution.

However, in biology ecology is also internal to a species (Brown 1995). In addition to the environment, it includes a number of factors within a species. In the case of language evolution, such factors include cross-dialectal and interidiolectal variation (insofar as they are considered parts of coexistent systems in a communal language), as well as the way structural principles coexist within a language. All aspects of variation accessible to speakers bear on choices that they make consciously or unconsciously in their speech acts, the part of the "invisible hand" that influences the evolutionary trajectory of a language. For instance, in AAVE, one has the option of predicating adjective and preposition phrases with or without a copula in the present tense, such that *Larry Ø tall/with Mary* is as well formed as *Larry's tall/with Mary*. Such copula-less predicative constructions are nurtured ecologically by the existence of other constructions such as the following in which the copula seldom occurs: *Tracy done gone* and *Tracy bin done gone*. Evolution toward predicative constructions in which the copula is required in the present tense would have to involve a restructuring of these aspects of AAVE's tense–aspect system too. That it is required in other American English dialects is not enough of an ecological factor to trigger a convergence of AAVE with standard or White middle-class English.

Linguistic features in a system also constitute part of the ecology for one another. Removal, insertion, or modification (of the role) of a variant affects the distribution of other variants in a subsystem, thus yielding a different kind of system overall. For instance, the addition of the flap [D] in the American English phonological system, in words such as *latter* and *ladder* (pronounced the same), has contributed to distinguishing this variety from others, as it has reduced the overall phonetic distribution of the alveolar stops [t, d] in its lexicon. Even features that are not variants form part of the ecology for each other. Thus, in some English dialects, the loss of the interdental fricatives /θ, ð/, as in *think* and *this*, has also affected the distribution of alveolar stops /t, d/, with the latter pair gaining a wider distribution than in other dialects. In this case, one depends more heavily on discourse context to distinguish words such as *tie* and *thigh*, or *den* and *then*, when they are produced indiscriminately as *tie* and *den* but not as *thigh* and *then*. In some other cases, it is the labiodental fricatives /f, v/ which occur where the interdental fricatives would be expected, with the words *Ruth* and *roof* pronounced alike as *roof*.

At the crossdialectal and interidiolectal levels, the mutual accommodations invoked in sections 1.3 and 1.4, which may cause changes within the system, are often the result of responses to species-internal ecological relations. Thus not only does the affected dialect or idiolect lose the interdental fricatives /θ, ð/ but it also gains wider distributions of the alveolar stops /t, d/ and/or labio-dental fricatives /f, v/ in its lexicon. In the case of the above examples, attempts to sound like, or to remain different from, other speakers influence some individuals' speech characteristics and act as an external eco-logical factor, while the coexistence of structural principles acts as an inter-nal one.

So, the fact that the lexifier of a creole, or any language undergoing change, was heterogeneous before the change is an important ecological factor that bears on its restructuring, which often results in the reallocation of expressive functions among units already in the system. For instance, on the plantations where English or French creoles developed, their lexifiers were typically incipient koinés from diverse dialects imported from the European metropole and from second-language varieties spoken by European indentured servants from other countries. Those who developed the relevant creoles were often exposed to more than one way of pronounc-ing the words *this* and *think* in colonial English or the word *trois* "three" in colonial French.

Thus, part of internal ecology in the evolution of a language lies in the actual structure of the language itself just before its restructuring: what units and principles were in place and how interrelated were some of them? Knowledge of the state of the language at that time would preempt unjus-tified explanations. For instance, knowing that pronunciations such as /gwot/ for *goat* and /pyɛ/ for *pear* were attested as alternatives to the more common ones in the colonial English to which non-Europeans were exposed – just as were lexical uses such as *learn* for "teach" and *thief* for "steal", and constructions such as *he was a-huntin* – would make it unneces-sary to seek exclusive non-English explanations in order to account for their presence in Atlantic creoles.

These examples are **not** intended to dispute the role of substrate languages (the other external ecological factor relative to the lexifier) in the selection of these peculiarities into Atlantic English creoles. As explained in Mufwene (1993b), **congruence** of features of (some) substrate languages with variants available in the lexifier often favored the selection of some features that could have been omitted, such as some of the above examples which did not find their way into noncreole varieties of North American English. Assuming that the local varieties of English which lexified the different pidgins/creoles were very similar (even if internally variable) in both the Atlantic and the Pacific areas, cross-area differences between these new varieties support the ecological role of the substrate languages in the selec-tion of particular features, including those originating directly in the sub-strate languages (for instance the DUAL/PLURAL distinction in Tok Pisin).

However, what must also be realized is that in most cases different selec-tions of features could have been made if in the first place the options now attested in a pidgin or creole had not been available in the lexifier. As the rest of the creoles' systems show, speakers of the substrate languages were definitely not determined to continue using principles of their ancestral languages by simply associating them with (the phonological forms of) lexical items from the lexifier (cf. Lefebvre 1998; Lumsden 1999). As much incontrovertible substrate influence as there is in Oceanic pidgins, these new varieties are not nearly as complex morphosyntactically as their substrate languages (Sankoff and Brown 1976, Sankoff 1984, 1993; Keesing 1988).

During the development of creoles, as of other new language varieties, the structural systems of the lexifiers were naturally undone and redone a few times, being gradually modified in the transmission process, consistent with Lass's (1997) principle of imperfect replication and with Meillet's (1929) and Hagège's (1993) observation that language transmission involves both inheritance and recreation. One can also argue that, by **the principle of least effort**, those who made the new varieties used materials already available in the lexifier (the inheritance part) and sometimes modified them unwittingly to produce (somewhat) different systems (the recreation part). The original system can hardly remain intact and the dynamics of the coexistent variants have a lot to do with the evolutionary path that a language takes. Overall, internally motivated change would be hard to explain, from the point of view of causation, without the kind of approach presented here. The agency of change lies definitely within the behavior of individual speakers, and causation partly in the mutual accommodations they make to each other while they are more intent on communicating effectively than on preserving idiolectal, dialectal, or language boundaries.

The following questions are relevant to understanding ecology: Were the evolutionary processes that produced the relevant new varieties random? What role did the combination of internal and external ecologies play in the development of all the new varieties of European languages since the seventeenth century? What does the development of creoles tell us about language evolution in general? The essays assembled in this book are intended to help us answer them or at least reformulate them more adequately. In some cases, they do no more than open a debate on issues that are much more complex than we may have imagined. In some others, they simply show that it may have been premature to declare or assume the case closed. The question of whether creoles are structurally and/or evolutionarily different from noncreole languages is quite open, just as is that of whether they are dialects of their lexifiers or separate languages (by any structural linguistic criteria?). How much has really been explained about language speciation? Can the role of contact be overlooked in the latter case? How are traditional questions of language evolution related to those of the "life of a language," which have to do with whether a particular language thrives or is doomed to extinction? How do competition and selection work concomitantly with language transmission? These are all questions that I hope this book makes more interesting for linguists to address.

2 The Founder Principle in the development of creoles[1]

The original title of this chapter was "the Founder Principle in creole genesis." I have modified it here because, as pointed out in the Preface, the established phrase *creole genesis* is misleading. Although there has been a great deal of interest in the origins of creoles' structural features, much of the research in genetic creolistics has been on the *development* of these vernaculars, which was a protracted process. Such scholarship has also focused on their identification as separate varieties, hence on the speciation of their lexifiers into diverse new varieties. The latter interest has justified discussing creoles' "life cycles" too, for instance whether or not they have "decreolized," i.e., lost their basilectal features and become structurally closer to their acrolects. These concerns all remain in the present chapter, and I find the term *development of creoles* truer to the subject matter.

This essay is not the first in which I have elaborated my population genetics approach. That distinction goes to "Creole genesis: a population genetics perspective," presented at the meeting of the Society for Pidgin and Creole Linguistics, at the University of Amsterdam in 1993, but published only a couple of months before this one, in 1996 (cited here as Mufwene 1996b). However, in the present essay, I had an opportunity not only to articulate my hypotheses more explicitly but also to sketch out a long-term research agenda with several questions and issues that I would address in later essays. Some of these are included in this book, but others are yet to be written. I was lucky to be prompted by one of *Diachronica*'s referees to define "restructuring," which I explained briefly in chapter 1 and elucidate below.

Characterizing the process of restructuring led me to think, from an ecological perspective, more about a language as a complex adaptive system. It is undone and redone several times during its transmission from one group of speakers to the next and thus keeps changing in various ways. For instance, it can lose features and/or acquire new ones, or it can exhibit different statistical distributions of the same features within its system, owing perhaps to changes in the relative weights of factors regulating the distribution of competing variants. Equally relevant is the fact that not all its modules need be affected (to the same extent) during the restructuring process. The morphology module may be restructured more extensively than the syntax or phonology subsystems, or vice versa, despite the interconnections between them. One module may be more influenced by the substrate languages than another.

As explained in chapter 1, it is through the spontaneous communicative acts of speakers that the restructuring is done. Otherwise, speakers typically do not plan to rearrange their language variety and give it "a new look." I found it necessary then to note the role of communication **networks** as points from which changes spread. Since everything begins with individual speakers, the role of mutual **accommodations** in regular verbal intercourses could not be overlooked either. These phenomena are reminiscent of breeding conventions in population genetics and their role in the selection and transmission of genes within a population. It is on this model that the dynamics of language evolution are presented here. I return to this subject matter in chapter 6, where I articulate more explicitly similarities and differences between the biological and linguistic species and argue that there are compelling reasons for approaching language evolution on the population genetics model. I argue that this approach amounts to doing population genetics of language evolution, transcending simple borrowing of concepts from biology and addressing questions more specific to the linguistic species. To date, mentions of "creole genesis" in historical linguistics volumes such as McMahon (1994) and Hock and Joseph (1996) are ambivalent, partly perpetuating the view that these vernaculars have not developed by the same evolutionary processes that have affected the lives of noncreole languages. I argue below for just the opposite interpretation.

The notion of accommodation is related to variation within a population, and this led me to think of the competition-and-selection condition of the ecologies in which creoles developed, and more generally, in which any language evolves. I had to articulate the manifold aspects of the competition, both ethnographically and structurally (an aspect of the subject matter to which I return in chapter 6). Then I still had to ask what principles constrain the selection processes that resolved the competition. Are all competitions usually resolved, and is such a resolution necessary in the first place? All in all, this chapter enabled me to show that the subject matter of the development of creoles is a much more complex process than the literature has suggested, especially when it is well anchored in the socioeconomic history that explains the relevant population movements and language contacts, as well as their consequences.

Compared to the original essay, this chapter has been adjusted not to overlap with chapter 1, in which the general background to its arguments are articulated. The notion of "Founder Principle" used here is similar to

Zelinsky's (1992) (1973) "Doctrine of First Effective Settlement," according to which

> Whenever an empty territory undergoes settlement, or an earlier population is dislodged by invaders, the specific characteristics of the first group able to effect a viable, self-perpetuating society are of crucial significance to the later social and cultural geography of the area, no matter how tiny the initial band of settlers may have been . . . in terms of lasting impact, the activities of a few hundred, or even a few score, initial colonizers can mean much more for the cultural geography of a place than the contributions of tens of thousands of new immigrants generations later. (1992 (1973):13–14)

However, I have been inspired almost exclusively by biology rather than cultural geography. The terms in usage there for the same idea are *Founder Principle* and *Founder Effect*. I am sticking to this model and will not refer to Zelinsky simply because I became aware of his work after the revised substance of this book was already in place. I will explore in later work ways in which it can improve my approach to language evolution.

2.1 Introduction

Genetic creolistics has focused more on the coexistence of languages in a population than on the actual contacts that take place in the minds of speakers. Contact at the communal level provides the conditions for the actual contact of linguistic systems in the minds of speakers, the loci of phenomena that have interested linguists. My primary concern in this chapter is creoles of the New World and the Indian Ocean, which the literature has made our heuristic prototypes. However, nothing precludes the main thesis of this chapter (stated two paragraphs below!) from applying to other contact-induced language varieties, especially those which have been lexified by non-European languages and to which the terms *pidgin* or *creole* have been extended (e.g., Kituba, Lingala, and Sango). Of first importance in all such cases is the contact origin of the varieties. The specific socioeconomic histories of their developments account for regional diversity in the outcomes of the restructuring of the same lexifier (Le Page and Tabouret-Keller 1985). They are part of the ecology of the restructuring process.

The term *restructuring* is used in this book in the sense of "system reorganization," comparable to "genetic recombination" in biology. However, what is reorganized in a language amounts to, for instance, phonological and morphological units and principles that regulate how they are used individually and in combinations with each other (chapter 1). My basic position is that during the development of an I-language at least part of the system associated with a communal language is undone and redone in ways that do not necessarily replicate the original or the target. Cumulatively such recreations may amount to a new communal system that is different from the target. The divergence which has resulted from such restructuring is characterized as a change.

A creole is a restructured variety of its lexifier. The latter was primarily the colonial variety which was spoken by the European colonists and was itself developing from the contact of diverse metropolitan dialects. It has often been identified as a koiné (e.g., Chaudenson 1992, Corne 1999).[2] As explained in chapter 1, this is in itself a restructured variety, which has also developed by competition and selection of features from the different dialects of the same language. This view definitely complicates things, but usefully, as it helps determine the particular role played by non-Europeans in actuating the changes that produced creoles. More and more detailed studies of nonstandard varieties of European languages have revealed features that are (partially) related to those of creoles. Note, for instance, uses of *done* as a PERFECT marker (Christian, Wolfram, and Bube 1988; Tagliamonte 1996), of *does* + Verb ([dəz] in Gullah) and *be* + V-*ing* or non-verbal Predicate as HABITUAL markers (Clarke 1997a), of durative *a* ("*a*-prefixing," Wolfram 1980), and of a null copula (Giner and Montgomery 1999; Martin and Tagliamonte 1999). Even the preverbal progressive marker [də] in Gullah ([dɛ] in other English creoles) is matched by basically the same construction in Newfoundland vernacular English (personal observation, August 1999).

Restructuring partly consisted in modifying functions of the grammatical features selected from a language into an emergent variety. For instance, the English preposition *for* participated in the restructuring that produced several English creoles. In addition to being selected as a purposive and causal preposition, it was also extended to function as a modal predicate and as a complementizer (Mufwene 1989a, 1996a). This extension was facilitated by the fact that a nonverbal item can be used predicatively without a copula in these new vernaculars. Thus, the same kinds of exaptations which are associated with grammaticization were applied in some syntactic environments to extend its basic purposive prepositional function to a modal one without necessarily changing its syntactic properties.

The reorganization also consists in recombining in a new system features which formerly did not belong in the same one, as may be determined by the diverse origins (dialect and language-wise) of several features of any creole. Such is the case with the collapsing of the ASSOCIATIVE PLURAL function – which is commonly expressed in most SubSaharan African languages – with the typical PLURAL function of nonstandard English *dem* in the same system.[3]

The term *Founder Principle* (Harrison et al. 1988), is used here, along with *founder population*, to explain how structural features of creoles have been predetermined to a large extent (though not exclusively!) by characteristics of the vernaculars spoken by the populations that founded the colonies in which they developed.[4] European colonies typically started with large proportions of indentured servants and other low-class employees of colonial companies (see e.g., Beckles 1990; Kulikoff 1991a, 1991b; Menard 1991), and thus with speakers of nonstandard varieties of the creoles' lexifiers. This proletarian background of the colonies generally explains the seventeenth- and eighteenth-century nonstandard origins of several features of creoles. Further, some features which might be considered disadvantageous in the metropolitan varieties of the lexifiers – because they were rare, not dominant, and/or used by a minority – may well have become advantageous in the speech of the colonies' founder populations. The founder population produced what Nettle (1999:15) identifies as "amplifiers of variation," with *variation* to be interpreted as "diversity," having to do with "differentiation" (p. 30). This is accomplished at least by accumulating new combinations of variants or by weighting them differently (p. 17), because of biases toward some variants or speakers (p. 25).

Examples include the PROGRESSIVE construction with *après* + Infinitive and the FUTURE construction with *pour* + Infinitive in nonstandard French, or locative–progressive constructions such as *be up(on)* V-*ing* in earlier varieties of English (now also attested as *be a-*V-*in* in some nonstandard varieties). For any subset of the reasons discussed below, these features have been selected into the systems of some creoles, although not necessarily with the same systemic distribution as in the lexifier.[5] Through transmission from one generation of speakers to another, they have become deeply entrenched, as predicted by Wimsatt's (1999, 2000) principle of "**generative entrenchment**." That is, barring some stochastic events in the evolution of a language variety, the oldest features have a greater chance of prevailing over some newer alternatives simply because they have acquired more and more carriers, hence more transmitters, with each additional generation of speakers.

The typical population-genetics kinds of explanations for the dominance of such would-be disadvantageous features in a (colony's) population are: (i) such features may have been reintroduced by mutation; (ii) they may have been favored by new ecological conditions in the colony; or (iii) the colony may have received significant proportions of carriers of the features, a situation which maximized the chances for their successful reproduction. I argue below that in the development of creoles the second and third reasons account largely for the restructuring of the lexifier. True mutations are rare, though there are plenty of adaptations. The developments of creoles are instances of **natural adaptations** of languages qua species to changing ecological conditions. In every colony, selection of the lexifier for large-scale communication in an ethnographic ecology that differed from the metropolitan setting called for adaptations that resulted in a new language variety.

The notion of "ecology" will be discussed in detail in chapter 6. Worth recalling here is the distinction stated in chapter 1 between species-internal and species-external ecologies. The former pertains to the coexistence of features in a language variety, whereas the latter subsumes, in our case, the contact of a linguistic system with another and the general ethnographic context in which it is used. The allocation of some factors to internal or external ecology also depends on the focus of the analyst. For instance, while discussing a language such as English brought to North America from the British Isles, dialectal variation can be considered internal ecology. On the other hand, the same variation can be considered external ecology if the analyst focused only on the London dialect coming in contact with British Southwestern English in, say, Virginia. The main idea is that when there are alternative strategies for the same or similar grammatical functions, each of the variants becomes part of the ecology for the others and each one of them can be affected by what happens to the others. Simple systemic relations among different aspects of a system are also part of this internal ecology. For instance, as shown above, whether or not the preposition *for* can develop into a purposive modal depends, from an internal-ecology perspective, on whether or not a nonverbal predicate phrase must combine with a copula in the emergent variety.

Except where considerations are obviously different, as between pragmatic and structural principles, there is no clearcut boundary between internal and external ecology. The notion of coordinate bilingualism in which linguistic systems are kept separate is a myth that is inconsistent with, for instance, the speed of second language acquisition compared to first language acquisition. The contact of language varieties, hence of linguistic systems, in the mind of a speaker produces a set-theory union of features that is analogous to a gene pool in population genetics. Nettle (1999:5) identifies it as a "linguistic pool," which unfortunately does not rule out languages as part of the pool. A more adequate counterpart to the notion of "gene pool" is perhaps "feature pool," although the concept of "feature" is not an ideal analog of "gene" either. However, as observed in chapter 1, there is no particular reason why every structural notion applicable to a biological species should also be applicable to a linguistic species, nor why the latter should be thought of in all respects like the former. I prefer the name "feature pool" to "linguistic pool" simply because the term "feature" refers more specifically to parts or components than the term *linguistic*.

The coexistence of linguistic systems in a set-theory union fashion (perhaps complemented by a tagging system for specific languages) seems in fact to be the simplest explanation for interference. Regardless of their origins, the coexistent features compete with each other. When the tagging conventions that associate them with different, yet overlapping, systems have failed, there is confusion, identified in the context of language contact as interference. That coexistence of features and its consequences is an important ecological factor that accounts for some of the evolutionary processes that produced creoles, ranging from the unrounding of French front rounded vowels in Haitian Creole to the extensive use of serial verb constructions based partly on models such as *aller prendre* "go get" in French itself.

Because several geographically distant metropolitan varieties of the lexifier came into contact with each other in the colonies (Le Page 1960; Le Page and Tabouret-Keller 1985), many features that distinguished them from each other were likewise engaged in the competition, once they formed a larger pool in the locus of contact (in the speakers' minds). The selection of those which became parts of colonial vernaculars often depended on congruence with features of some substrate languages (see below). An ecological approach helps us determine which factors in individual contact arenas favored the selection of advantageous features into creoles' systems. My ecology-sensitive model of markedness (Mufwene 1989c, 1991a) was designed to answer some of the questions regarding feature selection.

As the ecological conditions changed over time (section 2.2), new features may have prevailed over some older ones, which in turn became disadvantageous. For instance, the habitual marker [dəz] in Gullah and its counterpart [dɔz] in Guyanese Creole may have developed under labor recruitment conditions that were different from those of the founder populations which had come earlier from Barbados. The later recruits from the British Isles would have created conditions more favorable to the prevalence of the habitual or consuetudinal *does* ([dəz]), then attested in the Englishes of Ireland and Southwest England (Clarke 1997a:284f). The fact that in other English varieties the periphrastic *does* has an EMPHATIC–HABITUAL function must have been an ecological factor favoring the selection of [dəz]/[dɔz] in Gullah and Guyanese Creole, which cannot have developed before the eighteenth century. In the first case the conditions for basilectalization did not obtain till after 1700, in the second the colony was not founded until 1740 (see below). The Barbadian basilectal creole texts studied by Fields (1995) and Rickford and Handler (1994) reveal no attestations of such a HABITUAL construction, which rules out the role of importation of the feature from Barbados by the original, founder populations of the South Carolina and Guyana colonies. Jamaican Creole, which must have developed earlier and also has some historical connection with Barbadian (Le Page and Tabouret-Keller 1985), has no such HABITUAL construction either. Neither does Saramaccan, which also has older genetic ties with Barbadian colonial English speech. We are left with the conjecture that the feature must have been brought straight from Southwestern England and Ireland, where consuetudinal *does* [dəz] was already established by 1700 (Clarke 1997a:284).[6]

Some new features may also have prevailed without eliminating any previous ones, with alternatives coexisting "happily" in the developing creole's system, providing stable variation. For instance, in Belizean Creole, the later ANTERIOR construction with *was* (Escure 1984) has not displaced the original one with [mɛ], the counterpart of *bin/ben* in other Caribbean English creoles. In such historical scenarios marked by continuous population contacts (Le Page and Tabouret-Keller 1985; Winford 1998), how an emergent vernacular is affected by new contacts depends in part on the makeup of the current system and in part on the new alternatives brought over by the new populations. For instance, did the new populations bring with them systems that are different from, or largely similar to, those of the local or target vernaculars? Factors such as regularity, semantic transparency, and perceptual salience also continue to bear, sometimes in conflicting ways, on the selection of features into a creole's system as it continues to evolve under changing contact conditions. Ethnographic factors such as the demographic proportion of the newcomers relative to the local populations, their attitudes toward each other, and their social status also bear on how the systems in contact emerge from the competition.

As noted in chapter 1, speakers are the agents of the selection processes invoked here. It is through their communicative acts that selective advantage was conferred on some structural features over competing alternatives. Their role as agents was made possible by the fact that their minds were the arenas of the feature competition discussed here. The plantations count as settings of contact at a second level, at which features not uniformly selected by individual speakers competed with each other for prevalence in the communal system. Factors such as frequency, which determine markedness values and influence feature selection, may prevail at this level, unlike structural factors. This distinction is important because, as in biology, the features that gain selective advantage at the level of individuals ("individual selection") need not prevail at the level of populations ("group selection"). It also allows variation within a population, as is typical of creole vernaculars.

Consequently, language contact is a more complex situation than has been assumed in the literature on the development of creoles. Any communal language exists because speakers using systems that are not necessarily identical interact with one another. In the process they accommodate each other in their speech habits. While still maintaining some idiosyncrasies of their own, they achieve what Le Page and Tabouret-Keller (1985) call "**focusing**." Creoles have developed both from individual speakers' attempts to speak the lexifier and through their mutual accommodations in the contact settings.[7] For convenience, we simplify this more complex picture of contact by focusing on the communal language level. In reality, however, the primary actions identified here through the notions of competition and selection take place in the minds of individual speakers. Recognizing the reality described in this section enables us to account for variation within the community.

2.2 The development of creoles: what the histories of individual colonies suggest

The purpose of this section is to dispel several unwarranted assumptions in studies of the development of creoles. I propose some alternatives that are critical to understanding how the Founder Principle works. I begin by showing why we need not subscribe to any of the dominant hypotheses to explain how creoles and other contact-induced vernaculars developed.

2.2.1 A brief survey of approaches to the development of creoles

Since about 1980, discussions of the origins of grammatical features of creoles have been polarized between substratist and universalist hypotheses, as well captured by the title of Muysken and Smith (1986): *Universals versus substrata in creole genesis*. According to substratists (e.g., Alleyne 1980, 1996; Lefebvre 1986, 1998; Holm 1988), these creoles owe most of their structural features to the influence of the languages previously spoken by the African slaves, who were the overwhelming majority on New World plantations, at the critical formative stages of these new vernaculars. According to some universalists, these new vernaculars owe their features to the language bioprogram, a blueprint for language, which putatively is most active in children. The latter innovated most of their grammatical structures, which helped remedy the deficiencies of their parents' pidgins while they acquired them as their mother tongues (Bickerton 1981, 1984, 1992, 1999). According to some other universalists, creoles owe their grammatical peculiarities to universal principles of (second) language acquisition, with adults being the (primary) agents of vernacularization (Thomason 1980, Sankoff 1984).[8]

Although quite strong from the 1920s to the 1960s, the view that the colonial varieties of the European languages played a critical role in determining not only the vocabularies of creole vernaculars but also their grammars has generally been downplayed since the 1970s. The legacy of Krapp (1924), Kurath (1928), Johnson (1930), Faine (1937), Hall (1966), and Valkhoff (1966), among others, has been barely noticeable in the context of Atlantic creoles. Exceptions include D'Eloia (1973) and Schneider (1989) regarding African-American vernacular English (AAVE), and Chaudenson (1979, 1989, 1992) in the case of mostly Indian Ocean French creoles.

Overall, superstratists claim that creoles have typically extrapolated, through normal adaptive processes, structural alternatives that were already present in metropolitan and/or colonial varieties of the lexifiers. The new vernaculars did not innovate much in the sense of *ex nihilo* or UG-based creations advocated by Bickerton (1984, 1992). Nor did they accept much substrate influence that did not have some model, however partial or statistically limited, in their lexifiers. However, Chaudenson (1989, 1992) and Corne (1999) recognize the role of substrate influence, without which creole vernaculars would be more similar to (ex-)colonial varieties of European languages spoken by descendants of Europeans, such as Québécois and Cajun French. Chaudenson takes creoles' lexifiers to have been approximations by slaves of colonial European speech of the late homestead phase, i.e., varieties that were not significantly restructured compared to European colonial speech. According to Chaudenson, during the **homestead phase**, identified as *société d'habitation*, all those born in the colonies spoke the same colonial varieties of European languages, regardless of race, because they all lived in the same integrated settings.[9] (This is an important point against arguments that creoles developed due partly to a break in the transmission of the lexifier. Transmitters of the lexifier need not have been European.)

Since the mid-1980s I have contributed to the "complementary hypothesis."[10] I argue that the only influences in competition are structures of the lexifier and of the substrate languages. The language bioprogram, which need not be understood to be operating exclusively in children, regulates the selection of structural features from among the options in competition among the language varieties in contact. It can incorporate my ecology-sensitive markedness model, according to which the values of the competing alternatives are determined by diverse factors, such as regularity or invariance of form, frequency, generality, semantic transparency, and perceptual salience, among apparently a host of other factors that future research is likely to uncover.

Along with Le Page and Tabouret-Keller (1985) and Chaudenson (1992), I criticize a shortcoming common in most studies, viz., the comparison of creoles' structural features with those of the standard varieties of their lexifiers rather than of their nonstandard varieties. The illusion that the Europeans with whom the non-Europeans interacted on the plantations spoke the standard varieties of their lexifiers is not consistent with sociohistorical information available about the beginnings of the colonies. Some seventeenth-century letters addressed to, for instance, the West Indian Company, the Virginia Company, the [Dutch] West India Company, or their other European counterparts reveal that their authors were typically low-ranking employees who had been sent on difficult ground-breaking missions in the colonies. They corroborate studies of Ship English, such as Bailey and Ross (1988:196–7), who argue that "most of the sailors were illiterate, including many of the captains and masters." According to this literature, the varieties spoken aboard the ships must have been more nonstandard than the ships' logs indicate, especially as the written medium may have skewed the samples in the direction of the standard variety.

These observations are consistent with historical accounts according to which large proportions of the immigrant European populations consisted of defector soldiers and sailors, destitute farmers, indentured laborers, and sometimes convicts. That is, the vast majority of the (early) colonists came from the lower strata of European societies. As much of their correspondence indicates (e.g., Eliason 1956), they spoke nonstandard varieties, inherited by the vernaculars of rural and low-income Whites in such locations as the Piedmont, Appalachian and Ozark Mountains in the USA. The same may be said of French varieties spoken on the Caribbean islands of, e.g., St. Barths and St. Thomas.

It has often been argued against the non-relexificationist version of the substrate hypothesis (represented chiefly by Alleyne and Holm) that the Africans could not influence the structures of the emerging creoles because of their extensively diverse linguistic backgrounds. However, as noted above, the European lexifiers themselves were typically heterogeneous. Several of their diverse dialects were brought into contact with one another in the colonies. As shown in chapter 3 regarding North America, the varieties spoken today in such former colonies are also outcomes of restructuring under contact conditions, regardless of the extent of their system-reorganizations. Contact-induced restructuring explains why none of the extra-European dialects is an exact match of any metropolitan variety. As shown in chapter 1, *koinéization* – if such a name is necessary at all – is the same kind of restructuring that produced creoles by competition and selection, except regarding whether the varieties in contact were genetically and/or typologically related, and whether the languages in contact were all European. (The latter is a shameful tacit assumption of creolistics that is hardly ever stated.) Investigating the development of (ex-)colonial dialects of European languages ecologically should be informative about the nature of feature competition and the factors which regulated specific selections in their respective settings. In relation to creoles, factoring in the relevant historical, socioeconomic information about the contact settings and speakers of these colonial varieties should also tell us a great deal about the origins of the typically nonstandard options which found their way into creoles' structures, even if only in modified forms.

2.2.2   The koiné lexifiers of creoles

A factor that has often been overlooked regarding both the European and non-European elements in the new vernaculars is the demographic signifi- cance of diverse ethnolinguistic groups and how it varied from one period to another during the development of these communities. This factor greatly complicates the language contact formula regarding when a partic- ular language variety was likely or unlikely to influence the development of a new vernacular. I return to this in section 2.3.

Hancock (1969) and Dillard (1972, 1985), among others, emphasize the contribution of an antecedent maritime, or nautical, English jargon to the development of the new colonial varieties. Like Le Page (1960) and Le Page and Tabouret-Keller (1985), Dillard (1985, 1992) invokes the high propor- tion of nautical terms to support this position. On the other hand, Buccini (1995) argues that the making of colonial varieties of European languages may have started in Europe. He presents port cities such as Amsterdam and Utrecht as contact settings where speakers of diverse Dutch dialects met before they sailed for the colonies. New varieties putatively developed there, triggering "**leveling**" processes (reinterpreted in chapter 1 as restructuring) which would continue up to the time of the colonies. It is not yet clear what role such diachronic processes, which must have taken place in other metro- politan port cities too, played in the development of nautical varieties.

It is plausible that these then-emergent port-city koinés and nautical varieties influenced the vernaculars that developed in the colonies. It is from the port cities, where they stayed for a while, that immigrants left for the col- onies; and they traveled by sea. It is just not clear whether the new metro- politan koinés had already normalized before the colonists emigrated, nor is it evident whether they were dominant among the varieties which were brought from Europe. What Buccini observes may simply boil down to this: precolonial population movements and contacts in Europe itself must have initiated language restructuring, and forms of these restructured varieties were brought over to the colonies, where the process would continue under new ecological conditions.

The above summarizes what is also suggested by the socioeconomic history of colonization, especially as described by Bailyn (1986) and Fischer (1989) in the case of the USA. They show how British emigrations to North America were basically extensions of population movements that were taking place in the British Isles, originally in the direction of industrial Southern English cities. These were settings of population and dialect contact, where much of the restructuring that would take place in the colonies began. This process is well evidenced by the changes undergone by English in the UK since the seventeenth century.

All the above observations show that there was independent ground for feature competition and selection among the European colonists themselves, as proved by, for instance, Québécois French and North American White English vernaculars. Regarding the development of creoles, the competition-and-selection situation was made more complex by the presence not only of Africans on plantations but also of other Europeans who did not speak the lexifier natively. In the case of the Chesapeake, numerous non-English-speaking Europeans, especially Germans, counted among the early indentured servants (Kulikoff 1991a, 1991b; Menard 1991). Based on Dyde (1993) and Beckles (1990), regarding St. Kitts and Barbados, respectively, one is led to speculate that the practice of recruiting labor from places other than the metropole of a colony was a common practice. Moreover, a closer examination of the linguistic histories of the different European metropoles reveals that not all their citizens or subjects spoke natively the languages which lexified the different creoles.

For instance, as pointed out in chapter 1, rural Ireland was just beginning to Anglicize when England engaged in the colonization of the Caribbean and North America. Chaudenson (1992) cites Father Labbat's observation that many French citizens (identified in French as "les patoisants") could be learning French from African slaves of the homestead phase in their Caribbean colonies. The observation suggests that indeed several indentured servants in French colonies were not (fluent) speakers of French. Some of the varieties then identified by Francophone French as "patois" were probably Celtic languages, just like Breton. Kibbee's (1999) "French language policy timeline" shows that in places such as the Midi and Brittany, French did not become a common vernacular until the twentieth century. Thus, in the colonies, much of the same kind of restructuring of the lexifier that took place among the Africans was also taking place among European colonists. An important difference regarding the restructuring of the lexifier among the Europeans and among non-Europeans is the following: after segregation was institutionalized, selective substrate influence must have applied along racial lines, except for common features that had been selected earlier and were deeply entrenched. That is, with the Africans then interacting more among themselves than with non-Africans, some linguistic habits were likely to develop among them that were not attested, nor significant, among other speakers, and vice versa. The nature and extent of such influence are yet to be determined.

Taking into account the following observations on how the colonies developed from homestead to plantation societies, the position that creoles' lexifiers were not metropolitan varieties is plausible. There must have been some already locally restructured varieties, and/or something in the process of development, spoken by the founder populations, including Europeans and non-Europeans, of the homestead phase (Chaudenson 1979, 1989, 1992; Le Page and Tabouret-Keller 1985:26).

2.2.3   Normal, uninterrupted language transmission and the development of creoles

Most genetic creolists have taken it for granted that New World and the Indian Ocean creoles developed "abruptly," within a human generation, after an initial phase during which a pidgin was spoken by adult non-Europeans. The position is also related to the stipulation since Polomé (1983), repeated by several other creolists, that there was a break in the transmission of the lexifier.

We must set aside some incorrect assumptions, for instance, that the lexifiers of creoles were monolithic and standard varieties. Then we can realize that the socioeconomic histories of the territories where these vernaculars developed do not support the pidgin-to-creole evolutionary scenario rejected in chapter 1. Contacts and communication in the homesteads were regular, not sporadic. To be sure, there must have been a lot of frustration arising from unsuccessful attempts to communicate in the beginnings. However, nothing in the ecologies of human contacts during the homestead phases of the development of the colonies suggests reliance on stable pidgins for the purposes of communication. Rather, speakers must have proceeded through normal adult interlanguage stages of second-language acquisition in naturalistic settings toward closer approximations of the lexifier.

Another incorrect assumption emerging from the literature is that colonial plantations developed overnight, so to speak, with all their peak population aggregates in place apparently since the foundation of the colonies, and with all the relevant non-European languages represented with their features competing concurrently. Instead, several important historical sources examined by, e.g., Baker (1990, 1993), Singler (1993, 1995), Migge (1993), and Mufwene (1992b, 1997c) confirm Chaudenson's position that the colonies developed gradually into plantation economic systems, although not necessarily at the same speed (see below). They suggest that creoles developed by continual restructuring of their lexifiers, subject to varying ecologies.

Baker (1996) observes correctly that the homestead phase lasted less time in Mauritius than in Réunion. Mauritian Creole would thus have developed quite early in the history of Mauritius and in a setting where, given the much smaller proportion of a founder population speaking colonial French, features that were congruent with those of non-European languages were favored. Hence the emergent creole diverged more significantly from the structures of its lexifier than Réunionnais.

The same can also be inferred from Le Page and Tabouret-Keller's (1985) history of Caribbean colonies and the development of their creoles (see also Williams 1985). For instance, Jamaica, which was colonized by the English almost thirty years later than Barbados (1655 as opposed to 1627), adopted the sugar cane plantation system about twenty years faster than Barbados. Its non-European population grew even faster. By 1690, thirty-five years after the English took Jamaica from the Spaniards (1655), the African population in Jamaica had grown to three times that of the European population: 30,000 vs. 10,000 (Williams 1985:31). The same year, Barbados had 50,000 Africans against 18,000 Europeans, at a ratio of less than three to one in sixty-three years (Williams 1985:31). By the mid-eighteenth century the proportion was over ten Africans to one European in Jamaica, whereas it did not exceed two to one in Barbados, even despite the continuous dwindling of the European population. Note also that in Barbados, the African population remained a minority for the first thirty years, whereas in Jamaica it surpassed the European population within the first twenty years. (More on demographic developments below.) Although Barbados **did** develop a basilect comparable to those of other Caribbean territories by the nineteenth century (Rickford and Handler 1994; Fields 1995) – probably later than Jamaica – it seems to have done so on a smaller scale, which accounts for its disappearance.

These historical observations also reveal that Africans from different regions and language families – often coinciding with different typological groups – became critical to different stages of the development of Atlantic creoles. Curtin's (1969) general demographic estimates in Table 1 (subject to conventional reservations on his figures) show that the proportion of Africans from the Windward Coast (speaking Mande, Kru, and Western Kwa languages) was significant mostly during the homestead phases of some colonies, e.g., South Carolina and Jamaica. However, it became significant in some other colonies, e.g., Barbados and Suriname, mostly during their plantation phases. Africans from the Gold Coast and the Bight of Benin (also speaking Kwa languages) became demographically significant during the early eighteenth century, when the basilectalization of several Atlantic creoles was underway. Features of the lexifiers which were Kwa-like were likely to gain selective advantage, barring other factors which may have influenced the restructuring differently (Mufwene 1989c, 1991a).

Map 1   Africa: some historical regions and major language groups

By the time the Central Africans (speaking Bantu languages) became demographically significant, during the second half of the eighteenth century, most of the creoles must have already developed the greatest and/or more fundamental parts of their structures and norms. By the Founder Principle, since such demographic significance did not obtain overnight, it was generally more cost-effective for subsequent generations of immigrants (free, enslaved, and indentured) to learn the emerging local vernaculars rather than to develop new ones from scratch. Thus a great deal of features which became associated with the creoles in those early stages became more and more entrenched through adoption by newcomers who targeted the current speakers (creole and seasoned slaves) and would later serve as models for future newcomers. The Founder Principle thus also

Table 1 *The English slave trade, 1680–1800, by African region of origin, expressed in percentages of varying samples, from Philip Curtin (1969:129)*

Period	Senegambia	Sierra Leone	Windward Coast	Gold Coast	Bight of Benin	Bight of Biafra	Central Africa	Other
1. 1680–85	12.0 }	(12.0)	27.3	20.9	15.7	6.7	12.0	5.4
2. 1688	12.0 }	(12.0)	38.0	18.4	12.3	5.2	11.3	2.8
3. 1713	14.6	4.2	10.4	31.2	39.6	—	—	—
4. 1724	6.4	10.6	5.3	38.3	21.3	3.2	14.9	—
5. 1752	7.0	{ 32.0 }	(32.0)		5.2	40.4	12.7	2.6
6. 1771	7.0	{ 25.4 }	(25.4)	16.0	{ 49.5 }	(49.5)	2.1	—
7. 1771	6.7	2.0	31.0	13.1	3.0	44.2	—	—
8. 1788	0.9	4.7	5.4	13.5	16.8	29.0	29.7	—
9. 1798		{ 6.2 }	(6.2)	6.8	3.0	38.2	45.8	—
10. 1799	0.3	{ 9.8 }	(9.8)	9.7	1.0	44.8	34.4	—

Sources: Data from Davies, *Royal African Company*, pp. 225, 233, 363; Le Page, "Jamaican Creole," pp. 61–65; Donnan, *Documents*, 2:308–9, 454–56, 598; Edwards, *British West Indies*, 2:56. See also text, pp. 130–32.

favored continual transmission of the gradually basilectalizing local vernacular over the often-alleged break in its transmission. Both sociohistorical facts and the evolutionary account proposed in this book make it unnecessary to posit an antecedent pidgin to the creoles which developed in European plantation colonies of the Atlantic and Indian Oceans.

We must remember that the mortality rate was very high among the plantation laborers, although this population continued to increase until the nineteenth century. This trend of rapid **population replacement** and growth (as compared to communities growing by birth) also favored continual restructuring of the extant vernaculars among non-Europeans, especially after segregation was institutionalized on the large plantations and the non-Europeans had less and less fresh input from (colonial) European varieties. Even though the most drastic restructuring may have taken place during the initial and critical transition to the plantation phase in every colony, the basilectalization process probably continued up to the abolition of slavery in the nineteenth century or up to the total collapse of the plantation industry, which entailed the end of the importation of indentured labor sometimes from the same places which had formerly supplied slaves. Having proved adaptive several times before (by Wimsatt's 1999a Generative Entrenchment principle), the features selected in earlier phases of plantation development stood a good chance of being selected for one reason or another during every round of the competition. However, there was always room for new selections to be substituted for, or added as alternates to, some older ones.

This is precisely the kind of evolutionary scenario that Le Page (1960:74–5) and Le Page and Tabouret-Keller (1985:47) suggest for Jamaican Creole. They divide the development of the colony in the eighteenth century into two major periods: the first half, marked by the prevalence of Kwa-speaking populations, especially Twi and Ewe; and the second half, marked by a significant Bantu presence. If we ignore the fact that Bantu morphosyntax is not exclusively agglutinating (Mufwene 1994b), the early Kwa prevalence would suffice to account for the selective advantage gained by the Kwa-like morphosyntactic features, most of them being (partially) congruent with patterns of some varieties of the lexifier. These features include the invariance of the verb regarding person and number, the periphrastic marking of tense and nominal PLURAL, the introduction of relative clauses with a complementizer (including Ø) rather than with a relative pronoun, and the significant presence of serial verb constructions.

The few exceptions to the putative selective advantage of Kwa-like features include Palenquero (Maurer 1987), São Tomense, and Principense (Ferraz 1979), whose initial creators included significant proportions of

Table 2 *The population of Suriname, 1652–1754 (from Migge 1993:28)*

Years	Europeans	Africans	Amerindians	Total
1652	200	200	90	490
1665	1,500	3,000	400	4,900
1680	438	1,010	50	1,498
1700	745	8,926	—	9,671
1715	838	11,664	—	12,502
1730	1,085	18,190	—	19,275
1744	1,217	25,135	—	26,352
1754	1,441	33,423	—	34,864

Bantu speakers. Consequently, they reflect Bantu influence. Le Page and Tabouret-Keller (1985) conclude that São Tomense must have formed around the mid-seventeenth century (almost 150 years after the first Bantu slaves had been imported from the Kongo Kingdom). This formation would have occurred after many Portuguese planters had left for Brazil, Portugal stopped sending convicts, and the demographic disproportion of Africans and Europeans increased dramatically in favor of Africans, with the Congo-Angola, Bantu-speaking region being the main supplier. The sugar cane plantation industry was then thriving and São Tomé continued to be an important slave depot. As a language contact setting under continuous dominant Bantu substrate influence, it developed a creole that selected Portuguese features more congruent with this linguistic ecology. These conditions account for structural differences between São Tomense and other Portuguese creoles which developed in places with less, or no, Bantu substrate input.

On the other hand, the developmental demographics of Suriname suggest that the restructuring of English into the present basilects of Saramaccan, Sranan, and its other creoles may have been quite advanced by the year 1700. This conjecture is supported by the settlement history of the colony as summarized below, as well as by Migge's hypothesis (1999, chapter 2) that (most of) the different Surinamese creoles may be traced back to the same "proto-creole" from which they separated between the late seventeenth and mid-eighteenth centuries. Table 2 shows that by 1700, the plantation phase must have been well underway. The disproportion between European and African populations was so great that, owing partly to the departure of most native English speakers, the restructuring of the local vernacular was inevitable. That is, in the very short time when English had established itself as the local lingua franca and/or vernacular, more and

Table 3 *Regional origins of slaves in the Dutch slave trade, 1658–89 (from Migge 1993:33)*

Years	Ivory Coast	Gold Coast	Slave Coast	Bight of Biafra	Loango	Total	Unknown Origin
1658–74	2,270	5,453	12,154	2,581	7,337	29,795	22,883
	(7.6%)	(18%)	(40.8%)	(8.6%)	(25%)		(43%)
1675–82	379	1,121	8,414	748	6,009	16,671	7,627
	(2.3%)	(6.7%)	(50.5%)	(4.5%)	(36%)		(31%)

more of those who served as linguistic models for the newcomers were non-native speakers and fewer and fewer of them were fluent in the original colonial koiné developed by the native speakers who had left. A rapid process of basilectalization was thus underway, leading to present-day Surinamese creole varieties with an interesting twist in the restructuring process, which is explained below.

Table 3 highlights the likely demographic prevalence of Kwa-speakers from the Slave Coast (Benin and Southern Nigeria), which would have favored periphrastic morphosyntax in the emergent local vernaculars. Kwa-like features prevailed not only because of the numerical dominance of the Kwa-speakers but also because several of the same features, which were congruent with alternatives in the lexifier, are attested disjunctively in some other languages, for instance, the Mande languages and, in some cases even the Bantu languages (Mufwene 1994b), as shown in section 2.3.2.

Table 4 underscores the role of the Founder Principle, suggesting that the later numerical significance of Bantu-speakers probably had little effect on the general developmental course of Surinamese vernaculars begun in the late seventeenth century. The fact that demographic dominance did not shift overnight may account for the closer structural proximity of Surinamese creoles to Kwa-like structures than to Bantu-like structures, i.e., for the greater impact of Kwa-like features on the selection of materials used in the basilectalization of the lexifier. By the Founder Principle, the linguistic features of the populations that preceded had a greater chance of prevailing, especially if the newcomers included children. From a structural point of view, several factors that determine markedness values would have favored the Kwa-like features independently, for instance, salience, semantic transparency, regularity, and certainly the sheer frequency of those features that were already entrenched among the preceding slaves who served as models to newcomers. After all, the newcomers intended to learn the local vernacular the best way they could and did not plan to speak it deliberately according to principles of their native languages or others that they had previously spoken. What they contributed to further restructuring the

Table 4 *Regional origins of slaves in the Dutch slave trade, 1739–74 (from Migge 1993:41)*

Years	Gold Coast	Slave Coast	Loango	Guinea General	Total	Unknown Origin
1739–59	8,332	530	15,895	23,692	48,807	67,300
	(17%)	(1%)	(33%)	(49%)		(58%)
1760–74	5,043	380	28,424	39,702	73,551	11,415
	(7%)	(0.5%)	(39%)	(53.5%)		(13%)

local vernacular was just a by-product of imperfect replication in their communicative acts.

The demographics of coastal South Carolina (table 5) suggest that the essence of Gullah's basilect may have formed during the first half of the eighteenth century, i.e., while the colony was shifting to the plantation industry as its most important economic activity and the slave population were growing rapidly. This development occurred especially after the institutionalization of race segregation in 1720, which reduced the amount of interaction between Europeans and Africans, making allowance for divergence between the colonial varieties spoken by their respective descendants. What table 5 does not show is that on the coast, where the rice fields and Gullah developed, the African population often rose to ten times that of the European population during the eighteenth century.

Taking into account structural facts, table 6 suggests that the Bantu presence in coastal South Carolina became significant (about 70 percent of the African population) perhaps toward the end of the most important phase of basilectalization.[11] This may explain why there is no identifiable Bantu influence in Gullah's grammatical system (except of course for features which were congruent with those of other languages). It is also possible that gradual basilectalization was still in process. If so, the nature of the linguistic feature competition, compounded with the short duration of the Bantu prevalence and with the non-negligible presence of West Africans speaking nonagglutinating languages (especially Mande and Kwa) during the second half of the eighteenth century, simply offset any potential for dominant Bantu structural influence on the then-emergent Gullah. Rawley (1981:335) observes that during 1733–1807 the South Carolinian colonists "secured about one-fifth of their slaves from Senegambia, one-sixth from the Windward Coast, and two-fifths from Angola." He also suggests that throughout the history of colonial South Carolina, "Guinea (from Gold Coast to Calabar)" – the Kwa-speaking area – remained a constant important source of slaves (441), which must have played an important role in giving selective advantage to Kwa-like periphrastic morphosyntax. The fact

Table 5 *Excerpts from Peter Wood's (1989:38) "Estimated southern population by race and by region, 1685–1790 . . . South Carolina (east of the mountains)"*

Year	1685	1700	1715	1730	1745	1760	1775	1790
White	1,400	3,800	5,500	9,800	20,300	38,600	71,600	140,200
Black	500	2,800	8,600	21,600	40,600	57,900	107,300	108,900

that Bantu languages do not totally lack periphrastic morphosyntax, as noted above, may have encouraged the offset.

Overall, in some colonies, such as South Carolina, Virginia, and Réunion, the Africans remained minorities for the first thirty to fifty years, whereas in others such as Suriname, Mauritius (Baker 1996), Jamaica, and apparently Guyana (Rickford 1987), the plantation phase came about rather rapidly and brought along an early slave majority.[12] In the particular case of Suriname, founded by the English in 1651 with an equal proportion of Europeans and Africans (apparently two hundred of each group), the proportion of Africans doubled by 1665 (3,000 against 1,500 Europeans, in fourteen years), and reached almost twelve to one by 1700 (8,926 Africans against 745 Europeans of mixed composition in about fifty years). In 1667 the Dutch took over Suriname and by 1670 (nineteen years after the foundation of the colony) almost all the English planters left, taking with them more than two thousand slaves. This change drastically reduced (by two thirds) the proportion of speakers of various approximations of English, while the local vernacular that had been developing from it was retained. (This vernacular was certainly already restructured and variable, but it is not clear to what extent it was structurally similar to today's Surinamese creoles.) Along with Arends (1986, 1989) and Plag (1993), I suspect that this local vernacular was gradually restructured further away from its lexifier with subsequent importations of slaves, although the essence of the basilects may have been in place by the end of the seventeenth century, and certainly by the first half of the eighteenth century, for which evidence is available in Sranan.

The removal of the Europeans' colonial varieties of English from Suriname is one of the most significant factors accounting for the notable divergence of basilectal Saramaccan from structures of colonial English varieties, a fact on which Alleyne (1980) and Bickerton (1984) agree. However, the former characterizes Saramaccan as the creole most influenced by African substrate languages, whereas the latter presents it as the most radical one, created, expanded, and stabilized by children. In reality,

Table 6 *Africans arriving in Charleston, South Carolina, March 1735–March 1740, by year, by origin of shipment, and by age group ("over age 10" vs. "under age 10")*

Periods	From Angola				From Gambia				From elsewhere in Africa				From the West Indies				Totals			
	Ship-ments	Over age 10	Under age 10	Total	Ship-ments	Over age 10	Under age 10	Total	Ship-ments	Over age 10	Under age 10	Total	Ship-ments	Over age 10	Under age 10	Total	Est. no. ship	Over age 10	Under age 10	No. slaves
1735–36	6	1858	171	2029	—	—	—	—	4	569	43	612	3	4	6	10	13	2431	220	2651
1736–37	12	2474	417	2891	2	163	25	188	1	196	28	224	3	22	1	23	18	2855	471	3326
1737–38	5	789	38	827	—	—	—	—	1	194	34	228	4	7	0	7	10	990	72	1062
1738–39	6	1276	330	1606	3	291	23	314	3	453	122	575	1	12	0	12	13	2032	475	2507
1739–40	2	590	102	692	2	178	25	203	5	894	186	1080	3	33	8	41	12	1695	321	2016
5-yr Total	31	6987	1058	8045	7	632	73	705	14	2306	413	2719	14	78	15	93	66	10003	1559	11562
% Slaves	69.6				6.1				23.5				0.8				100			
Avg. size ship	260				101				194				7				175			
% 10+	86.9				89.7				84.8				83.9				86.3			
%10–	13.1				10.3				15.2				16.1				13.5			

Notes:

The "Totals" columns represent the estimated number of shipments, the totals by age group, and the total numbers of slaves. The bottom three rows represent, according to region and by age group, the percentages of slaves imported and the average size of shipment (adapted from Wood 1974: 340–341).

Source: From *Black Majority* by Peter H. Wood. Copyright © 1974 by Peter H. Wood. Reprinted by permission of Alfred A. Knopf, a division of Random House Inc.

the new ecology after the Dutch took over Suriname made a lot of room for restructuring away from the lexifier, under the influence of other languages, including the Portuguese-based vernacular brought from Brazil and elsewhere (see below). However, this ecology does not suggest that there was a break in the transmission of the lexifier; it merely suggests that the lexifier was transmitted in a (perhaps significantly) restructured form.

In South Carolina, the first colonists, who arrived from Barbados in 1670, started with small farms and deer skin trade. They typically lived in homesteads until the dawn of the eighteenth century, when the rice fields were grown. These became the primary industry by the middle of the century. Large plantations developed with segregated patterns of interaction between the African slaves and the European colonists (including indentured servants), especially since 1720, when the territory became a crown colony (Wood 1974). As indicated above, the Africans did not become the colonial majority, with about 90 percent of them living on or along the coast, until about 1715. The institutionalization of race segregation must have expedited the basilectalization process, although the earliest available written evidence of Gullah dates from the nineteenth century, with Simms (1839). Here too the contact ecology suggests transmission of a gradually restructured lexifier, through generations of creole and seasoned slaves, rather than a break in its transmission.

The development of the Guyana colony is partly reminiscent of plantations in the Suriname interior, except that, unlike the Portuguese-speaking Jewish planters in Suriname, the British ultimately gained the political rule of Guyana from the Dutch. According to Rickford (1987:51f), English planters originating in Barbados, Antigua, and St. Kitts began to settle in Essequibo and Demerara, then parts of the Dutch colony that extended all the way from Suriname, in the 1740s. Holm (1989:462) reports that "by 1760 the British outnumbered the Dutch in Demerara; in 1774 the colony established its own administrative capital, Stabroek," the antecedent of today's Georgetown. According to Rickford, "English military forces were in control of the colonies after 1796" and the Dutch "ceded the colonies to England in 1814" (p. 51f). After the British won the rivalry, there was "a great influx of slaves from the British West Indies and West Africa that quadrupled the slave population in the British Guiana colonies before the slave trade was declared illegal" (Holm 1989:462).

There is little in this scenario that suggests a different pattern of plantation and language development in Guyana. One possibility is that a Dutch creole, similar to Berbice Dutch, had already developed by the first half of the eighteenth century. This vernacular would gradually be replaced by Guyanese English Creole, which developed subsequent to the English economic, and later military and political, colonization of present-day

Guyana. Berbice Dutch would thus be a relic of a contact-induced, restructured Dutch vernacular spoken over a wider territory. Another possibility is that, consistent with the scenario developed here, Berbice Dutch developed concurrently with Guyanese English Creole, as the plantations grew bigger. The trend was for European colonial languages appropriated by the slaves to basilectalize as the size of the slave populations increased more by importations than by birth, segregation was institutionalized, and the proportion of second-language speakers exceeded that of creole slaves, the native speakers of colonial vernaculars.

There is now evidence, from Samuel Augustus Matthews' (1793) *The lying hero* that a basilectal Kittitian Creole was in existence by the second half of the eighteenth century. However, this does not entail that one was in existence during the first half of the same century or earlier (Corcoran and Mufwene 1999). Nor is it evident that the English colonists who came from St. Kitts necessarily brought with them slaves who spoke basilectal Creole (*ibid.*). The colonists who brought slaves from earlier Caribbean colonies are likely to have been those who owned small farms and were being bought out, or put out of business, by the expanding plantation estates (Mufwene 1999b). Their slaves came from intimate contact settings of homesteads which did not favor the development of basilectal creoles, although the lexifier was generally being restructured in the colonies, among Europeans and Africans and the like. On the other hand, the growing plantation industry during the English colonization of Guyana, with the increasing massive importation of slaves from Africa during the second half of the eighteenth and first quarter of the nineteenth centuries, favored the development of an English creole in the direction of the basilect.

Without demographic data, I cannot determine how different the development scenario proposed here for Guyanese Creole is from that of Gullah. In South Carolina, the evidence suggests that among Africans the local vernacular started to basilectalize perhaps fifty years after its foundation, regardless of whether or not some of the original slaves may have spoken a basilectal variety on leaving Barbados. During the homestead period those who came speaking a basilectal variety had no reason for preserving it, as well recognized by Winford (1993) in the context of the development of AAVE. (I articulate in Mufwene 1999b all sorts of sociohistorical arguments against the speculation that Caribbean English creoles had deterministic influence on the development of Gullah and/or AAVE.)

Overall, nothing in the development of these colonies suggests a break in the transmission of the lexifier, only that the ever-changing ecology favored its gradual basilectalization at different stages, and more and more restructured varieties, along with earlier less restructured varieties, served as targets for newcomers. This accounts for the continua associated with creole speech communities, as well explained by Winford (1997b).

2.2.4   The post-homestead phase and the varying basilectalization phase

It appears that during the initial, homestead phase of each colony's development, most of the slaves lived on small farms or at trade posts, rather than on the handful of then-burgeoning plantations. It is very unlikely that anything close to today's creoles was then developing on a large scale, even if subsystems close to those of today's basilects may have been shaping up on the plantations or in the speech of some individuals. Rather, approximations of European speech are likely to have been the trend among the non-Europeans living fairly closely with the European colonists. There is no reason why mentally normal non-European laborers living intimately, and/or interacting regularly, with European indentured servants would of necessity have developed different speech varieties during that period, especially the children. All the non-native speakers must have spoken approximations of the local colonial koinés.

After the colonies switched to the second, agricultural-economy phase, the sugar cane plantations or rice fields claimed 80–90 percent of the slave populations. As these economic systems needed intensive labor to prosper, this period is marked by a general increase in slave imports, which led to a typically overwhelming slave majority on the plantations, on many of which they easily constituted the 80 percent of the population stipulated by Bickerton (1981) as a condition for the development of creoles.[13] The increased importations of slaves to meet the labor demands on plantations also brought with them the fear of a "black majority" (Wood 1974) and the concomitant institutionalization of race segregation. As the working conditions on the plantations became harsher, life expectancy dropped, and the mortality rate (even among children) increased. Consequently, the plantation populations increased more by importation of new labor both from Africa and Europe than by birth. This rapid rate of population replacement bore on the restructuring of the laborers' vernaculars by creating situations in which fewer and fewer speakers that were sufficiently fluent in what they had found locally served as linguistic models to those who came after them.

Several censuses reveal a high proportion of children (up to fourteen years of age) on the plantations, although many of them were not locally born. During the second half of the eighteenth century, more and more children in the same age group were imported, particularly from Bantu-speaking Central Africa (Lovejoy 1989). This situation may indeed be interpreted to provide support for the language bioprogram hypothesis, since I argue that the basilects of creoles such as Gullah, Jamaican Patwa,

Bajan, and even those of Suriname probably did not develop before the eighteenth century. However, more consistent with the hypothesis of gradual restructuring away from the lexifier is the following alternative: as in any other speech community, the children were relatively successful in acquiring the local colonial vernacular (however variable it was), restructuring it the least (except in favoring some of its own variants) and thus helping its features become more and more entrenched. Thus, children must have slowed down the ongoing restructuring of the local vernacular.

Overall, the above post-homestead situation entailed several things:

(i)   Outside work time, the African slaves had limited contacts with even the European indentured servants who worked with them.

(ii)   The newly arrived Africans learned the colonial vernacular mostly from the creole and "seasoned" slaves.

(iii)   After the creole populations became the minorities on the plantations, continually restructured varieties often became the models for some of the newcomers. This restructuring process led to the basilectalization of the colonial vernacular among its segregated users, i.e., the emergence of sociolects identified as basilectal.[14]

(iv)   The basilectalization process, whose social concomitant was the disfranchising of the new varieties as creoles, was typically gradual after the initial critical phase of drastic restructuring, probably lasting until after the last non-European indentured labor were imported.[15]

(v)   In the history of each creole, there is a particular period during which the most significant part of basilectalization must have taken place under the dominant influence of speakers of some languages, typically those speaking Kwa languages in the case of Atlantic creoles.[16]

(vi)   Basilectalization must have halted near the end of the plantation economic systems, during the second half of the nineteenth century, and with the stabilization and growth of populations of African descent by birth.

(vii)   Finally, increased post-formative cross-plantation contacts may have allowed (more) mutual influence of creoles on each other, perhaps leaving fewer differences among vernaculars which in the main developed independently, even in parallel and similar, though not identical, fashions.[17]

The last statement makes it normal for creoles that developed on different plantations and in different colonies to differ from one another, which they normally do. On the other hand, it also makes it surprising that they do not differ more than they do, which has prompted Bickerton (1981 and later works) among others and, before them, Coelho (1880–88), to invoke a language(-acquisition)-universal account. This is by no means the only explanation. First of all, there is no compelling reason for downplaying differences in favor of similarities (Alleyne 1980, 1986); both are all equally significant.

Second, typological similarities among the languages in contact are equally significant (Sankoff and Brown 1976; Muysken 1983; Thomason 1983; Sankoff 1984; Mufwene 1986b; Keesing 1988; Singler 1988; and Corne 1999). No (major) restructuring of some subsystems of the lexifier was necessary if these were (partially) shared with most of the substrate languages. Thus the overlap in function between distal demonstratives and definite articles accounts for the common choice of the former when the definite article system was not familiar to substrate speakers. Likewise, crosslinguistic similarities in the meanings of PERFECT explain why a verb meaning "finish" (the case of *done* in English) has typically been selected to mark PERFECT when, for one reason or another, the morphosyntactic convention available in the lexifier's standard variety (*have* + Past Participle in English or *avoir/être* + Past Participle in French) was disfavored.

When structures of most of the substrate languages were very similar typologically, their common features often prevailed over alternatives provided by the lexifier. Sankoff and Brown (1976) show this phenomenon well with the bracketing of the relative clause with the demonstrative *ia* (< English *here*) in Tok Pisin. Sankoff (1993) shows the same regarding the alternative structure of focus markers in Tok Pisin, for instance when speakers leave the focused noun phrase in situ and postpose the marker *yet* to it. The same kind of explanation applies to the fact that Melanesian English pidgins have a DUAL/PLURAL distinction in the noun phrase, an INCLUSIVE/EXCLUSIVE distinction for nonsingular first-person pronouns, and a transitive marker on the verb, as these distinctions are shared by most of the substrate languages (Keesing 1988). Corne (1999) shows similar development with Tayo. Interestingly the contact settings where these creoles developed are closer to those that Chaudenson (1979 and later works) characterizes as endogenous, as opposed to the exogenous settings of the Atlantic and Indian Ocean plantation colonies.

In learning an umpteenth language speakers typically apply the principle of least effort, trying to identify things that are the same in the lexifier and the languages they already speak, or settling for alternatives that cause no communication problems and/or satisfy their traditional communicative needs. When there was more typological diversity, competition of features was more likely to be resolved by factors other than congruence (alone), e.g., by the salience or regularity of a particular marker. This was the case, for instance, in marking nominal PLURAL in Atlantic English creoles with *dem* rather than with the suffix {-Z}. (The role of the lexifier or some of the substrate languages is never to be overlooked!) Variation often followed from such typological diversity. While the number of alternatives could be reduced, mutual accommodation among speakers by no means entails the elimination of diversity. One way or another, typological kinship or lack thereof bore on the development of the new vernaculars.

Given the role now assigned to the pre-plantation, homestead phase of the colonies in the development of creoles, typological similarities among the European languages are especially significant (Thomason 1980, 1983). Several shared features of the European early colonial speech were likely to be selected by the slave founder populations in similar ethnographic ecologies. As the founder populations' speech became the target of subsequent arrivals of slaves, at least some of the same features became more and more entrenched as they were passed on through successive selections and adaptations marking the gradual developments of the new vernaculars in the direction of the basilects.

This picture does not suggest complete chaos. Rather, the contact scenario advocated here is one in which individual speakers' strategies of communication competed with one another, and those which appeared less marked prevailed over others (Mufwene 1989c, 1991a). Except in cases where the newcomers had significant linguistic homogeneity and where, almost overnight, they prevailed demographically over the creole and seasoned populations, the more deeply entrenched features had a greater selective advantage over new features. (This scenario would not have prevented some of the new features from being retained as alternatives and perhaps eventually replacing some of the older ones.)

As observed above, most basilectal features date from the early days of the new vernaculars. As shown by Baker (1995a, 1995b), they go back to the earliest days of contacts between Europeans and non-Europeans. Basilectalization as a communal process amounts to the change that showed dense clusters of basilectal features in the speech of many slaves. The proportion of basilectal speakers may have never been higher than today (Mufwene 1994a), in part because basilectalization did not entail generalized shifts in speech patterns for all slaves. Instead, the evidence collected by, e.g., Brasch (1981), Rickford (1987), and Lalla and D'Costa (1990) suggests that the creole speech continuum dates probably, and naturally, from the early colonial days, as suggested earlier by Alleyne (1980) and explained later by Winford (1997b) in the context of the Caribbean. My guess is that the mesolects must have always been the dominant varieties everywhere. The basilectalization I advocate thus amounts to the consolidation of basilectal features into clearly identifiable sociolects, without ruling out the gradual introduction and integration of new alternatives. Also, the building materials – "matériaux de construction" in Chaudenson's 1992 terminology – were not new. They have merely been put into new uses by exaptation, thus producing new construction types. As has been shown in the literature on grammaticization, the principles used were often, if not typically, extensions of models available in the lexifier (Chaudenson 1989, 1992) and were consistent with patterns in any of the other languages it came into contact with (Mufwene 1989a, 1996a).

2.2.5   Continuity from lexifiers to creoles

It is convenient to start this section with Bruyn's (1996) and Plag's (1999) claim that there is no grammaticization in creoles. Contrary to Mufwene (1996a), they assume that this diachronic process is strictly internally motivated and that any structural development which started before the identification of a vernacular as a creole is not to be associated with the latter's history. The position is obviously based on the mistaken assumption that creoles are not continuous evolutions from their lexifiers.

As argued briefly below and in chapter 3, much of the so-called internally motivated change is contact-induced, particularly because several changes affect dialects before they spread to whole languages. Since the distinction between dialect and language is not structural, it is difficult to take their claim seriously when we consider what has been learned in recent decades from historical dialectology (e.g., Trudgill 1986). Ironically, the processes that Bruyn and Plag claim started in the languages out of whose contact the relevant creoles developed are the very ones which seem to have led linguists to single them out as separate languages rather than as dialects of their lexifiers. They are also the very processes that led Chaudenson (1989, 1992) to argue that the grammatical strategies associated with creoles are extensions of principles that already applied under some constraints in the lexifier. If anything, Bruyn's and Plag's observation should be used to argue that creoles are normal outcomes of language evolution.

These considerations make more compelling the case for approaching the development of creoles' structures in light of the literature on grammaticization. Certain items and constructions in the target language are put into new, exaptive uses within the constraints of the evolving grammar, representing an ongoing modification of the target. No particular age group seems to be privileged for such innovations, and contact as a cause of such exaptations is not necessarily precluded, since interference is normal in the speech of multilinguals.

As shown by several papers in Traugott and Heine (1991), especially those by Hopper and by Lichtenberk, grammaticization (a form of restructuring) is a concomitant of shifts in patterns of usage. As explained in chapter 1, creoles' structural peculiarities have developed largely by exaptive processes, thus similarly to grammaticization processes. Some brief examples will suffice here in which emphasis lies more on Chaudenson's "**matériaux de construction**" than on how the selected materials were exapted. In several English creoles, the general PERFECT-marker *done* may easily be derived both in function and in meaning from constructions such as *I'm done* "I have finished" and from its clearly PERFECT function in the lexifier, as in *you've done broke it now*.[18] The fact that in the emerging vernaculars copula-less nonverbal predicate phrases, as in *dem tall* "they [are] tall," were becoming the norm rather than the exception made it possible to use *done* predicatively without a copula in PERFECT constructions. A contributing factor to this evolution is the reanalysis of *done* as a verb meaning "finish," as in *mi don mi jab* "I (have) finished my job." The normal option of using it with a verbal object produced constructions such as *mi don taak* "I have finished talking" which would be exapted to express PERFECT. All happens within the limits of what either the lexifier or the new system evolving from it allows (including in this case the absence of any inflections on the verbal complement of *done* in creoles, although there are fossils of this such as *im don lef/gaan* "he/she has left/gone"). In AAVE, the verbal object of *done* is still required to be in the past participle or past tense, as in *he done eaten/ate/?*eat* or *I done did/done/*do it*, just as in other nonstandard English vernaculars.

Likewise, the HABITUAL marker [dəz] in Gullah and [dɔz] in Guyanese may not only be derived etymologically from English *does* [dʌz, dəz] but may also be related to its function as an EMPHATIC HABITUAL marker with nonstative verbs, as in *Mary does say those kinds of things*. More significantly, Ihalainen (1991) documents nonemphatic periphrastic *do* constructions with a GENERIC/HABITUAL meaning in East Somerset, Southern England, and observes that "although the periphrastic use of *do* is a provincialism today, it was common in Standard English until the end of the 18th century" (p. 148). If *does,* in the unstressed form [dəz], did not already function as a HABITUAL marker in some of the English dialects to which those who developed English creoles had been exposed (e.g., British Southwestern and Irish Englishes, cf. Clarke 1997a), patterns of usage of emphatic *does* could still have independently favored its grammaticization into a HABITUAL marker in creoles. This may indeed be what happened in the development of uses like this in such English dialects in the first place, possibly under Celtic substrate influence.

In the same vein, taking into account the consequence of the loss of verbal inflections, serial verb constructions in creoles show some etymological connection with Verb + Verb sequences such as *go/come get, went 'n'got,* and *go fishing* in English or *aller/venir prendre* in French. Substrate influence notwithstanding, the presence of constructions such as [*take* NP *and* Verb] and [Verb NP *and give*] in the lexifier is not entirely irrelevant to the development of "instrumental" and "dative serial verb constructions," especially when *and* is reduced to a mere nasal consonant in such combinations. (More on this syntactic construction below.)

Research on creoles contributes the following observation to the literature on grammaticization, viz., the sources of the "matériaux de construction" need not be the sources of the principles for using them. Thus grammatical substrate influence is not incompatible with items from the lexifier which have only partially congruent patterns. This accounts for the wider systemic distribution of serial verb constructions in creoles, in which there are uses without models in the lexifier. Take for instance "dative serial verb constructions" with the serial verb "give," as NP_1 BUY NP_2 GIVE NP_3 "NP_1 BUY NP_2 FOR NP_3." The same kind of explanation applies to the postnominal use of *dem* in Jamaican Creole, in combination with a prenominal definite article, as in the *di bway dem* "the boy-s," a pattern that is different from nonstandard English *dem boys* "those/the boys." In addition, note in almost all Atlantic English creoles the postnominal usage of *dem* with proper names for ASSOCIATIVE PLURAL, as in *Kate (an) dem* "Kate and company," "Kate and her associates," or "Kate and her family/ friends." However, Tagliamonte (1999) reveals that such independent, though perhaps not widespread, uses of ASSOCIATIVE PLURAL have been attested in some dialects of British English. Their prominence in AAVE and English creoles spoken by descendants of Africans may thus be more a matter of congruence of patterns than exclusive substrate influence.

2.2.6   Diversity in the selection of features

This topic is elaborated in chapter 5. Here I present only a sketch of diversity in varieties from which the model features were selected and of the role of markedness in regulating the process.

There is no reason for expecting all the grammaticized morphemes to have been selected from the same dialect of the metropolitan ancestor of the lexifier, or for expecting features of any new (ex-)colonial English dialect today to have evolved from one single ancestor. And there is no *a priori* reason why some features could not have been selected from substrate languages, except possibly that targeting the lexifier disfavored the substrate languages. The contact settings brought together speakers of different dialects of the lexifier (Le Page 1960; Le Page and Tabouret-Keller 1985; Algeo 1991; Chaudenson 1992); thus their features collapsed into one larger pool in which they competed with each other.

The mixing of grammatical features suggested above falls out happily from the natural selection of features advocated by the ecology-sensitive model of markedness proposed in Mufwene (1991a). In a nutshell, markedness values are not predetermined by Universal Grammar, but rather by several factors, some structural and some others nonstructural, which give selective advantage to one or another of the competing forms or structures. At the ethnographic level of competing languages, the vernacular or lingua franca associated with the group in power typically had a selective advantage over other languages, as explained below. Consequently most of the lexical "matériaux de construction" were selected from the lexifier, according to the model proposed above and illustrated in section 2.3.2. As observed in chapter 1 and earlier in this chapter, the lexifiers of creoles were truly set-theory unions of competing varieties and, later, of koinés which developed locally. During the formation of these creoles, the more common or frequent, the more salient, more regular, or more transparent alternatives were favored over the less common or frequent, the less salient, the less regular, or the opaque alternatives in the disjunctive pool of morphosyntactic features. For instance, PERFECT with *done*, which cannot be contracted in English, must have been more salient than the alternative perfect construction with *have* + Past Participle (in which *have* is often reduced) or the alternative with Past Tense only.

Assuming these factors, we can explain selections which might otherwise be surprising. Frequency may account for why the forms *lef(t)* and *dead* are more common than the base forms *leave* and *die* in English creoles, if the verbs were used more often in the PERFECT function. This state of affairs apparently led to their reanalysis as base forms. Thus it is quite normal in most of these creoles to say *wi go lef/dead* "we will leave/die." Sometimes functional specialization followed from equally frequent alternatives, such as *do* and *done*, with only the latter used in English creoles for "finish" and PERFECT. The weaker form of *does* [dəz], which is consistent with its phonological representation as [dɔz] in creoles that do not have a schwa, has specialized for HABITUAL, whereas *did* is the mesolectal marker of PAST, as an alternative to *bin/ben/men/en*. Another example is the pair *go/gone*, in which case only *go* was grammaticized as a FUTURE marker and *gone* (pronounced [gaan] in West Indian varieties) is typically used in completive constructions without a stated GOAL argument, as in *im gaan* "he has gone, he (has) left."

We can now return to the selection of "matériaux de construction" and their exaptations to meet the communicative needs of the emergent vernaculars. As much as we have been haunted by the "Cafeteria Principle," neither the building materials nor the principles for using them need have originated in the same sources.[19] Assuming that creole vernaculars developed by the normal process of language change in contact ecologies, some heterogeneity in the sources of structural features must be allowed both from within the lexifier and from the substrate languages. The challenge we cannot continue dodging is that of coming up with adequate explanations for this recombination of features. The question here is: what principles or constraints regulate the selection of features from these competing sources into the new vernaculars' systems? The summary of Mufwene's (1991a) ecology-sensitive model of markedness presented above is an attempt to address the question, although much more work remains to be done. There is no empirical reason for expecting the sources of creoles' features to be any more homogeneous than those of, for instance, English and the Romance languages are. (See, e.g., Nagle 1995; Wright 1995; Posner 1996; and Kroch, Taylor, and Ringe 2000.)

Among the advantages of the proposed approach is that the explanations are consistent both with the settlement histories of the different colonies in which creoles developed and with the emergence of varieties such as Newfoundland vernacular English out of the contact of dialects of the same language, in this case primarily British Southwestern and Irish Southeastern dialects of English (Clarke 1997a). Trudgill (1986) presents a survey of such dialects, sketching out a selection account which anticipated Mufwene's (1991a) ecology-sensitive markedness model. According to this, the markedness values of the different features are determined relative to their other competitors in the contact setting rather than to whatever options happen to be available worldwide, a number of which are unknown to those appropriating and restructuring the lexifier. These selection constraints apply any time there are elements in competition, throughout the gradual evolution of the lexifier into the new vernacular. The constraints also make allowance for preserving variation, especially when factors determining markedness values are in conflict and none is more heavily weighted than the other alternative(s). We can account for this peculiarity by observing that creoles' systems are typically **nonmonolithic** (Mufwene 1992a), which has led several creolists since DeCamp (1971) to misguidedly posit a process of "decreolization" as debasilectalization rather than as "loss of a vernacular's social status as a creole."

At the population level, not all speakers need select from the same range of alternatives. Thus, more than one morphosyntactic strategy may have been selected into a creole for more or less the same function. For instance, Gullah has retained the PROGRESSIVE construction [də] + Verb along with the typically copula-less Verb-*in* alternative. Sometimes it combines them both as [də] + Verb-*in*. Likewise, Jamaican Patwa has the alternative FUTURE constructions *gwayn* + Verb, *a go* + Verb, and *wi* + Verb. Such alternatives also exist in other nonstandard vernaculars. Newfoundland vernacular English too has an alternative progressive construction with [də], just like Gullah, aside from its regular *be* + V-*ing* construction. All such similarities in contact settings and in the principles which regulate the restructuring of a language into a new system make it unnecessary to treat creoles as atypical cases of language evolution. This is a conclusion to which I return in some of the following chapters.

2.2.7   Summary

I have argued that the histories of the colonies in which creoles developed suggest that no language-development processes were involved that were unique to these new vernaculars, just the same ones usually assumed in historical linguistics, with the exception of the lopsided emphasis on language contact. Since in each case the lexifier was being appropriated by nonnative speakers who spoke diverse languages, we cannot deny that it was influenced by these other languages, just like several noncreole languages have been influenced by others in their histories. More strikingly, varieties such as Irish English, which need not, in fact should not, be called creoles, owe many of their peculiarities originally to appropriations of English by nonnative speakers and thus to substrate influence (e.g., Odlin 1997, forthcoming). This was part of the restructuring process.

In investigating the developments of these new vernaculars, we must remember that their lexifiers were nonstandard. This fact should enable us to gauge more accurately the extent to which the targets have been restructured after being appropriated by new groups. We must also remember that these lexifiers were not communally monolithic but instead consisted of varieties that developed out of contacts of several metropolitan varieties. For many European speakers these dialect contacts were being experienced for the first time in the colonies, despite Buccini's (1995) otherwise plausible remark that the restructuring of the lexifiers probably started in metropolitan port cities. This position also accommodates claims of influence of nautical varieties on colonial koinés. The contact-based nature of the lexifier is also made more complex by the presence in the colonies of large proportions of indentured Europeans who were not native speakers. It is debatable to what extent non-Europeans could (consistently) distinguish native from nonnative speakers of the lexifiers among the Europeans.

The colonies also shifted gradually to plantation economy at variable speed, depending in part on whether they were first-generation colonies (like Virginia, Barbados, St. Kitts, and Réunion) or **second-generation colonies** (like Mauritius, Guyana, Jamaica, and South Carolina), according to Chaudenson (1979, 1992). Second-generation colonies were settled from first-generation colonies and benefited from infrastructure-development experience acquired in the latter. Thus, the homestead phase ("société d'habitation") lasted longer for first-generation colonies than for second-generation colonies. However, these are matters of degree. One is certainly justified in identifying **third-generation colonies**, such as Georgia in relation to South Carolina, based on the development of rice fields, although its founder population originated in Europe. Overall, later-generation colonies benefited from the experience of colonists and slaves who migrated from previously settled ones and developed their economic infrastructures faster toward the plantation system.

This shift to the plantation socioeconomic system was marked not only by segregation between Europeans and non-Europeans but also by rapid population replacements which facilitated continual restructuring of the local vernaculars, fostered by the increasing attrition of proficient speakers. A concomitant of the socioeconomic change was the basilectalization of the local vernaculars appropriated by non-Europeans. A sociolect emerged that was structurally more and more divergent from the original lexifier. However, because the rapid population replacement proceeded incrementally, most features of every preceding population's vernacular had selective advantage accorded them by the simple fact that the local vernacular was being targeted. This explains the Founder Principle, according to which structural features of today's creoles were largely determined by those that were produced by the founder populations. Especially during the homestead phase, when the population increased by birth and by moderate rates of immigrations of settlers and/or importations of labor (Thomas 1998 in the case of Virginia), every new group of speakers of the locally evolving vernacular increased the number of transmitters of the founder population's speech. This increase was accomplished particularly through those who acquired it almost natively and restructured it little. Through them the founder features that survived successive layers of transmission became more and more deeply entrenched, and thus more likely to maintain selective advantage over, or keep up with, alternatives brought later.

As a concept, the Founder Principle, is adopted here rather loosely to underscore the influence of earlier populations in every colony, not always those who founded the colony. Because newcomers and children born in the colony targeted the local vernacular, the basilectalization process was more a by-product of imperfect acquisition of the target by second-language learners, which was to be expected under the conditions of population replacement explained above, than any attempt to develop a separate means of interethnic communication (cf. Baker 1997). Still, all newcomers, like locally born children, aimed at speaking the local vernacular the best way they could, though not everybody was equally successful. The fact that it was already variable also made it impossible for learners to acquire it with all its variants. The selections made by the different learners made ample room for divergence from the status quo. One must also remember that as time went by the models available to the newcomers were not all equally fluent, which made more room for divergence.

The varieties that were basilectalizing did not necessarily replace the mesolectal ones nor the earliest approximations of the European languages which developed earlier. As newcomers were exposed to variable targets, they probably also developed a sense of those varieties that were rated better socially. This factor must have prevented the replacement of earlier approximations of the lexifier by later varieties. Consequently, the effects of the varieties that developed during the **critical periods** of the transition into the plantation phases should not be over-rated. Assuming that these critical periods in the basilectalization process are analogous to the critical period in ontogenetic language development, I surmise that the rest of the gradual restructuring was only minimal, although it must have continued up to the end of the plantation economic systems. This is the period of increased non-European indentured labor after the abolition of slavery, which is worth more attention.

Chaudenson (1992) observes that the Indian indentured servants in Mauritius do not seem to have contributed significantly to the development of Mauritian Creole's structures. As noted above, this view is not contradicted by Rickford's (1987:65–9) position that the development of Guyanese Creole must have continued up to the post-emancipation time, when the East Indian indentured laborers became the majority working on the plantations. Although today's East Indians are very much associated with basilectal Guyanese Creole, because they are the majority in the rural areas where it is typically spoken (Edwards 1975, Rickford 1987), the features associated with the East Indian influence are rather minimal compared to Indic influence on, for instance, South African Indian English as described by Mesthrie (1992a). Rickford cites from Devonish (1978:39–42) an Object + Verb word order and the transitive verb marker. However, the evidence is so minimal that we can also agree with Winford (1997b:245) that "the Indians on the plantations acquired the basilectal creole spoken by Africans, and continued to preserve it (as did rural Africans) as the rural creole that survives today."

The histories of the European colonies in which creoles developed also suggest that their ethnographic ecologies relative to the same lexifiers (at least by name) did not replicate each other. Despite those similarities on which most of the literature has dwelled, ecological variation in structure-internal and external factors accounts for cross-territorial structural differences among the creole vernaculars which developed. An important factor to bear in mind in all such settings is the extent of typological kinship among the language varieties that came into contact. In the next section, I focus on some preliminary details of the Founder Principle.

2.3   Evidence for the Founder Principle

The evidence for the Founder Principle is twofold: ethnographic and structural. This section is accordingly organized into two subsections that highlight this aspect of the development of creoles. Each one remains programmatic. I leave it up to future research to flesh out details of the hypothesis. What follows should, however, suffice to validate the main tenets of the approach advocated here.

2.3.1   Ethnographic considerations

Little discussed in connection with the development of creoles is the competition that took place among the languages and dialects that came in contact and the nature of the selection applied among them. Yet several European languages other than the lexifier were spoken by indentured servants and other immigrants in the colonies during the homestead phase and even later on the plantations. One of the pieces of evidence for the Founder Principle lies in the selection of a particular language as the local lingua franca which eventually became the vernacular and gradually displaced and/or replaced the other languages. In the case of North America, for instance, English came to prevail at the expense of African, Native American, and other European languages. One can in fact argue that the present condition of endangerment of Native American languages is a belated consequence of those early selections made tacitly by the founder population. I return to this question in chapter 6. Here, I focus on other ethnographic aspects of the Founder Principle.

The relevant evidence is manifold and begins at the macro-level of the contact of languages and with the European:non-European founder population ratios. Cross-territorial differences in the proportions of speakers of the lexifiers and of the substrate languages within the founder populations account for a large amount of variation from one creole to another. This alone may account for some differences between Bajan and other Caribbean English creoles, between Réunionnais and Mauritian, between Martiniquais and Haitian, between Gullah and Jamaican, and between Gullah and AAVE. Greater European:non-European population disproportions obtained (faster) in Mauritius than in Réunion, in Haiti than in Martinique, in Jamaica, Guyana, and – to a lesser extent – Coastal South Carolina than in Barbados, and in Coastal South Carolina and Georgia than in Virginia and the American hinterlands. This variation explains why, although each of these regional vernaculars has its basilect spoken by a small proportion of the overall population, Réunionnais diverges less from its lexifier than Mauritian does, Martiniquais less than Haitian, Bajan less than Jamaican and Guyanese Creoles, and AAVE less than Gullah. Everywhere, the majority of the population speaks some level of the mesolect.

The difference in the duration of the initial European-majority phase is also an important factor bearing on cross-creole variation. The initial European majority lasted longer in Barbados and Virginia than in Jamaica, Guyana, and Coastal South Carolina. In fact, it was never reversed in Virginia. In coastal South Carolina, rice fields reached and held much higher African:European population disproportions than the cotton plantations of the American Southeastern hinterlands. There were also many more small farms maintained in the hinterlands than on the coast. These factors explain why Gullah is confined to the coastal area. (For South Carolina, see Wood 1974; for Georgia, see Coleman 1978; and for Virginia, see Kulikoff 1986.)

The duration of the initial, homestead phase – with an African demographic minority before the transition to the plantation economic system – is significant in a second way. The longer the initial phase lasted, the larger became creole slave populations whose speech was targeted by those non-Europeans who came during the plantation phase. The larger the proportion of creole people inherited from the homestead phase, the more transmitters there were of the local colonial koinés, hence the longer it took before the noncreole "seasoned" slaves became the majority of transmitters of the local vernacular. The longer it took the composition of the slave population to change in the above manner, the less extensively the local vernacular basilectalized. Recall that among the newcomers children typically acquired the local vernacular with only minimal deviations, if these were significant at all. So, they contributed more to stabilizing it than to restructuring it under the influence of substrate languages. Had all strictly linguistic considerations been equal, the above factors alone would account for regional variation among creoles lexified by the same European languages.

Chaudenson (1992) invokes differences in the duration of the homestead societies to account for lack of Spanish creoles (qua systems associated with extensive restructuring of the lexifier) in Latin America. For instance, Cuba remained for about 150 years in the homestead phase before getting into the sugar cane plantation industry. More intimate interracial relations, which account for the Hispanic ethnic phenomenon, also account for why Cuban Spanish has been treated as a closer analog of the white North American varieties of French and English than of the African-American varieties. The fact that during the long homestead phase Spanish missionaries engaged more in the Christianization of their slaves and taught them Castilian Spanish certainly bears on the fact that the restructuring of Spanish in Latin America has not proceeded along racial lines. In contrast,

French missionaries would later use the emerging creole to Christianize slaves in French colonies.

Places like Brazil make variation in the nature of interracial interaction a relevant factor. The more regularly or intimately Europeans and non-Europeans interacted with each other during the formative periods of the colonial vernaculars, the less evidence there is for diverging ethnic varieties.

However, the overall situation was more complex. For example, the fact that a lot of French planters left Haiti from the beginning of the nineteenth century affects the proposed parallelism between the relation of Réunionnais to Mauritian and that of Martiniquais to Haitian. Likewise, the fact that the British planters left Suriname while its English-lexicon creoles were still developing and being retained – despite the change in acrolectal language from English to Dutch – accounts in part for differences between these vernaculars and their counterparts in Anglophone territories.[20] Thus every creole vernacular has to some extent a unique development history, despite similarities with other situations (Le Page and Tabouret-Keller 1985:23).

An important macro-level difference which the Founder Principle may also help explain is associated with the composition of non-European populations in different colonies. As Ferraz (1979) and Maurer (1987) point out, some structural differences among Iberian creoles may be attributed to the composition of the slave populations during the critical stages of the development of these vernaculars. A case in point is the sentence-final position of the negator in Principense, São Tomense, and Palenquero. It is apparently related to the heavier presence of Bantu speakers among those who developed these vernaculars. As in the case of Kituba and Lingala, which emerged out of the contact of primarily Bantu languages (Mufwene 1994b), those who developed these Iberian creoles selected a strategy patterned on the salient, free, sentence-final negative correlative in several Bantu languages over the preverbal clitic marker.

The Founder Principle also helps determine what particular members of the founder population participated in, rather than simply witnessed, the development of the new vernaculars. This view suggests that speakers of the lexifiers must typically **not** have been passive by-standers with a role limited to making their language available for appropriation by non-Europeans. Since the Europeans brought with them diverse metropolitan varieties, they accommodated each other and produced new colonial, koiné varieties. As already suggested by Schuchardt (1909) for Lingua Franca, the Europeans also accommodated non-Europeans and thus helped them restructure the lexifier, though not necessarily in the way claimed by proponents of the Baby Talk hypothesis, such as Baissac (1880), Vinson (1882, 1888), and Adam (1883).

The role of speakers of the lexifier must also be seen in relation to the attitude of those holding political power. In this context, the Dutch colonies of Suriname and the Netherlands Antilles deserve a brief discussion. Regarding the Netherlands Antilles, it is unlikely that Papiamentu developed during the earlier rule of Curaçao by the Spaniards (1499/1527–1634). Three reasons particularly justify this inference: (i) no Atlantic creoles developed that early in time; (ii) very few creoles lexified by Spanish have developed in the New World, in great contrast with the large number of territories which the Spaniards colonized; and (iii) no plantations or big mines were exploited in Curaçao, which was initially a rest station. According to Goodman (1982:55), "very few slaves had been introduced [to Curaçao] before the fall of Brazil, perhaps not even before 1657." Goodman (1982), Maurer (1988), and Holm (1989) all claim that Papiamentu developed during the Dutch rule (since 1634), which was marked by immigrations of Portuguese-speaking Dutch and their slaves from Brazil, from which they had been expelled by the Portuguese in 1654. Along with these populations came several Portuguese-speaking Sephardic Jews and their slaves. Bearing in mind that no major Portuguese Creole extensively restructured away from general Brazilian Portuguese has been documented, we can conjecture that a restructured Portuguese vernacular – perhaps corresponding to Chaudenson's less restructured "approximation of the lexifier" – was imported with these immigrants (especially with the slaves) to Curaçao. Having been adopted as the local vernacular, this ancestor of today's Papiamentu must have been further restructured by new slaves brought from Africa – under conditions of rapid population replacement, as it was primarily a slave depot – and it seems to have been affected in a different way by increased trade with Spanish-speaking mainlanders of South America (Goodman 1982, Holm 1989). As in Suriname, the Dutch welcomed this new vernacular.

The linguistic parallelism between Curaçao and Suriname is enhanced by the development of Saramaccan, which contains a more prominent Portuguese element than, for example, Sranan, even though they both were lexified first and primarily by English. Unlike Sranan, which has a stronger Dutch element, Saramaccan developed in the Surinamese interior, where most of the Portuguese Sephardic Jews ultimately coming from Brazil developed their plantations. Here in the interior, the Jews constituted three fourths of the white population in the late seventeenth century (Price 1976:37–8, cited by Goodman 1982:58). This situation favored retentions from their Portuguese-based vernacular. According to Goodman (1982:59), "the English Creole gradually supplanted the Portuguese influenced one on the plantations, but the latter survived among the Saramaccans."[21]

Goodman's hypothesis does not conflict with the assumption that, with the selection of restructured English as the vernacular among slaves in the Dutch colony (a confirmation of the Founder Principle), the coexistence of English-speaking and Portuguese-speaking slaves on several plantations led variably to the Saramaccan phenomenon. Because speakers of restructured Portuguese were demographically significant in Suriname's interior, the presence of the Portuguese element was bound to be more evident there. On the other hand, in Paramaribo and on the coast, where there were more Dutch speakers, the Dutch element became more conspicuous in Sranan. Contrary to several claims in the literature, maroonage may thus not be a primary sociohistorical factor in the development of Saramaccan, although it may have fostered further basilectalization. The early departure of native speakers of the lexifier was in itself significant enough to account for why basilectal Saramaccan is the most different from English of all the English creoles. Discontinued supply of native speakers and rapid influx of non-English speakers combined to favor more sub- and adstrate influence from the other languages that the early Surinamese colonial English koiné came in contact with.

The situation in the Dutch colonies must have been favored by the Dutch disposition to adopt the local lingua franca where one was already developing or had already developed. This conclusion is contrary to the claim that the Dutch deliberately kept their vernacular as "a 'caste' language which slaves were not allowed to know" (Voorhoeve 1964:236, quoted by Holm 1989:435; see also Holm 1989:313). Even though there may be partial justification for this claim, note that where the Dutch were involved in the original contacts, as in the Virgin Islands and on the Berbice River (in today's Guyana), Dutch creoles did develop, viz., Negerhollands in the former and Berbice Dutch in the latter.

The case of Berbice brings up additional supportive evidence for the Founder Principle. According to Robertson (1993:300), the Ijos constituted the dominant African majority in the Berbice colony during the second half of the eighteenth century. Their incontrovertible influence on Berbice Dutch lies in several structural features, such as tense suffixes, sentence-final negative markers, and postpositions. This is one of the rare cases among creoles where substrate influence is evident even in the form of grammatical morphemes not selected from the lexifier. (For more information see Kouwenberg 1994.)

Louisiana Creole also turns up as an interesting illustration of the Founder Principle considered ethnographically. The French colonization of Louisiana, which then included plantations at and near the Mississippi River Delta, as well as trade posts in a corridor that extended from the Delta to the Canadian border and between the Appalachian and the Rocky

Mountains (excluding Texas), was interrupted by four decades of Spanish rule (at least in its southern, coastal part). The Spanish rule lasted from 1769 to 1803, after which the French sold the colony to the Americans. However, in parts of present-day Louisiana colonial French and the creole then developing from it were maintained as the primary local vernaculars, which continued to be spoken long after the "Louisiana Purchase" (1803). The development of AAVE in the area did *not* amount to a relexification of the restructured French varieties spoken before English replaced French as the official language and as the vernacular spoken by large proportions of subsequent immigrants and their descendants. Thus, in present-day Louisiana changes in political and economic realities have been slow to affect the legacy of the founder populations. To date, the state continues to bear French cultural elements. Similar observations may be made about the survival of French creoles in Dominica, St. Lucia, and Trinidad, although there is ecological variation which explains some differences in the ways these vernaculars have survived.

2.3.2 Structural considerations

At the structural level, an apparent counter-argument to the Founder Principle might be misconstrued from the fact that creoles share several morphosyntactic features with each other. Although the features do not single them out as a typological or genetic group apart from other languages, *pace* McWhorter (1998), this condition has indeed prompted the competing genetic explanations that were summarized in section 2.2.1. The Founder Principle is of course not intended to replace any of these hypotheses. The best of substratist and superstratist accounts for features of individual creoles can coexist happily, assuming at the same time that the language bioprogram qua Universal Grammar is the body of principles which, like a **filter**, have regulated how elements from the different language varieties in contact got selected and recombined into these new vernaculars' systems. This chapter is intended to enrich this basic position of the so-called complementary hypothesis.

To reiterate my thesis, several, if not most, of the deeply entrenched features of creoles' structures originate in the founder populations' linguistic peculiarities. A useful starting point is the makeup of the lexifier, which typically consisted of a set-theory union of diverse nonstandard dialects which may not even have coexisted locally or regionally in the metropolis. Different subsets of these varieties were represented on the same plantations in the colonies and developed into local koinés. A concomitant of the situation with the lexifier is the mixed ethnolinguistic makeup of the slave population during the critical stage(s) of the formation of a creole.

Together, all the colonial varieties of the lexifier and the diverse languages spoken by the slaves constituted new, disjunctive pools of features competing for selection into the developing creoles' systems, on the model of gene pools in biology, as explained in chapter 1.

Making allowance for exaptations, I argue that with regard to form or distribution of morphemes, there are scant features of creoles that did not have (partial) models in the language varieties represented in the contact settings. As shown in section 2.2.5, after a form or construction was selected into the emerging system, there was room for exaptive innovations. Thus the development of creoles' grammatical patterns can be related to various processes of grammaticization. I show below that several of the morphosyntactic strategies invoked to support diverse positions on the development of creoles are intimately connected to the Founder Principle.

2.3.2.1 Serial Verb Constructions (SVCs) in Atlantic creoles are a convenient starting point. Substratists have used the presence of SVCs in several African languages, especially those of the Kwa group, in contrast with the rarity of SVCs in European languages, to argue that creoles owe the constructions to substrate influence. The significant demographic presence of Kwa speakers in several plantation colonies during the critical periods of the development of the new vernaculars has been used to justify this genetic position. In some cases, more specific claims for the dominant influence of particular groups have been made, for instance, for Fongbe influence in Haitian Creole (e.g., Lefebvre 1993, 1998) and for Twi influence in Jamaican Creole (Alleyne 1993).

On the other hand, advocates of the language bioprogram hypothesis have invoked absence of such constructions in, for instance, the Bantu languages – whose speakers were in proportions higher than, or (almost) equal to, those of Kwa languages on some plantations – to argue that SVCs in creoles must have been innovated by children. They argue that if a construction was not shared by all African languages in the contact setting, there was more room for the bioprogram to kick in and produce this allegedly more basic and less marked structural alternative, relative to options specified in Universal Grammar.

All the above positions call for some corrections, especially if a close correlation is held to exist between changes in external ecological conditions and the restructuring of the lexifier which resulted in the creoles. The "matériaux de construction" involved in the restructuring were present in the founder populations' speech. As far as English creoles are concerned, colloquial English has serial-like constructions such as in *let's **go get** the book* and *every day I **come get** the paper* (Pullum 1990). Although these are restricted to combinations with *go* or *come* as heads and to base forms, they are frequent enough to consider their presence in the nonstandard lexifiers of creoles relevant to the development of SVCs.

Regarding French creoles, we should not take too rigidly Seuren's (1990) observation that SVCs are not attested in French and should not be confused with constructions with infinitival complements, such as *va chercher ton couteau* "go get your cutlass," which he prefers to call "**pseudocomplements**." The French constructions share some superficial similarity with SVCs in terms of Verb + Verb sequences, just as do English constructions such as *go fishing*, which Seuren and most creolists justifiably rule out from the category of SVCs. However, what matters is not the status of such constructions in the lexifiers, but how they were analysed by those who targeted them. As inflections were generally not selected into the creoles' systems, the distinction between SVCs and pseudocomplements was likely to turn into a moot matter of details that were insignificant to speakers of the new vernaculars.

Regarding the Bantu languages, it is not accurate to flatly deny the existence of SVCs in them. Varieties of ethnic Kikongo have serial-like constructions in the historical present, which have survived in the narrative tense in Kituba (Mufwene 1988:41), as illustrated below:

(1)   a **Kikongo**:
       María ú+bák+a   mbeele, ú+lwek+a   bákála   di+ándi
       Mary AGR+take+TA cutlass AGR+cut+TA husband AGR+her[22]
       A. "Mary took a cutlass and hit her husband."
       B. "Mary hit her husband with a cutlass."
       b. **Kituba**:
       María báka mbelé búla yakála na   yándi.
       Mary take cutlass hit husband CONN her
       A. "Mary took a cutlass and hit her husband."
       B. "Mary hit her husband with a machete."

Thus, almost all the language varieties in contact seem to have conspired to favor the selection and variable development of SVCs in Atlantic and other creoles. Speakers apparently selected options that were identified as less marked for any number of reasons, including crosslinguistic congruence, semantic transparency, salience, and frequency. More or less the same factors seem to have favored the development of SVCs, not *ex nihilo*, in Kituba as in Atlantic creoles. While factors can be used to argue that the role of Universal Grammar should not be overlooked in the development of creoles, the point of invoking the Founder Principle here is to show that for whatever reason SVCs became so prominent in creoles' systems (unlike in AAVE), there was no scarcity of models in the language varieties that came into contact in the settings in which they developed. No children need be invoked as a *deus ex machina* to account for the presence of this syntactic construction in almost all creoles. The role of Universal Grammar in this particular case may have been limited to constraining the selection of particular grammatical strategies.[23]

The relation between creoles' SVCs and their possible sources is complicated by constructions in which a serial verb meaning "give" alternates with, or is used instead of, a dative prepositional construction. This serial pattern, which is used only in some creoles (such as Haitian and Saramaccan), is not attested in the European lexifiers; nor is it used in all serializing African languages. Such variation underscores the need to examine the development of every creole separately, in its specific contact ecology. Of course this ecology need not be completely isolated from similar developments elsewhere; I advocate paying attention to similarities and differences alike.

2.3.2.2 The structure of negative constructions is another interesting structural feature. In all the relevant creoles, neither the form of the negator(s) nor its/their position is novel. In the case of Atlantic English creoles, the negator and its position are generally from the lexifier, selected undoubtedly with the conspiracy of the pre-predicate position of the negator in several African languages. Note that although several Bantu languages of the Congo-Angola region have a free clause-final negative marker, many of them also have a negative verbal prefix, which co-occurs with the former but may also be used alone (i.e., without the sentence-final correlate) in some languages. Although the dynamics of the developments of Kituba and Lingala out of the contact of primarily Bantu languages favored the selection of a free clause-final negative morpheme, nothing would have made it too difficult for speakers of such languages to adjust to one single pre-predicate negator during the development of the English (and French) creoles' systems. With regard to Bantu speakers, it appears that different ecologies led to different selections out of the preverbal and sentence-final alternatives.

The particular selections made into English creoles regarding form and position underscore the significance of what forms and strategies were competing in the lexifier. All the creoles' negators, viz., *no, don* [dõ], *ain* [ɛ̃], and *neba* "never," are from English. The main difference is that in the creoles these negators have syntactic distributions and semantic functions which are sometimes not identical with those of their etyma. For instance, *no* is no longer limited to noun phrases (narrow scope) or to elliptical/anaphoric contexts in which the speaker chooses not to repeat the whole sentence. It also occurs freely before the predicate in Caribbean English creoles, as in *im no (ben) kom* "he/she did not come." In Gullah, *ain* is used not just before nonverbal predicates and as an alternative to *have not/do not have* but also in completive constructions, before a verb stem, as in *he ain come* "he/she has/did not come." Likewise, *don* typically functions as a HABITUAL negator, as in *he don come* "he does not come," in addition to where it is used in other varieties of English. Even these new uses show undeniable connections to the lexifier, as *ain* also alternates with *hasn't* and *haven't* in some British nonstandard dialects (Cheshire 1991) and may very well have been extended from *hasn't/haven't come,* given the time-reference ambiguity of the PERFECT construction (Tagliamonte 1996). Likewise, *do not* is HABITUAL with nonstative verbs in almost all English dialects. The challenging questions are: why are these particular selections made and why do they vary from creole to creole?

Note that with regard to selecting from competing strategies in the lexifier, the situation in Kituba, Lingala, and English is not so different from that of French creoles, even though French offers a seemingly variable system in which the more common negator *pas* of colloquial French (typically used without *ne*) follows finite and present participial verbs but precedes infinitival and past participial verbs, for example, *je (ne) viens pas* "I am not coming" and *ne travaillant pas* "not working" vs. *pas fini* "not finished" and *elle (ne) peut pas venir* "she cannot come" (Mufwene 1991c). The regularization of its pre-predicate position in French creoles is obviously not entirely independent of French itself (Hazaël-Massieux 1993; Spears 1993), although the congruent influences of several African languages following this pattern must be acknowledged. Loss of inflections and selection of verbal forms which are not clearly distinct from the infinitive and the past participle seem consistent with the selected preverbal position of the negator *pa* in creoles. Not only did the morpheme for negation come from the lexifier but so did the model for its syntactic distribution. Even forms that might appear to be exceptional may be traced to French, e.g., *te pas la* (formerly a variant of the today's regularized *pa te la*) "was not there" and *ve pa* "don't want" are frozen retentions from *(n')était pas là* and *veux pas* with the same meanings (Hazaël-Massieux 1993). (For more details on how negation works in Haitian Creole and may have developed, see DeGraff 1993.)

On the other hand, São Tomense and Palenquero (discussed above) followed the Kituba and Lingala option under ecological conditions of dominant Bantu influence (Ferraz 1979; Maurer 1987), contrary to the preverbal position of the negator in other Iberian creoles. These facts converge with those of French creoles in suggesting that specific ethnographic and linguistic dynamics of the founder populations more or less determined the directions of the restructuring of the lexifiers into diverse creoles.

2.3.2.3   The role of the INDIVIDUATED/NONINDIVIDUATED distinction in the noun phrase of most creoles (Bickerton 1981, 1984; Mufwene 1981, 1986c; Dijkhoff 1983) has been invoked to support the language bioprogram hypothesis (Bickerton 1981, 1984).[24] Taken together with the absence of (definite) articles and the phrase-final position of the deictic marker *la* in Haitian and other French creoles, this delimitative system has been adduced also to support African substrate influence (Alleyne 1980). However, a closer examination of facts reveals that the INDIVIDUATED/ NONINDIVIDUATED distinction is inherent in both English and French, as well as several other languages. English has constructions such as *go to church*, *beware of falling rock*, and *boy meets girl*, which are relevant to the selection of nonindividuated noun phrases in creoles for MASS uses of nouns and for GENERIC reference. This may be doubly illustrated with the Jamaican Creole proverb *daag no nyam daag* "[a] dog_1 does not eat dog_2 [meat]" (GENERIC$_1$ ... MASS$_2$).

As different as it may seem from English in this respect, French also has constructions which may have influenced the development of an INDIVIDUATED/NONINDIVIDUATED   system   in   the   creoles   it   lexified. Constructions such as *crime de passion* "crime of passion" and *avoir faim* "be hungry," in which the object of the preposition or verb is nonindividuated and used without an article, are relevant. Valli (1994) uncovers inconsistencies in the uses and omissions of articles in fifteenth-century French texts, as shown below, a practice that he justifiably suspects may have occurred in colonial French:

(2)   a. *Les princes ont **charge politique**.*
          "The princes are in charge of politics."
       b. *... Dieu vous y a deja donné **bon commencement***
          "... God has already given you a good start"

All the above facts highlight the role of the founder population's language in the development of creoles' systems. Facts on French creoles' deictic marker *la* speak even louder in support of this position. This marker is extensively used in nonstandard French, making the definite article superfluous in constructions such as *l'homme là* "the/that man." It is also more salient, being normally stressed in its phrase-final position. In addition, hardly any African languages have an article system. They mark definiteness by extending the use of a distal demonstrative to this function. At least among the Bantu languages, the marker typically has a phrase-final position, like the distal demonstrative *là* in French. All these factors conspired to favor the selection of French NP-final *là* over the definite article as a marker of definiteness in Haitian Creole.

Again, features of the founder populations' linguistic systems deter-mined the alternatives selected into the relevant creoles' structures. Innovations *ex nihilo* are an exaggerated account, whereas innovations as traditionally invoked in historical linguistics are consistent with the Founder Principle.

2.3.2.4 The STATIVE/NONSTATIVE distinction, which is useful in explain-ing the differing interpretations of predicates used in the NONDURATIVE and NONANTERIOR – as in *im come* "he came/he has come" and *im laik filfulfə sing* "he/she likes to sing" in English creoles – has also often been invoked to support the language bioprogram hypothesis. The typical reason invoked is that in the lexifiers and several substrate languages the interpretation of time reference does not depend as much on this lexical aspect (Aktionsart) opposition.

Such an observation is unfortunately not so accurate regarding the lexifi-ers. For instance, in English, the temporal interpretation of *Paul likes wres-tling* is not the same as that of *Paul works here*; the difference follows from the fact that *like* is a stative verb, whereas *work* is nonstative. The same is true of the French translations *Paul aime la lutte* and *Paul travaille ici*. The main difference between the relevant constructions in these languages and their counterparts in the creoles they lexified lies in the preferred interpreta-tion of the constructions in the absence of adverbials. In an English creole *im come* "he/she came" or "he/she has come" is typically assigned a COM-PLETIVE interpretation (referring to the past) in such cases, whereas *im laik* "he/she likes" receives a CONCOMITANT interpretation (typically referring to the present).

If we take the general absence of inflections in creoles into account, things fall out neatly, consistent with a distinction which is available in the lexifiers, even in the case of French creoles. In most of the language varieties that came into contact (with the exception of standard French, if it is at all relevant), a nonstative verb must be in the PROGRESSIVE in order to refer to the present. The construction *être après de* + Infinitive was attested in non-standard French for basically the same PROGRESSIVE function as its adap-tation *ap(e)* + Verb Stem serves in French creoles. Such a requirement for morphosyntactic delimitation does not hold for stative verbs. Since nonsta-tive verbs are typically used with an aspectual marker to refer to the present, bare verbal forms are interpreted as referring to the past. Common usage of the HISTORICAL PRESENT in spoken language may very well have been an important factor. The application of a similar grammatical system in several West-African (not just Kwa) languages would have favored selection of nonstative verb stems, over other alternatives, for completive reference.

This development is different from, for instance, Kituba (Mufwene 1990b) and Lingala because the latter vernaculars developed in ethnographic ecologies in which they were bound to be heavily influenced by Bantu morphosyntax.

Thus, much of what was innovated in Atlantic and Indian Ocean creoles was inspired by several of the languages spoken by the populations in contact, including the lexifiers, during the critical periods of their developments. Since Bantu-speakers were likely to exert a significant influence on the development of Mauritian (Baker 1994; Corne 1999), it appears that the lexifiers themselves played a greater role in the development of creoles than is often suggested in the literature. A convenient example may be cited from the **fusion** of articles with nouns in Mauritian, though less extensively in other creoles, as discussed by Baker (1984, 1994). For instance, the partitive French article *du* – unrounded to [di] among nonnative speakers – has been fused with *blé* "wheat" in *diblé* "wheat," with the consequence of preventing homophony with *blé* from *bleu* "blue" (also produced as [ble] among non-native speakers). The new forms are clearly patterned from forms/constructions which occur in French, which can also be observed in such a Mauritian item as *zanfan* "child," which has kept only the end of the definite article in *les enfants* [lɛzɑ̃fɑ̃] "children." This explanation does not necessarily contradict Baker's (1984, 1994) invocation of Bantu influence in the selection of this particular solution, given the existence of agglutination in the Bantu languages. The only problem is that one would have expected Bantu speakers to be more attentive to form variation and be able to identify the stems. It is also debatable whether speakers *deliberately* prevented the proliferation of homophones in Mauritian Creole by fusing articles and nouns into new lexical items. However, the result is undeniable. Other examples, among many, include the following:

(3)   Fusion of Article + Noun in Mauritian
       lari "street" (< *la rue* [laRü]) vs. *diri* "rice" (< *du riz* [düRi])
       lavi "life" (< *la vie* [lavi]) vs. *vi* "sight, view" (*la vue* [lavü])
       laser [lasɛr] "flesh" (< *la chair* [lašɛR]) vs. *ser* [sɛr] "sister" (*la soeur* [lasœR]).[25]

Still, the "matériaux de construction" came from French itself, in which the article and the noun or nominal it modifies are typically pronounced as one phonological word.

2.3.2.5 Generally, most grammatical features of a creole can be explained in the way sketched above, which is essentially in the traditional spirit of historical linguistics taken to intersect with language contact. In many ways, the features are not faithful copies of their etyma or models. They involve exaptations to new functions, as happens in the evolutions of other languages too. There is really no particular reason why the developments of creoles should not be treated as consequences of normal linguistic interactions in specific ecological conditions of linguistic contacts involving not only speakers (as in any monolingual speech community) but also different language varieties. Creoles should prompt us to rethink some established assumptions about language change and the role of ecology.

2.4 Conclusions

The Founder Principle is not a hypothesis on the development of creoles in the same way that the universalist, substrate, superstrate, and complementary hypotheses have been claimed to be. Like the markedness model that I have often invoked in this discussion, it is one of several principles that must be considered as we try to account for the development of creole vernaculars.

One of the flaws of genetic creolistics lies in the all-too-common comparison of creoles' structural features with those of the standard varieties of their lexifiers. The social histories of the relevant colonies suggest that the varieties to which the makers of creoles were exposed and which they restructured were nonstandard. Thus it is with them that comparisons must be made to develop an adequate picture of what was restructured and how.

I have also argued that several structural features of creoles' systems are not the kinds of innovations claimed by the language bioprogram hypothesis, though they involve exaptive innovations. Many such innovations have been extended from strategies which were already available in the lexifier. Others have originated in some of the language varieties with which the lexifier came into contact and whose features competed with its own during the development of the new vernacular. Structural congruence (often only partial) between the lexifier and the substrate languages was often an important factor, but it may not have applied in all cases nor independently of other factors. In emphasizing that models of many of creoles' structural features were attested in the speech of the founder populations, the Founder Principle shows that the development of creoles may be explained with the same kinds of principles generally invoked in historical linguistics. We simply must interpret every set of restructuring processes that resulted in a creole within the relevant sociohistorical ecology.

The focus on the founder population, when European colonists still interacted regularly with the non-European laborers, also makes it inaccurate to invoke a break in the transmission of the lexifier as a reason for the restructuring of the latter into a creole. After the creole non-Europeans appropriated the lexifier in basically the same form as the European colonists did (viz., a colonial koiné), they functioned as the linguistic models for the non-Europeans who arrived later in the colonies. There was thus no time when the lexifier was not normally transmitted from one group to another, even as it was restructured in the process. We should ask ourselves whether there are cases when a language is not restructured even minimally while it is acquired by another group or generation of speakers. Even language transmission through the scholastic medium has not prevented restructuring, as discussed in chapter 4.

The Founder Principle does not preclude later influence as the ethnographic conditions of the contact setting changed during the gradual and protracted development of the new vernacular, especially during its basilectalization phase. However, during this process, features of the founder variety often had selective advantage. A partial explanation is that populations did not double or triple overnight; growth was achieved by installments, each of which generally brought a group which was a minority relative to the local creole and the already seasoned slave population. Under such circumstances, it must have been more cost-effective to try to speak the local vernacular as such, even if not so successfully, rather than to try to modify or replace it. This caused the founder population's features to be more and more entrenched within the language community.

Admittedly, in situations such as the development of Saramaccan, the new group consisting of slaves speaking (restructured) colonial Portuguese varieties did significantly influence the development of what had started from an English lexifier. However, such situations are uncommon and correspond to massive influxes of newcomers including new managers of the economic system (e.g., the Shephardic Jews who brought slaves from Brazil). All this happened also thanks to a transition from English to Dutch domination during which the system left behind by the English colonists was both inherited and modified. The adoption of the English-based lingua franca itself is evidence for the Founder Principle.

The Founder Principle can also be invoked to explain the retention of French creoles in territories that the French colonial system lost, e.g., Mauritius, Dominica, and St. Lucia: the extant local vernacular just prevailed. Likewise, it accounts for the survival of a French creole in Trinidad, though an interpretation more sensitive to the beginning of the British colonial regime is required here to make sense of the process. According to Holm (1989), there was massive immigration of planters and their slaves from neighboring francophone islands in 1763. One wonders whether the francophones were not integrated with the anglophones, at least for a significant while.

It should also be emphasized that structural features need not have been selected into a creole with their forms or functions preserved intact

(Boretzky 1993). Chaudenson's trope of "matériau de construction" is particularly apt because it does not preclude alterations for the purposes of meeting communicative needs in the new vernacular. For instance, loss of the copula in several syntactic environments and of inflections in the emerging creoles was bound to affect the selection of some constructions from the lexifiers for tense and aspect. Thus French *être après de* + Infinitive was adapted to the copula-less *ap(e)* + Verb Stem in Haitian Creole.

Regarding function, the reinterpretation of the STATIVE/NONSTATIVE distinction is noteworthy. As habits are typically expressed with either specific adverbials or special preverbal markers, the distinction has been reassigned to interpreting time reference for predicates in the absence of inflections and any other indicators of time. In the domain of nominal number, the absence of an INDEFINITE PLURAL in most of these new vernaculars has caused NONINDIVIDUATED to subsume GENERIC reference too. Other noteworthy developments include the clause-introducer *sɛ* (< English *say*) in English creoles, which, while retaining its quotative function, has also acquired a complementizer function (Mufwene 1989a, 1996a). Likewise, based on (partial) models in English itself, the morpheme *fi/fu/fɔ* (< *for*) has not only retained its basic function as a preposition, but also developed modal and complementizer functions (Mufwene 1989a, 1996a). The models include constructions such as *I'd like for John to come* (with the complementizer *to* generally dispensed with) and *this is for you/cleaning up* (with the copula and the gerund -*ing* marker also omitted in the emergent vernacular). The same principles which apply in the context of grammaticization to exapting uses of extant constructions and making them consistent with the rules of the extant grammar appear to have also applied in the development of creoles. As noted above, the development of each creole seems to have involved several concurrent restructuring processes, with a number of them conspiring to produce new grammatical peculiarities.

Whether or not creoles are treated as dialects of their lexifiers – an issue that is highly political – the structures of these vernaculars can be interpreted as having resulted in part from several concurrent processes of grammaticization. The whole evolutionary trajectory from the lexifier to specific creoles was continuous. Grammaticization is of course not the full story, since other evolutionary processes took place, starting with the simple selection and reintegration into one system of forms, structures, and principles which did not use to form one system even in the lexifier itself. Sylvain (1936), which could well be interpreted as one of the best defenses for combined superstrate and substrate influence, shows clearly how many diverse varieties of nonstandard French were the sources of several of Haitian Creole's forms and structures. For instance, Sylvain relates *kišoy* "something" to Norman *qui chose* [ki šoz] (p. 53); *yo* "they, them" directly to Gascony and Auvergne *yo* rather than the standard French *eux* "they, them" (p. 65); *yõ* "one" to Norman *yon* (p. 74); the anterior marker *te* to Picardy *té* (past participle of *être* "be") (p. 138); and the PERFECT marker *fin* to similar uses of *fini* in central France dialects (p. 139). Much remains to be understood about the principles which, at least at the communal level, permitted such diverse sources to contribute to the development of the new vernacular.

Unfortunately, the above kind of explanation has been hurriedly dismissed by misinvoking the Cafeteria Principle. Yet, there is no empirical evidence for the tacit assumption that a language is transmitted wholesale from one group of speakers to another. Even children acquire it piecemeal, unpacking it and recreating it with variable degrees of success. Since linguistic contact (at the level of idiolect, dialect, or language) takes place in the minds of individual speakers and there is no reason why the coexistent systems must be kept (neatly) apart, there is no particular reason why "matériaux de construction" cannot have been selected from different sources initially for the purposes of establishing successful communication, with the unplanned result of producing a new language variety. Nettle (1999:5) apparently espouses the same view in observing that "Languages are not phylogenetically homogeneous units; instead their traits often derive from multiple sources in a way that depends on the origin and cultural affiliation of their speakers." The literature on code-mixing suggests that this should be part of normal evolution. What we have always needed to account for the development of creoles is a set of principles that account for how competing forms and constructions have been selected into the new vernaculars.

I have proposed the Founder Principle, like the ecology-based model of markedness, to articulate more explicitly what is involved in the development of creoles according to the complementary hypothesis as characterized in section 2.2.1. In my version of this position, substrate and superstrate elements are the only ones involved in the competition of features, especially as far as structural principles are concerned. The language bioprogram qua Universal Grammar functions as a body of principles regulating the selection of features into creoles' systems, like into those of non-creole language varieties. Much remains to be articulated about the nature of Universal Grammar itself, including the selection principles I have been alluding to.

The status of the markedness principles in Universal Grammar is discussed in Mufwene (1991a). There I argue that markedness values are determined relative to the ecology of restructuring by diverse factors which sometimes yield different selections in different contact settings. Sometimes the factors also conflict naturally with each other in the same ecology. In such cases the more heavily weighted factor may prevail; but the competing alternatives may also be retained, producing normal variation in the system. Neither the weighting nor the values are determined in Universal Grammar, although the factors determining the values may be identifiable by it. The Founder Principle is likewise an ecological factor external to Universal Grammar, but it works concurrently with it in constraining the restructuring which results in a creole or any other restructured language variety. In relation to the complementary hypothesis, the Founder Principle helps define the pool of competing features from among which a subset is selected into a creole's system.

In this context, we may also examine the question of whether restructured varieties of European languages previously spoken in Africa, e.g., Guinea Coast Creole English (GCCE), may have served as the basis from which English Atlantic creoles of the New World would have been developed (Hancock 1980; McWhorter 1995, 1998). Several questions arise which can be formulated but not answered here. First, what was the form of GCCE? Second, were its speakers among the founder populations of English colonies? Third, what proportion did they represent of subsequent populations during the basilectalization phase of the creoles? Fourth, did GCCE have any chance of being preserved during the homestead phase of the development of the colonies?

If one could speak of perfect language acquisition at all, let alone of perfect second language acquisition among adults, patterns of interaction during the homestead phase could have favored such linguistic developments. However, although discrimination existed, it was less race-based and not compounded with segregation. There is no evidence that non-European non-native speakers of the lexifier had less linguistic success than European non-native speakers under the same ethnographic conditions. One must wait until the eighteenth century for suggestions that non-Europeans spoke the colonial lingua franca differently. Further, such divergent speech is usually associated with slaves who were born in, or had recently arrived from, Africa. Otherwise, the silence on language can be interpreted to suggest that during the homestead phase non-Europeans did not speak the colonial lingua franca differently from European speakers, matching locally born with locally born and nonnative speakers with nonnative speakers in each case. Sometimes one comes across explicit references to Africans speaking the lingua franca well, such as the observation by Father Labbat cited earlier and the following from Kulikoff (1986:317) who quotes Jones (1724) as saying that "slaves born in Virginia 'talk good English, and affect our language, habits, and customs'" (1956 edition, pp. 75–6). The creole non-white children certainly spoke the same colonial (koiné) varieties of the lexifiers as the creole white children did and they became the models for subsequent immigrants, especially after segregation was institutionalized.

So, are there any particular ethnographic reasons why GCCE would have prevailed as a founder variety and would have influenced the development of particular creoles? We can refer this question to Le Page and Tabouret-Keller's (1985:26) position that the development of most creoles could not escape the influence of previous lingua francas used before the development of New World communities and the like. However, like Rickford (1987), I find no evidence in the history of the slave trade that suggests that even a significant proportion of slaves imported from Africa during the seventeenth and early eighteenth centuries would have been familiar with GCCE. It is not even clear how widespread this variety was during that time. Huber (1999) argues that it was not and that Portuguese was more commonly used as a trade language in the region.

The Founder Principle thus offers us some ways of addressing in an enlightening fashion this important genetic question about whether GCCE played a central role in the development of Atlantic creoles. Similar questions could be raised about the role of varieties used in contacts between the Indians and the Europeans in the New World before the Africans became the primary component of the labor populations (Emmanuel Drechsel, p.c. October 1994; Baker 1996). History suggests that the role of pidgins used in European–Native American interactions would be negligible, primarily because those contact varieties were typically based on Native American languages, not on European languages (Goddard 1997; Buccini 1999). A second reason is that colonial communities during the homestead phase developed on concessions in which the Africans and Europeans lived more intimately with each other than with the Native Americans with whom some of them traded. The Africans need not have depended on Native Americans to appropriate the language varieties spoken by the Europeans.

To close, the Founder Principle offers a useful perspective from which we may address various, though not all, aspects of the complex question of the development of creoles as mixed languages, with features coming from diverse sources and possibly at different stages of their gradual and protracted development. It enriches the complementary hypothesis by providing it more solid grounding in the socioeconomic history of the development of creoles and by directing attention to specific critical periods, even if these may not literally involve founder populations.

3 The development of American Englishes: factoring contact in and the social bias out

In this chapter I take up some of the positions and issues not elaborated in chapter 2, especially the assumption that koinéization played a role in the development of White American English vernaculars (WAEV). I maintain that they are contact-based and developed by the same restructuring processes which produced the vernaculars called creoles. The myth that WAEVs have been inherited almost intact from England, whereas African-American English (AAE) varieties represent their corruption by contact with African languages cannot remain unchallenged. The fact that no single WAEV is a match of any British English vernacular, although many of their features can individually be matched across both sides of the Atlantic, deserves an explanation. Part of the explanation lies in the competition-and-selection process submitted in chapters 1 and 2. Contact of dialects and of languages was as much a factor in the development of WAEVs as of AAE.

3.1 Introduction

This chapter is largely programmatic. I primarily intend to be provocative and invite readers to re-examine several poorly justified assumptions about the status and origin of American English varieties. I do not provide (conclusive) answers to several questions I raise, although I suggest new research avenues. The term *American English* is pluralized in the title, on the model of the more common term *new Englishes*, simply to emphasize diversity over the typically suggested uniformity in the anglophone linguistic universe of the USA. Thus I expect to be consistent with research in American dialectology. After all, the unifying singular term makes more sense to one who wishes to compare national varieties than to one who focuses on variation within a polity.[1]

The variation which I discuss is primarily ethnic. I focus especially on African-American and white nonstandard varieties. This simply reflects the background of my scholarship on Gullah, a by-product of rice agriculture, and on African-American vernacular English (AAVE), a by-product of tobacco and cotton agriculture. Sometimes I do not distinguish these vernaculars from each other, typically when I discuss points which apply equally to both as being English varieties appropriated by descendants of Africans in the United States. Thus I use the name AAE. This lumping is justified by several features which they share (Mufwene 2000b). Ironically, it is also suggested by the position of some creolists (e.g., Holm 1988, 1991) and dialectologists (e.g., Schneider 1990), who identify AAVE as a semi-creole in relation to Gullah – presumably a *bona fide* creole – and thus suggest a common "creole(-like)" element. See Mufwene (1997a) for further reasons.

Among the questions addressed in this essay are the following. Why are WAEVs not characterized as creoles? Why has the term *creole* been applied only to Gullah and maybe also to AAVE?[2] Why does the literature suggest, and why do most lay people assume, that WAEVs are more natural offspring of English than AAE is?

According to Algeo (1991:637), WAEVs differ from varieties of English in the UK because the British settlers in North America no longer communicated regularly with their relatives in the motherland, because "changes in the English of England were slow to reach America," because "the colonists were forced to talk about new physical features, flora, and fauna," because "they had to talk in new ways in order to communicate with their new neighbors" who spoke, or had spoken, Native American languages, French, Dutch, German, or African languages, and because "the settlers [who] had come from various districts and social groups in England" and lived and interacted together "came to talk more and more like one another and less and less like any particular community in England. All these influences combined to make American English a distinct variety of English."

Do the above causes of the distinctiveness of WAEVs, relative to British varieties, differ in nature from those which account for the distinctiveness of AAE varieties? Can extent of restructuring alone justify characterizing Gullah in particular as a separate language and not a dialect of English? Or does the appropriation of a language by a segregated ethnic group justify treating it as a less natural, if not less legitimate, offspring of its lexifier? In other words, may linguistic research have contributed to disfranchising a particular ethnic group?

Like AAE, WAEVs and other varieties of English in the USA are outcomes of language contact (Mufwene 1999d). They are all outputs of the same restructuring equation; differences among them can be explained by assigning different values to its variables. I am still unable to formulate the equation – which is very likely **nonlinear** – in a specific algebraic formula; but I have a sense of some variables it must include, for instance, the nature of the diverse dialects of English brought over by the British colonists, the coexistence of English speakers in the colonies with speakers of other languages, the demographic proportions of speakers of the language varieties in contact during the critical periods of the development of new English varieties, the kinds of social contacts between the different social and ethnic groups during the formative stages of the new varieties, the structural features of the varieties that were actually in contact, the rate of immigrations after the (original) formative stages, the origins of the new immigrants, their social status (which may be correlated with prestige or lack thereof), their proportions relative to the preceding populations, and the patterns of integration within the extant populations.

The above are not by any means all the variables which form part of the relevant ecology. However, they give us a sense of how, *ceteris paribus*, the same language appropriated in the colonies by different groups – which were not equally integrated in the broader American speech community and which did not form the same intimate communication networks – has developed different varieties. The more variables differ in their values, the more cross-systemic variation in outputs of the restructuring is undergone by the lexifier. Using the term *equation* as an informal reference to the complex of interactive factors affecting the development of a language within a particular ethnographic ecology (chapter 6), I submit that the same equation may be used to account for the emergence of the varieties generally identified as American.

3.2 Why are WAEVs (White American English Vernaculars) not creoles?

I assume here the definition of *creole* summarized in section 1.2. It is worth repeating here, however, that nowhere is it explicitly stated in the histories of the relevant territories what requisite structural features a colonial vernacular lexified by a European language must possess in order to be identified as a creole. History and European linguistic systems suggest that in most cases the adjectival uses of the term *creole* meant no more than the association of a vernacular or animal or vegetal species with the colonies, aside from the fact that they exhibited differences from the Old World models. In the case of language varieties, characterizing them adjectivally as creole was a vague way of acknowledging that they had diverged structurally from their lexifiers.

Since the noun *creole* was used as much for people of European descent as for those of African descent – from mixed and nonmixed parents – born in the colonies, the adjective could equally well have been extended to colonial varieties spoken by descendants of Europeans. Thus, WAEVs and other colonial varieties spoken by descendants of Europeans could have been identified as creoles too. This has, however, not been the case.

To be sure, in the English New World, the noun *creole* was typically not used for descendants of either Africans or Europeans born in the colonies, despite Berlin's (1998) uses of the term, almost exclusively in reference to Blacks in the English North American colonies. Diverging linguistic features of European colonists were attributed by default to influence of the Africans whom they had as nannies or interacted with. It is in part against this gratuitous explanation that Krapp (1924), Kurath (1928), Johnson (1930), and Crum (1940) speak when they argue that the descendants of Africans speak the kind of nonstandard English that their ancestors learned from the indentured servants they interacted with. Thus, in English, as in other European languages, there has been an interesting development of the meaning of *creole* which has associated the word more and more with people who did not descend (fully) from Europeans and were not indigenous to the colonies; their language varieties were disfranchised by the same term.[3]

This practice, which is simply social, does not rule out the conclusion suggested by the socioeconomic history of North America (grounded as it is in population movements and contacts), viz., that WAEVs have also developed from dialect and language contact. Much of the confusion over the development of WAEVs seem to come from unjustified attempts in linguistics to characterize creole vernaculars structurally and to treat their formation as untypical of presumably natural and/or regular historical developments, free of influence from language contact. Some unjustified working assumptions, on which I focus in chapter 5, have led linguists to present WAEVs as results of normal transmission from their British ancestors, but creole vernaculars as those cases that regular diachronic processes cannot account for. As explained in section 2.2.3, there is no sociohistorical backing for the often-repeated claim that creole vernaculars developed in settings in which there was a break in the transmission of the lexifier from one group to another. Despite the institutionalization of race segregation early in rice field colonies and much later in the cotton plantation states (in the late nineteenth century), the lexifier need not have been transmitted through European speakers. There was no break in the transmission of English to and among descendants of Africans at any point in time, despite the continual restructuring of the lexifier into AAE.

Linguists' attempts to characterize creole vernaculars structurally – as if any noncreole languages or nontypological groups of languages could be so defined – have failed miserably. The only valid reasons for discussing them as an interesting group of languages are the sociohistorical conditions of their development (Mufwene 1986a, 1997a) and any opportunity they may give linguists to note and further investigate matters that have been overlooked in the diachronic and synchronic study of other languages.

Such opportunities arise any time one verifies a universal or typological claim against any particular language, especially those that have been rarely investigated. From a diachronic perspective, knowledge gained from understanding the ecologies in which creoles developed and the impact of such conditions on language evolution should lead us to re-examine our hypotheses on language evolution, including some of our working assumptions.

I should emphasize that an attempt to account for the development of WAEVs from the perspective of population movements, language contact, and the ensuing restructuring does not entail that they too must be treated as creoles. Had it not been for the particular sociohistorical circumstances which brought about the term *creole*, we would still be facing the same diachronic facts calling for a more adequate correlation of ecological conditions and structural change. I show in the next chapters that evidence of contact-induced language restructuring can also be found at any stage in the histories of languages, for instance in the development of Romance languages, in the emergence of Old English, and in the respective speciations of Bantu and Indo-European languages. There is no particular reason why ecological factors should have been given more attention in the case of creoles than in that of noncreoles (with the exception of Trudgill 1986 and a handful of others). Nor is there any justification for assuming *a priori* that it is mostly internally motivated change in the case of WAEVs but externally motivated evolution in the case of AAE, contrary to what the socioeconomic history of the region suggests.

The same language restructuring equation applies to both cases, except that different values are assigned for each variety to (some of) the algebraic variables. The rest boils down to the saying "What's in a name?" As a Gullah speaker told me in 1986: "You call [our vernacular] Gullah; we call it English." Siding with this Gullah speaker, I submit that creole vernaculars are legitimate offspring of their lexifiers, assuming that genetic ties have been determined to date not necessarily by structural similarities but firstly by the lexical kinship of the relevant language varieties (chapter 4).

Some scholars may not agree with me, but it remains that AAE developed from English around the same time as WAEVs. For several practical reasons which I will not detail here, those who developed AAE varieties meant no more than to speak as their vernacular the politically dominant language of the then English colonies. That their varieties became different is as much an academic curiosity as the divergence of WAEVs from British varieties of English. Hence we have nothing to lose in attempting a methodology which sheds light on diverse factors which bear on language restructuring, which is the case for all American Englishes. The challenge is to articulate differences in the values assumed by some structural and ethnographic variables of the proposed language contact equation. I assume that differences in the variables' values account for differences in outputs, in this case, AAE and WAEVs. I show below that these assumptions are well justified sociohistorically.

3.3   The development of AAE (African-American English)

I have reviewed the debate on the development of AAE in Mufwene (1992c, 1997c, 1999b). Here I will limit myself to a statement of the major issues and my own conclusions, including an articulation of the questions which must be addressed in order to adequately account for the divergent developments of Gullah and AAVE.

Among the most commonly debated questions are the following: (i) Did AAVE start from a Gullah-like creole formerly spoken by all African Americans in the United States (Labov 1972a, 1982; Fasold 1976, 1981; Rickford 1977; Cassidy 1986a; Hancock 1986b; Winford 1992)?[4] If so, when did the debasilectalization process which putatively produced it stop and when did its recently claimed divergence from White vernaculars begin (Labov and Harris 1986; Bailey and Maynor 1987)? (ii) Did AAVE start from a West African pidgin English, which "creolized" first and later "decreolized" (Stewart 1967; Dillard 1972)? (iii) Does the development of AAVE amount to some sort of relexification of West African languages (DeBose and Faraclas 1993)? (iv) Did Gullah develop primarily according to structures of (West-)African languages (Alleyne 1980; Wade-Lewis 1988)?[5] (v) Does AAE reflect retentions from nonstandard varieties of colonial/British English and has it therefore been influenced more by these varieties than by African languages (Krapp 1924; Kurath 1928, Johnson 1930; Crum 1940; D'Eloia 1973; Schneider 1982, 1983)?[6] I will try to answer these questions briefly and then state what I take to be the most adequate explanation of the genesis of AAE, accounting differentially for the developments of AAVE and Gullah and allowing congruent and/or complementary influences from both the lexifier and the substrate languages.

3.3.1   A critique of the literature

3.3.1.1   The "**creole origins hypothesis**," according to which AAVE developed from an erstwhile Gullah-like creole, is a convenient starting point. An important motivation behind this position, also known as the "decreolization hypothesis," has been similarities noted since Beryl Bailey (1965) between AAVE and Caribbean English creoles. Later studies pointing out such similarities include Stewart (1967, 1968, 1969, 1974), Holm (1976, 1984), Rickford (1977), Baugh (1980), Mufwene (1983b), and Winford

(1992, 1993). Except for Mufwene (1983b), which suggests that the relation may be simply typological, and for Winford (1993), which reinterprets "decreolization" as a shift from the creole previously spoken by some slaves to the new vernacular that was just emerging, these studies generally suggest that there was a common or identical basilect from which all New World English creoles started and from which they have been changing.

Structural similarities alone do not lend strong support to the creole origins hypothesis, because those similarities could also be due to similarities of inputs and circumstances of development. The conditions do not necessarily suggest a parent-to-offspring relation between AAVE and a Gullah-like ancestor. History suggests that because the contact conditions in different territories and on different plantations were not identical, AAVE must have started quite different from, though related in some respects to, Gullah and Caribbean creole kin. For instance, not all plantations started at the same time, under the same population disproportion conditions, with identical compositions of the founder populations, or with the same terms of interaction between Europeans and Africans. Nor did change occur within the same period of time from the homestead setting to the plantation setting. Their populations grew neither at the same rate nor with identical ethnolinguistic additions within the plantation phase.

As shown in chapter 2, sugar cane plantations in Guyana seem to have developed faster than did rice fields in coastal South Carolina, within about twenty years. Recall, however, the Guyanese colony started later, around 1740, as opposed to 1670 for the South Carolina colony. The African population of South Carolina remained smaller than the European population for the first twenty-five years and became its double only after fifty years, around which time segregation was institutionalized. It is in the second half of the eighteenth century that the African:European disproportion started decreasing in favor of the European population. As shown in table 5 (in chapter 2), by the late eighteenth century, European Americans became the majority again and things have not since changed. The exception remains the coastal area, where African Americans remained a significant proportion of the population (though no longer the majority) in some counties where the rice agricultural industry boomed, until probably the early twentieth century.

Yet in Guyana, as in other British Caribbean colonies, the proportion of populations of British and other European origins has remained a very small minority since the eighteenth century. These language-external ecological differences alone account for some of the structural differences between, on the one hand, AAE and, on the other, Guyanese and Caribbean English creoles. When AAE started developing, perhaps toward the end of the seventeenth century, the socioeconomic conditions in

Barbados (then the major supplier of slaves to English colonies) favored both the exportation of slaves who had come freshly from Africa and the emigration of homestead slaves with owners who had been put out of business by the growth of large plantations (Mufwene 1999b).

That is, if Caribbean creoles had already developed by the same period, very few slaves speaking them would have come to North America. Moreover, soon after the early eighteenth century, only a very small proportion of slaves came from the Caribbean: 10 percent for Virginia and only 15 percent for South Carolina (Rawley 1991). The bulk of slaves during the formative years of AAE came from Africa. During the seventeenth century, Virginia relied primarily on European indentured labor, and South Carolina's Europeans did not have enough capital to launch into the plantation industry and import slaves. They lived in small homesteads, where the integrated living conditions were not conducive to the development of a creole. Even those slaves who may have spoken Creole had no reason for sticking to it, and their children certainly did not inherit it. In Virginia, where the majority of Africans lived on small farms or worked as domestics during the seventeenth century, a period during which the slave population grew more by birth than by importation (Thomas 1998), there is no reason why (most) Black native-born children would have developed a creole. What little evidence we have from advertisements on runaway slaves suggests that those born locally spoke English well, albeit the same nonstandard koiné varieties that the mostly proletarian European colonists spoke. All the above ecological conditions argue against a dominant influence of a Gullah-like creole on the development of AAVE. Gullah itself must have started developing later than AAVE, as the South Carolina colony started much later.

In general, the agricultural settlements were demographically smaller in North America than in the Caribbean (Curtin 1990). Cotton plantations required fewer laborers than tobacco plantations, and these in turn required fewer laborers than rice fields. Sugar plantations, which were almost the norm in the eighteenth-century Caribbean, required even more laborers. Although Barbados was colonized early, soon after Virginia, it started with tobacco cultivation and only later got into sugar cane agriculture. This suggests that Barbadian Creole, for which there is nineteenth-century evidence (Rickford and Handler 1994; Fields 1995) may not have developed there as early as has been suspected. Besides, as suggested above, it is misguided to assume that importing slaves from a previously developed plantation or colony to develop another one necessarily entailed the continuation of the variety spoken in the previous plantation or colony. While this was true of the Netherlands Antilles, where the slaves imported from Brazil maintained what developed into Papiamentu (Goodman 1982), it was not true of Suriname, where Portuguese-speaking slaves imported from Brazil around the same time (section 2.1.1) shifted to the local English vernaculars. (Part of the evidence for this view lies in the contribution of Portuguese to, for instance, Saramaccan, up to 30 percent of which is composed of Portuguese lexical items, according to Byrne 1987.)

The influence of the relocated slave populations depended very much on what the initial demographic size and composition of the new plantation or colony were like, how long this initial phase lasted, whether or not there was a founder slave population, and what patterns of interaction were present between this founder population and its European counterpart during the initial period. More or less the same considerations apply even when no slaves were relocated from a previous colony or plantation.

Although my conjecture still depends in part on missing diachronic linguistic evidence, history suggests that no common cross-territory English basilect could possibly have developed that was spoken universally by Africans and their descendants in all British colonies. Invoking decreolization qua debasilectalization to account for variation today among creoles, and between them and AAVE, is also inconsistent with the observation that the new vernaculars developed in the direction of basilectalization. As argued in chapter 2, the more intimately the Africans lived with the Europeans, the more similar their vernaculars must have been to those of the indentured servants with whom they interacted on a regular basis, typically before the institutionalization of segregation or its *de facto* adoption as a *modus vivendi*. The high proportion of mulattoes during the early stages of colonization (Wood 1974; Berlin 1998) is evidence of the less restricted relations between the mostly European indentured servants and the African slaves during those initial periods.

In the United States, history also suggests that we not lump together the development of Gullah and AAVE. Gullah was a special rice field phenomenon, which developed in conditions similar to sugar cane plantations, which required large slave labor and produced the most drastic disproportions between Europeans and Africans. In British North America (especially in the eighteenth century), these conditions obtained only in coastal South Carolina and Georgia. According to some historians (Wood 1974; Coleman 1978), 85–90 percent of African slaves in the eighteenth century lived in the coastal plantations owned by about 5 percent of the European colonial population.

The Virginia colony, from which most of the laborers were (originally) imported to work on the cotton plantations of Alabama and Mississippi, with which no Gullah-like creole is associated, was developed almost half a century before South Carolina. According to Kulikoff (1986) and Perkins (1988), most of the Virginia planters preferred indentured servants and did not use much African labor until 1680, seventy-three years after this first British North American and Caribbean colony was founded. At the peak of slavery, the Africans hardly exceeded 40 percent of the total Virginian colonial population. Overall, the tobacco and cotton plantations used less labor than the rice fields of coastal South Carolina and Georgia. Besides, the slaves in Virginia were integrated for a longer time than in the other two states. The initial homestead living conditions lasted longer in Virginia, in which the overall contact ecology does not seem to have been conducive to the extensive restructuring of the lexifier associated with creoles.

Even if part of the original slave populations in the South Carolina and Georgia hinterlands, and later in Alabama and Mississippi, had come from creole-speaking settlements in the West Indies, is it justified to assume that these people would have stuck to the varieties of their backgrounds while living in settings in which they were minorities and in conditions which might have motivated them to speak in new ways? Is it not more plausible to assume, like Winford (1993), that creole speakers would have then shifted immediately to something closer to present-day AAVE, or closer to the current approximations of the lexifier?

It seems that different ethnographic conditions led to the development of different vernaculars. In new settings where interactive conditions were different – as on the cotton plantations – and in which new language varieties were developing, even people who had spoken creoles previously would have had to adjust to the emerging systems, with their children more likely to acquire the local vernacular quite successfully. This scenario is different from "decreolization" as a wholesale gradual restructuring of a creole or its basilect in the direction of the acrolect.

There is little, if any, diachronic evidence for debasilectalization (Lalla and D'Costa 1990; Mille 1990; Mufwene 1991d, 1994a). Even the changes reported by Rickford (1987) about Guyanese Creole can be reinterpreted as the normal changes which occur in a particular language (Mufwene 1989c:126, n. 2), regardless of whether or not it is subordinated to another. There are in any language forms and constructions which older speakers used but which have fallen out of fashion. One of the strongest arguments against debasilectalization, and one which has hardly been considered, is that members of lower classes do not organize their cultures by emulating those of the upper classes, although they learn to accommodate the latter while interacting with them. With or without success, they do this by code-switching (Mufwene 1999c).

Another important motivation behind the creole origins hypothesis has been variation not only in AAVE but also in the creoles themselves, in relation to which the terms *basilect* and *mesolect* were originally coined. The evidence about this remains controversial. The Samaná and Nova Scotia evidence (Poplack and Tagliamonte 1991, 1994; Tagliamonte 1988, 1993) suggest no debasilectalization. Poplack (1999) is especially informative. The comparisons with West Indian creoles seem misguided, in part because they gratuitously assume a common basilect for the varieties compared and in part because the West Indian creoles are not related to AAE in the same way that Samaná and Nova Scotia AAE varieties are. The latter represent AAE varieties that were exported to enclave communities in which the influence of the local vernaculars has been minimal. The West Indian slaves who came to North America joined both the local slaves who preceded them and the more numerous groups that were being imported from Africa during the eighteenth century.

What should also retain our attention in the debate based on evidence from offshoots of AAE is what is suggested by the Liberian Settler English data (Singler 1991a, 1991b), viz., that the nineteenth-century AAE which was taken over to Liberia was not as communally homogeneous as is typically assumed. This does not contradict Poplack and Tagliamonte, although Charles DeBose (p.c., 1994) believes that such a conclusion depends on what sample one collects in Samaná.

Misunderstandings about how creoles began account largely for the unjustified assumption that basilects are homogeneous and creoles started with them. To begin with, monolithic languages without variation, if there are any natural ones, fall into the category of exceptions. The history of the development of creoles presented in chapter 2 suggests that there must have been a lot of variation at the beginning and even after the creoles had normalized. In the particular case of AAE, it is significant that the sources researched by Brasch (1981) not only expose variation in its structure in the mid-eighteenth century but also suggest that the basilect did not consolidate until toward the end of the century, contrary to Brasch's own interpretation.[7] Thus both Poplack and Tagliamonte's and Singler's analyses seem consistent with the Brasch materials.

History suggests that divergence, however minimal at first, between varieties spoken by descendants of Africans and those spoken by descendants of Europeans started some time in the late seventeenth or early eighteenth century, depending on the location. Similarly, there is no particular reason for assuming debasilectalization to have affected a putative Gullah-like variety formerly spoken by all Africans and maybe some of their descendants all over the initial USA, or perhaps just in the southern states, to have debasilectalized. Note also that the slave populations were stratified in ways that provided variable access to colonial native varieties of the lexifier. Accordingly, the house slaves for instance had more exposure to it than the vast majority of field hands (Herskovits 1941; Dillard 1972; Alleyne 1980; Joyner 1984). Another reason is that, disregarding variation in individual skills, much depended on whether one interacted the most with and learned the local vernacular from creole or seasoned slaves. At all phases in the development of the colonies, conditions of interaction favored intra-communal variation.

The position summarized above does not of course entail that the Caribbean colonial vernaculars which some slaves brought with them (regardless of whether or not they were already identified as creoles) did not contribute anything at all to the development of AAVE and/or Gullah. Just the opposite. However, their influence competed with those of the more numerous African slaves who were being brought to the North American colonies during the same period. Together, these competing influences were rivaled by the structures that were already emerging locally and had an advantage conferred on them by the Founder Principle (as explained in section 2.2). This is apparently the sense in which Rickford's (1998) position regarding some merits of the creole origins hypothesis must be interpreted.

As the debate continues, it should be remembered that Caribbean and North American English vernaculars developed concurrently. It is misleading to assume that structural features associated with creoles today were necessarily typical of these vernaculars in the seventeenth and early eighteenth centuries. Quite relevant in this respect is also the fact that the creole origins hypothesis does not provide an account of the sources of what have been identified in the literature as "creole features." Cursory analyses such as presented in chapter 2 and much of the ongoing research in English historical dialectology suggest that they had models, at least partial, in the lexifier. The substrate languages played a critical role in their selection and their coevolutionary adaptations to the emerging systems. Thus, structural similarities between especially AAVE and Caribbean creoles do not prove the creole origins hypothesis.

3.3.1.2 Rickford (1998) and Bailey and Thomas (1998) reiterate the position that AAVE is a Southeastern phenomenon which spread northwards and westwards. This view is supported in part by greater similarities between AAVE and Southern White nonstandard varieties of English (McDavid and McDavid 1951, Wolfram 1974). It is also backed by the history of settlements in the USA. The African-American population was of very low density in nonplantation states until the late nineteenth century. The collapse of the Southeastern plantation system in the second half of that century, the increased need for labor in Northern states during World War I, and the economic depression that followed it all encouraged massive African-American exoduses from the Southeast northwards and westwards. This **Great Black Migration** from the rural South[east] continued into the 1960s, making northern and western American cities the new

"focal points of black life" (Katzman 1991). These new populations over-
whelmed the original ones, especially in the ghettoes which perpetuated the
segregation system of the South (Lemann 1991). One thing that was bound
to happen in this transplanted Southern social ecology was an opportunity
for Southeastern AAVE varieties to consolidate among themselves (and
perhaps with local varieties) into an urban variety claimed to be relatively
homogeneous throughout the USA (Labov 1972a:xiii). With a largely
southeastern origin, AAVE normally continues to share several features
with Southeastern English varieties.

However, while the above historical considerations support assuming
that Southeastern AAVE varieties must have influenced the present shape
of AAVE, little is known about what Northern African Americans spoke
before the Great Migration. So, what we learn is only a partial, recent
history of the development of AAVE. Moreover, we learn nothing about its
genesis qua original development, to which I return below.

3.3.1.3 The hypothesis of the Southeastern origin of AAVE is closely
related to the claim since Krapp (1924) that AAE is an archaic retention of
what was spoken by low-class Europeans, largely the indentured servants
with whom the Africans interacted regularly in colonial days. This position
has developed into the "dialectologist position" (Mufwene 1992c, 2000b),
according to which most of the features which make AAE distinctive are of
British and/or colonial English origin. One shortcoming of this genetic
interpretation, at least in its original form, was its claim that the African
contributions to AAE were marginal. McDavid (1950) and Schneider
(1993) correct it by making allowance for substrate influence, but one can
still detect a general misunderstanding of how substrate influence operates.

We cannot deny that colonial English as spoken by native and non-native
speakers was targeted by newcomers to British North American colonies.
However, while the earlier speakers set the standards, there were no safe-
guards against restructuring as the language was being appropriated by
non-native speakers as a vernacular for communication more among themselves than with native speakers. As in several such situations around the
world, features of English had to compete with those of substrate languages. Selection principles consistent with the markedness factors summarized in chapter 2 determined whether structural patterns of the lexifier
or of some of the substrate languages would prevail. Because there was
variation even within the lexifier itself, the contribution of African languages must often have consisted in determining which particular variants
of its structural options would prevail, consistent with the principle of **convergence** qua congruence advocated by Thomason (1983) and Thomason
and Kaufman (1988).

For example, attributing to African substrate influence NOMINAL PLURAL with *dem* in AAE, as in *dem boy(s)*, does not entail that such a plural was not attested in varieties of British or colonial English. Rather, it means that the congruence of such a strategy with the pattern in the Mande and Kwa languages of West Africa to mark NOMINAL PLURAL with a third person pronoun adjoined to the head noun favored it over the other English alternative of marking NOMINAL PLURAL by simply suffixing {Z} to the noun. It means that if English had come in contact with languages which did not have the West African patterns, the chances are that this alternative might not have been chosen, as may be observed in some varieties of Melanesian pidgins, which have another strategy for marking NOMINAL PLURAL.

Substrate influence becomes more obvious through the extension of the strategy to mark the ASSOCIATIVE NOMINAL PLURAL, as in *Rita (an) dem* "Rita and family/company." The influence is more general in this case, because in most African languages this semantic delimitative strategy is available, although it may not be implemented in exactly the same way. For instance, in the Bantu languages, the only morphosyntactic requirement is to pluralize the proper name, just like any other noun, in order to convey the ASSOCIATIVE PLURAL meaning. Even in this case, as Talgliamonte (1999) shows, there is a model for the Proper Name + *an' dem* construction in Yorkshire nonstandard vernacular English, although it is not common. Assuming that the pattern is attested in other nonstandard British vernaculars, it is likely to have been in use in (early) colonial English and thus to have been favored by the congruent pattern in African languages over the longer alternative [NP *and company/family*]. The way things worked out in the case of NOMINAL PLURAL also underscores the selective way in which substrate influence applies, showing that even among the African languages themselves there was a competition of features for prevalence in AAVE's and the creole's systems.

Several other examples could be added here to show that among non-native speakers the "matériaux de construction" from the lexifier, were not necessarily used literally according to native principles, and these non-native patterns ultimately crystallized to make AAE varieties distinctive. I will give only one more example here, from Gullah's serial verb constructions. It is true that constructions such as *go/come get* are common in colloquial and nonstandard English. However, these varieties have nothing similar to *Uh tell um come kyah me home* "I told him [to] come [and] drive/take me home." The common usage of serial verb constructions in Kwa and Mande languages and the more restricted usage of similar constructions among Bantu languages (Mufwene 1988a, 1997d) must have favored the extension of the *go/come get* pattern to other verb combinations, a process certainly aided by the loss of verbal inflections in Gullah. It is informative that in those cases where Africans had relatively greater exposure to the English spoken by Europeans, as in the case of AAVE (basically the by-product of tobacco and cotton plantations), serial verb constructions are just on the basic English pattern. This observation underscores again the role of external ecological factors in the development of AAE varieties, as of other contact-induced varieties.

3.3.1.4 In the case of Gullah, Turner (1949) adduced African linguistic evidence to dispute the early and strong dialectologist position that AAE was archaic colonial English which low-class European Americans had presumably abandoned. Since the early 1970s, the substrate hypothesis has been advocated mostly in reference to creoles. However, the following references are noteworthy: Alleyne (1980, 1996), Allsopp (1977), DeBose and Faraclas (1993), Holm (1988, 1993), Wade Lewis (1988), and Selase Williams (1993).

Among the greatest merits of Turner's (1949) thesis are his own conclusion that "Gullah is indebted to African sources" (p. 254), and his observation that one cannot draw genetic conclusions about Gullah or any other AAE variety without paying attention to structures of African languages.[8] Note that, although he devotes the whole book to demonstrating African linguistic contributions to Gullah, Turner nowhere claims that the entire grammatical system of this vernacular is African. It is his followers who have promoted substratism as if it alone could account for every aspect of New World creoles. They have given the false impression that the Africans and their descendants were resolved to preserve their African speech habits intact and develop new language varieties that would be unintelligible to speakers of their lexifiers.[9] As explained in previous chapters, these new vernaculars were simple accidents of the ways the lexifiers were appropriated by the Africans in settings in which they were not (fully) integrated in native speaker communities, and by the principle of imperfect replication.[10]

One of the strongest criticisms of substratists has focused on their failure to explain whether the influences attributed to diverse and competing African languages was principled (Bickerton 1981; Mufwene 1991b). They seldom made reference to selection principles. Invocation of areal features such as by Gilman (1986) does not account for features which have been central to the debate on creole genesis, such as time reference, serial verb constructions, and nominal number. Until the early 1990s, little reference was made to historical accounts of the timing and patterns of slave importations in North America (e.g., Wood 1974; Rawley 1981, 1991; and Lovejoy 1982, 1989), in order to justify, if only partially, invocations of some African languages or ethnolinguistic groups (especially the Kwa group) in accounts of substrate influence (e.g., Mufwene 1992b). Likewise, substratists have not really articulated the kinds of conditions that are likely to favor such influence. Comparisons with central-African contact-induced varieties such as Kituba should shed light on this subject matter, since Kituba's morphosyntax diverges in several respects from the Bantu canon; this despite the fact that it developed in a Bantu ethnographic ecology and out of the contact of primarily Bantu languages (Mufwene 1994b). By the same token, comparisons with Melanesian pidgins would help; for instance, they display incontrovertible substrate features which make them structurally different from Atlantic creoles. Keesing (1988) and Corne (1999) make excellent demonstrations of the role of the ethnolinguistic–ethnographic ecology of language contact in demonstrating substrate influence.

3.3.2   What history suggests: a Feature-Competition Hypothesis

Having critiqued conventional accounts of the genesis of AAE (often in the general context of New World creoles), I now wish to propose an account of my own for its development. I focus first on Gullah and its socioeconomic ecology in the rice fields, and sometimes on sugar cane plantation phenomena, for the sake of generality and/or comparison. Then I turn to AAVE, the tobacco and cotton plantation phenomenon. I do not overlook the effect of the "Great Black Migration" mentioned above.

Recall that the plantations of the New World developed in phases, beginning with small homesteads, in which Africans and Europeans lived fairly intimately (Wood 1974). Thereafter, some of the homesteads gradually evolved into large plantations. Though there are exceptions, it generally took thirty to fifty years for a territory to switch from a predominantly fur trade and small farming system to the plantation system as the dominant industry and the principal employer of slave and indentured labor. The plantations used most of the African slaves, 85–90 percent in the American Southeast by the mid-eighteenth century (Coleman 1978). However, the other 10–15 percent were on small farms or lived with fur traders and interacted regularly with Europeans. Segregation was institutionalized first on the coastal plantations of South Carolina and Georgia, where the Africans gained an early majority.[11]

With segregation began separate developments of Black and White speech varieties, although they were bound to share a few features not only because of interactions between the two groups at work but also because they shared basically the same lexifier consisting originally of nonstandard varieties of English. Among the coastal Africans, the basilectalization of the lexifier must have peaked during the periods of maximal growth for the plantations, typically before the abolition of slavery and when the plantation populations grew more by importation of new slaves than by birth. As explained in chapter 2, this is also a period when the mortality rate was high, among both adults and children. The influx of newcomers, who quickly outnumbered the creole populations, favored the basilectalization process. Demographic ecological differences between rice fields and cotton plantations explain why basilectalization started earlier and proceeded farther in Gullah than in AAVE. AAVE has remained closer to other American nonstandard vernaculars, especially those of the Southeast, in part because the population disproportions in the hinterlands were rarely in favor of the Blacks and because segregation was institutionalized with the passage of the **Jim Crow laws** in 1877, after over two hundred years of shared history between the Black and White populations, despite the practice of discrimination in the colonies since the early seventeenth century.

On the other hand, social stratification among the slaves, with some of them interacting more regularly with the European colonists than others did, produced lexical variation spectra known as (post-)(creole) continua. The fact that not all African slaves lived on plantations also favored the development of variable speech patterns among African Americans. The concentration of rice fields along the coast of South Carolina and Georgia thus laid the groundwork for differences between Gullah and AAVE as regional AAE varieties. The fact that in the eighteenth century a large proportion of the African captives were children (Lovejoy 1989) must have slowed down the wholesale restructuring, as the children were more likely to acquire the local (internally variable) varieties successfully. Thus the development of AAE was not a uniform process.

One must also pay attention to the ethnolinguistic composition of the African slave population. Interestingly, the initial substantial regional investment in rice cultivation (during the second quarter of the eighteenth century) was concurrent with the importation of the vast majority of slaves from central Africa, where the Bantu languages are spoken. This fact raises interesting questions about the high proportion of structural parallelisms with Kwa features rather than Bantu features. For instance, let us consider again the generally periphrastic nature of AAE (and New World creoles) with regard to NOMINAL PLURAL and the tense–aspect system, as well as the prominence of serial verb constructions in Gullah and its Caribbean kin. The earlier Kwa prevalence may be ruled out as irrelevant, because their dominance was during the homestead phases of the development of the colonies. During this period, the slaves spoke closer approximations of the lexifiers (Mufwene 1992b) and Black children certainly spoke the same colonial vernaculars as their White counterparts. We thus must think of feature-selection and principles regulating this process on the model of population genetics.

The proposed approach is favored also by the fact that new language varieties which developed out of the contact of mostly Bantu languages such as Kituba are less agglutinating and thus do not reflect the complex morphosyntax typically presented as the Bantu canon (Mufwene 1994b). Likewise, features of Melanesian pidgins that reflect Melanesian linguistic influence are not as morphologically rich as their models in the Melanesian languages. The numeral classifying system is very much impoverished in the pidgins.

As things stand, the most plausible interpretation of substrate influence in AAE is "the role played by substrate languages in determining which features of any of the languages in contact would be selected into the emergent vernacular." The proportion of features which can be traced exclusively to substrate languages seems to be limited and sometimes confined to some lexico-semantic domains. As discussed in chapter 2, such influence varies from one language variety to another, depending on diverse ecological factors.

An interesting aspect of this model is that it makes the best use of the notion of mixing, on the model of **blending inheritance** in biology. In the animal species, blending inheritance means that an offspring naturally inherits genes from both parents. In other kinds of species (including langue as described in section 1.1), this can be interpreted as follows: an offspring inherits, selectively in the case of idiolects or languages, features from the varieties out of the contact with which it developed. The model proposed here supposes that there was no problem with selecting features from diverse linguistic sources and reorganizing them into a new mixed system, as long as the selection was principled.

However, note that the above seemingly straightforward formula for the development of AAE and other New World creoles is complicated by other factors, including migrations. Intra-national migrations bear especially on the development of AAVE and the cross-regional morphosyntactic homogeneity that some scholars have claimed about it, from the inner cities of the North and West to rural areas of the Southeast.[12]

3.4   The development of WAEVs: a creole perspective

As stated in section 3.2, approaching the development of WAEVs from a language contact perspective does not entail that they are creoles. The history of colonial and postcolonial North America involves population movements and contacts, even among populations of European descent alone. Reference to creoles in this context has to do only with the fact that we have learned more about language evolution under contact conditions in creolistics. Despite the publication of Trudgill (1986), the literature has continued to suggest that WAEVs have developed by internally motivated change, whereas, like its Caribbean creole kin, AAE has developed from language contact. None of the genetic explanations proposed above for AAE rests on the premise that they are creoles, only on the premise that they are contact-induced varieties (Mufwene 1997a). My proposal is to also discuss WAEVs as contact phenomena, sometimes with more emphasis on dialect than language contact, in the spirit of Trudgill (1986). My primary purpose is to highlight similarities and differences in the geneses of AAE and WAEVs.

What initially prompted this perspective is the fact that WAEVs are different from British English varieties, just as they differ from AAE. Interestingly, in several parts of the Southeast, including South Carolina, Alabama, and Mississippi, Europeans and Africans arrived at more or less the same time, although this is literally truer of South Carolina than anywhere else. It has often been claimed that the differences between WAEVs and AAE in the Southeast are slight, but Rickford (1985) shows that the similarities may be superficial only, at least in the Gullah-speaking area. These seemingly similar ethnic vernaculars may well be underlain by different grammatical systems. Wolfram (1974) suggests the same thing for the hinterlands varieties.

Also, despite my observation above that AAE varies regionally, it is still less diverse from one region to another – especially if one focuses on AAVE. There is much more variation among WAEVs, apparently corrresponding to different settlement and contact patterns. These are reminiscent of ecological differences that account for variation between Gullah and AAVE or among Atlantic creoles. Approaching the development of WAEVs in the way we have investigated that of creoles can shed some light on how their structures were formed. Moreover, a comparison of the ways they and creoles developed should shed light on how languages evolve, subject to varying ecological factors. Although this question is the focus of chapter 5, we will anticipate its discussion here.

We may start by trying to answer the question of why outside the American Southeast AAE and WAEVs are so different from each other. Interidiolectal and intra-variety similarities are fostered by regular interactions among speakers. African Americans have not interacted with European Americans in the same way that members of each ethnic group (grossly defined!) have interacted among themselves. Segregation has prevented them from developing identical ethnic varieties. Although language contact was involved in both cases, it was not the same kinds of languages that were involved and would therefore be likely to bear significant consequences in the vernaculars of both groups. African languages were more likely to influence structures of AAE one way or another than they were to influence WAEVs.

However, there are other questions to address, especially because WAEVs have generally been considered less restructured than AAE. If this observation is accurate, how can we account for differences – however slight they might be – between WAEVs and British English dialects? Why are there no identifiable WAEVs that are parallel to specific British English vernaculars?[13] And why did German, Dutch, and French, which were spoken in some areas in (the early) colonial years, apparently not affect English in the same way or to the same extent as the African languages seem to have among African Americans?

Note, for instance, that New Netherland (including parts of New Jersey and New York) was initially a Dutch colony and its trade to the English did not entail that the Dutch, Germans, and French who were in the colony left it (Dillard 1992; Buccini 1995). As noted by several historians, including Kulikoff (1991a, 1991b) and Menard (1991), the Germans were among the early indentured servants in other North American colonies such as Virginia. Are the structures of German and English typologically so similar that German could not influence some WAEVs as significantly as African languages have among African Americans, or are there important ethnographic ecological differences which prevented a similar kind of influence?[14] Or is there significant influence, nonetheless, but less conspicuous in general American English and more manifest in varieties such as Old Amish vernacular English? Or is it that early influence is less distinct than later immigrant influence such as can be observed in Yiddish English?

There is one significant factor that should not be overlooked: in general, living conditions did not prevent immigrants from continental Europe from having constant exposure to native varieties of English. Ethnic divisions among Europeans do not seem to have been so prohibitive to the acquisition of native-like English as was segregation between people of European and African descents.[15] Besides, there are several typological similarities among Western European languages (Thomason 1983), perhaps more than with the African languages they came in contact with in the New World. For instance, African languages are generally tonal, whereas European languages have stress systems. This alone may account for prosodic differences between WAEVs and AAE, although neither Gullah nor AAVE is a tonal language variety (contrary to Sutcliffe and Figueroa 1992). Western European languages have largely similar tense–aspect systems and a syntax in which the copula is routinely used in main clauses to form a verb phrase when the semantic predicate phrase is headed by a nonverb (e.g., predicative adjective, as in *Mary is pretty*). A large proportion of African languages do not share these typological features. Moreover, several of them have very elaborate aspectual systems. Such typological differences between the European and African languages that came in contact with English made allowance for different features to be selected into AAE and WAEVs, although the origins of the selections lie in colonial English koinés.

Note also that during the critical periods when AAE and creole varieties developed, the Africans who were not born in the colonies quickly dominated demographically, creating the right conditions for extensive restructuring of English among them. On the other hand, the massive continental European immigrations of the nineteenth century took place more gradually and white colonial varieties of English may have already stabilized. By the Founder Principle, whatever changes some newly arriving groups effected on the local varieties may be considered peripheral, under circumstances in which the founder populations were not suddenly eclipsed demographically by the newcomers.

Nonetheless, Kulikoff (1991a, 1991b) and Menard (1991) suggest that the Germans constituted a non-negligible proportion of the indentured servants of the seventeenth century in the Chesapeake colonies, the period in which we may locate the founder populations. Leaving alone the Old Amish vernacular English, what German contributions can be counted in the structure of general American English? Similar questions may be asked of the Dutch and the French, who may be considered the founder populations of some parts of the United States, viz., New Jersey and New York for the Dutch and Louisiana for the French. Is there German influence as significant in the WAEVs of Virginia, Pennsylvania, and North Carolina as African linguistic influence is in AAE? *Mutatis mutandis* for Dutch and French. Did these founder populations contribute to the development of WAEVs in ways that dialectologists or genetic linguists may have paid little attention to?

Can we answer the question of why WAEVs are different from British English varieties without addressing these aspects of the founder populations and their effects? Under the circumstances, can some of us continue to assume that American Southern English, as the variety spoken in the American Southeast, is what it is only because of the influence of the Africans, even when at least 80 percent of the white population's children did not have African-American nannies?

Southern English set aside, it has often been claimed that WAEVs are vestiges of English varieties in the British Isles during the colonial period. Supposedly isolation by the Atlantic Ocean made it impossible for the Americans to participate in the changes that have affected British English. There are undoubtedly some regional varieties in which influence from particular parts of the British Isles is significant, for instance, Appalachian English (Montgomery 1989, 1995, 1996; Montgomery, Fuller, and Paparone 1994). Still, one must not only determine whether the global systems of their vernaculars match those of the regions from which most of their speakers came but also account for what happened in urban centers such as New York, Chicago, Boston, and the like. So far no answers have been provided to these questions.

We also hear a great deal about the influence of Irish and Scots-Irish English on WAEVs, which accounts for some features selected by several of the vernaculars. However, what factors account for interregional differences among the WAEVs which are claimed to have been influenced by these same ethnic groups? Would it not be informative to learn what favored the selection of *some* (Scots-)Irishisms but blocked other influences (not necessarily the same everywhere!) which the same ethnic varieties could have exerted on all relevant WAEVs?

In other words, did WAEVs not develop as contact phenomena, like AAE and its Caribbean creole kin, consistent with the observations cited at the outset of this essay from Algeo (1991)? This question is addressed by Montgomery (1995, 1996). He argues correctly against claims that colonial American English was homogeneous. He concludes that "the hypothesis of an American colonial koiné is questionable on both philological and linguistics grounds. Colonial American English was probably not a koiné in many places; rather, dialect diversity, especially reflected in style shifting, was the rule (1995:233)."[16]

The claim of a homogeneous cross-regional koiné is equally disputed by what the history of settlements tells us about the typically isolated nature of plantations and small farms, the social and linguistic contrasts which must have existed between these communities, and the fact that, as Montgomery also observes, new immigrants tended to go where they had relatives or people from the same background. However, small-scale koinés must have obtained everywhere speakers of different English dialects came to interact regularly with, and accommodated, one another.

I have insisted on the effect of the founder populations not because this is the only phase that matters in the development of WAEVs and AAE but because it makes their developments more manageable in starting from the first phases and retracing history. I am sure the migrations of the nineteenth century have also affected WAEVs. The question is: how or to what extent? (Perhaps post-Civil War immigrations from Europe, mostly those from after the passage of the Jim Crow laws, can contribute to explaining the divergence of European and African-American vernaculars, aside from the effects of segregation and the end of importation of labor from Africa.) Adding to complexity in this genetic scenario is what influence was exerted on English in states such as Louisiana and Texas, where French and Spanish speakers had to shift to colonial English which had already crystallized in the original United States. Are these later shifts different from that of the Dutch in New Netherland in the seventeenth century?

As stated at the outset, I have no answers to most of these questions. Research on AAE, as on creole genesis in general, has helped me tease out the above relevant aspects of the development of WAEVs. Without having to characterize them as creoles, we cannot deny the fact that we are dealing here with contact-induced varieties. Therefore the same considerations which have helped us understand what seems to have happened in the development of AAE and New World creoles may very well help us understand how WAEVs have developed. The research avenues opening up here should shed light not only on the formation of these particular vernaculars but also on the dynamics of language speciation, in this case, those which have produced diverse daughters of the English language around the world.

3.5   Conclusions

The position of this chapter on the development of WAEVs can be summed up as follows. Since the early colonial days, English in the USA and the New World in general has been used in novel kinds of ethnographic settings characterized not only by its contact with other languages but also by the way dialects from the British Isles came to coexist with each other. The British dialects no longer had the same geographical distributions as in the metropole. In the colonial ecology, demands of communication set their features to compete with each other in ways which produced new colonial varieties. For instance, the high visibility or prominence of the (Scots-)Irish demographic element in some parts of the USA increased the likelihood of its linguistic influence. In addition to this competition of structural features among varieties of English, we must also consider the presence of several non-English language varieties, other European languages in the case of WAEVs, which must have influenced the selection of features into the emergent vernaculars. Variation in the demographic representations of different language varieties must have led to differences in the specific subsets of features selected into the new colonial varieties; and variation in the selection of features must account for differences between the new English vernaculars. Virtually the same language-contact equation and the same selection principles applied in the formation of WAEVs and AAE. Differences among them arose in part from the diverse pools of features in competition in the development of each of these subsets of vernaculars. Combined with other ecological factors, they amount to varying values of the same **nonlinear** equation yielding different individual varieties.

Focusing on competition of linguistic features, it is worth noting in the case of speakers who were shifting to English that they aimed at speaking a language other than their own, however vaguely defined the target may have been for members of the same group. The awareness of this shift, as a factor, must have reduced the possible influence from their ethnic languages to cases of interference which they could not repress. The role of competition from these languages consists primarily, though not exclusively, in how they influenced the selection of features from among the competing features from the British varieties in different settings. In other words, form and structure competed in the case of dialects from the British Isles, whereas mostly structure bore on the competition in the case of language varieties from outside the British Isles. Otherwise, specific ethnolinguistic groups of speakers exerted different influences on the emergent vernaculars, depending on their demographic significance in a particular colonial setting and on the typological homogeneity of their substrate languages. These are among the ecological factors which assign markedness values to competing structural alternatives (Mufwene 1989c, 1991a).

Another important factor in all this is whether a particular ethnolinguistic group was or was not part of the founder population. This affected the conditions under which it may have influenced the emergent English varieties, creole and noncreole. We must of course keep in mind that particular kinds of interethnic interaction – for instance, whether or not the groups were segregated – generally affected the linguistic restructuring process. This factor determined whether or not (significant) influence from an ethnolinguistic background would prevail in a particular variety. Thus the segregation of the Africans maximized the role of African languages in shaping AAE, especially during the rapid population replacement trend of the eighteenth century. On the other hand, the same segregation lessened the influence of African languages on WAEVs, although it did not of course prevent similar features from more or less the same lexifier from being selected into their structures.

One important aspect of the development of American English varieties which is suggested by the citations from Algeo (1991) but not discussed in this essay is the contribution of Native American languages to their structures. This remains an "unknown quantity" about which there is only confusing information so far. The confusion follows from the **marginalization** of Native Americans during the colonial development of especially the plantation states. There was marginalization to the extent that Native Americans did not form part of the regular residents of the colonial homestead and plantations, and there is really no evidence of Africans having benefitted from "seasoning" by Native Americans in their interactions with the European colonists.

On the other hand, some European colonists were engaged in trade with Native Americans. One is now tempted to ask whether either AAE or WAEVs would not have been influenced by some English pidgin that would have developed in the less regular trade contacts with Native Americans.

However, the development of varieties such as Chinook Jargon, Delaware Pidgin, and Mobilian Jargon suggests that trade was conducted more in restructured varieties of Native American languages than in contact varieties of European languages. Native Americans had the advantage of being at home and were under less pressure to accommodate the foreigners, except in modifying their own languages.[17] They were not even under pressure to learn the language of the new rulers, or shift to it, until the new socioeconomic system started to integrate them, gradually undermining their own traditional systems, despite the institutionalizations of the Indian reservation system. English pidgins among Native Americans seem to be later, at best concurrent, colonial developments that simply had no bearing on the development of English in North America. Nothing comparable to AAE seems to have developed until the late nineteenth century (Mithun 1992). However, there is undeniable evidence of motivated lexical borrowings from Native American languages as part of the adaptation of English to its new physical and cultural ecology. In any case, these are just some preliminary speculations that will hopefully be verified by future investigations.

4   The legitimate and illegitimate offspring of English[1]

In this chapter I extend the discussion of chapter 3 to the broader context of Englishes around the world. I start with the question of what criteria have been used to name and assign them to different categories. I show that there is a social bias behind the labels used to distinguish "**new Englishes**" from each other. The term *new English* applies technically to all those varieties that have resulted from the English colonial expansion, although British English today is as new as the other varieties. I also argue that mutual intelligibility between speakers of different varieties is not a reliable criterion for determining whether or not they are separate languages. This especially regards the way English pidgins and creoles have been disfranchised from the group of Englishes, except when it is necessary to determine what proportion of the world's population is anglophone. The question of social bias is discussed mostly regarding the distinction "native" vs. "non-native Englishes," with the adjectives *native* and *non-native* used as modifiers of language varieties rather than of the competences of speakers. I show that language contact has been a relevant ecological factor in the evolution of English since its inception.

Much of the debate about the above distinction between Englishes is indirectly related to norm-setting. Chaudenson (1992) argues convincingly that much about the identification of creoles as separate languages has to do with their **autonomization**, i.e., the ability of their speakers to develop norms that are community-based rather than imposed by speakers of other varieties of the lexifier. The same is true of indigenized Englishes. This observation raises the unsettling question of whether native speakers are really **norm-setters**, as assumed to date in linguistics. As I show in Mufwene (1997b), it is those who speak a language on a regular basis – and in a manner they consider normal to themselves – who develop the norms for their communities. Where indigenized Englishes are spoken, it is second-language speakers who develop the norms, while the children enculturated to their varieties perpetuate these norms, subject to imperfect replication. It seems that the same argument can in fact apply to communities where "native Englishes" are spoken. Children who acquire them perpetuate the norms developed by earlier speakers, although they contribute to the evolutions of their varieties by the principle of imperfect replication. To be sure, non-native speakers have recently not reached the right critical mass to impact the evolution of native Englishes, but such was not the case in the seventeenth to nineteenth centuries. Contact had a role to play in the development of their norms, especially in settlement colonies.

This essay was originally written for a meeting of the International Association of World Englishes, before which I had already presented a paper on criteria used for distinguishing first between "native" and "indigenized" Englishes, and then between them and English pidgins and creoles. This explains why section 4.1 does not show immediate continuation from chapter 3. However, as in the previous cases, every effort has been made in this edition to reduce the amount of overlap between the contents of this and the preceding chapters.

4.1   Introduction

I argue in Mufwene (1994c) that the naming practice of new Englishes has to do more with the racial identity of those who speak them than with how these varieties developed and the extent of their structural deviations. It has little to do with how mutually intelligible they are. In this essay I pursue some of the questions discussed in that article. The title is just a caricature of the position suggested by how we have distinguished between the different varieties, especially regarding their developments. We have typically downplayed the role of contact in the case of "native" Englishes but have routinely invoked it in the case not only of creoles but also of indigenized Englishes.

The distinction in the title is also negatively correlated with how much we have learned about the development of "new Englishes" (Mufwene 1994c). I claim that we know more about the varieties which our practice has presented as "illegitimate offspring" or "children out of wedlock," i.e., creoles and the indigenized varieties, than we do about the "legitimate" or "native" varieties. Among the reasons for this disparity seems to be the following: in the case of indigenized Englishes, curiosity about how and why they deviate from the native varieties has led us to investigate all sorts of ecological factors that can account for their structural peculiarities. In the case of native Englishes, we have downplayed their divergence from British English(es) and the role of contact in their development, assuming that they reflect "normal" evolution according to the single-parent filiation suggested by the tradition in genetic linguistics. I return to this question in chapter 5.

My position here is the same as in chapter 3, viz., that the same kinds of restructuring processes are involved in the development of both kinds of varieties, subject to varying ecological conditions, in which new dialect and language contacts play an important role. I continue to assume that, although there is no consensus on how creoles have developed, what we have learned in discussing them should help us more adequately approach the development of other English varieties.

I see an undeniable correlation of race of speakers with the distinction presented in the title of this paper. The legitimate offspring are roughly those varieties spoken typically by descendants of Europeans around the world, whereas the illegitimate ones are those spoken primarily by populations that have not fully descended from Europeans. Those who are not happy with this dichotomic distinction may also consider distinguishing the offspring of English on a continuum. One of its poles consists of varieties which are spoken typically by descendants of Europeans and whose legitimacy has hardly ever been disputed. The other pole consists of English pidgins and creoles, which have been stipulated as separate languages, despite their speakers' claim that they too speak English (Mühlhäusler 1985, Mufwene 1988b).[2] In the middle range come varieties characterized as "non-native" or "indigenized."[3] Below, I show how pernicious this practice is, starting with how the different varieties are named.

4.2   An insidious naming tradition

The labeling of nonpidgin and noncreole varieties spoken primarily by non-Europeans tells much of the story. The term *non-native* is one for disfranchising the relevant varieties as not really legitimate offspring of English, because their norms are set by non-native speakers. Indeed most of the children born to such communities, as in India and Nigeria, inherit the norms set by their second-language-speaker parents, thus making clear that native competence has to do more with norm-preserving than with norm-setting (Mufwene 1997b). On the other hand, the term *indigenized* reflects the struggle for legitimizing them, a stand that is consistent with the position that every dialect has its own set of distinctive features and norms by which a speaker is identified as a typical or nontypical member of the community with which it is associated. Within this medium range of the continuum also fall varieties such as African-American vernacular English (AAVE), whose status has been alternately associated with creoles (hence the term *semi-creole* given it by Holm 1988 and Schneider 1990), or with nonstandard dialects of English (e.g., Labov 1972a:36–64, 1982; Fasold 1981).

I submit that the main reason for this apparently nonlinguistic classification of offspring of English lies in the tradition of genetic linguistics of assuming only a single parent in the filiation of languages. Accordingly, the speciation of mother languages into daughter languages has been discussed under the assumption that no intercourse was necessary with other languages prior to the production of offspring. The typical explanation for innovative or novel structural features has been internally motivated change. That is, the relevant language has generally not been affected by the peculiarities of the other languages it came in contact with. For instance, Thomason and Kaufman (1988) argue that Old English would have undergone several of the changes that affected it independently of its contact with Old Norse and Norman French. Interestingly, Kroch, Taylor, and Ringe (2000) argue just for the opposite conclusion, consistent with the ecological approach to language evolution advocated in this book.

Even contact among dialects within the relevant languages (see e.g., Trudgill 1986 regarding especially Australia and the Falkland Islands, and Algeo 1991 regarding North America) seems to have been of no significant explanatory interest in traditional genetic accounts of new native Englishes.[4] Accordingly, the Germanic languages are different among themselves presumably by some accident of patterns of speciation. Contact with other genetically unrelated languages (particularly the Celtic languages in whose territory the Germanic populations were dispersing) may putatively be overlooked, because it apparently did not affect their evolution. Neither does it seem to have mattered at all in this tradition that Proto-Germanic itself must have been internally variable, like Proto-Indo-European (Trubetzkoy 1939). Such internal variation must also have been the case later within West-Germanic and subsequently in the languages which the Jutes, the Angles, and the Saxons brought to England. Little attention has been paid to subsequent contacts among these languages in England that must have produced Old English, even if contact with Celtic languages in England could be overlooked during this founding period for English.[5] In the same vein, it seems to have been of little significance to Anglicists that the Celts inhabited England before the Jutes, Angles, and Saxons colonized it and imposed their language varieties. Thus, it is disputable that internally motivated change and ecology-free speciation have explained everything about the evolution of English. Unfortunately, the same tradition has led them to suggest in the development of new, "native" and "non-native," Englishes processual differences which are artificial from a genetic point of view. I return to this matter below.

4.3 How language contact has been downplayed

Cases where it is undeniable that speakers of the mother language came in contact with speakers of other languages which disappeared but left substrate influence on the superseding language have been treated as rather exceptional. Such is the case of the Romance languages, which developed from Vulgar Latin. Even in such cases, more often than not, only internally motivated linguistic processes have been invoked to account for the evolution of the mother language into its offspring. Thus little is usually said about the contributions of Celtic languages to the structures of Romance languages.

Treated more exceptionally in this tradition are the Balkan languages, in which evidence of intense and multilateral population contacts over centuries cannot be denied and have become the classic explanation for the convergence of their structural features.[6] Regardless of the increasing number of such cases (see, e.g., Gumperz and Wilson 1971 for India), contact and convergence have become the plausible *exceptional*, rather than normal, explanation (e.g., Hock and Joseph 1996). One may thus understand why *contact*, rather than possible extensions of principles occurring in the lexifier (under specific ecological conditions), has also been the explanation for the definitely *untypical* and *would-be unnatural* development of pidgins and creoles, and maybe also of indigenized Englishes.

Thus, as far as English as spoken by descendants of Europeans is concerned, it has been normal not to discuss whether or not it has been influenced by its Celtic substratum in England. Likewise, experts have seldom addressed the question of why Celtic influence in British varieties of English is confined to those which developed after the Old-English period and why it is perhaps most striking today in those which developed since the seventeenth century (in particular Irish and Scots-Irish Englishes). Other varieties that bear such conspicuous influence are those outside Europe whose developers included speakers of Irish and Scots-Irish Englishes.[7] According to Montgomery (1989), Appalachian English is one of these non-British varieties with Celtic influence. Newfoundland vernacular English (NVE) is another where such substrate influence is to be expected, despite Clarke's (1997a) capitalization on the Southwestern English sources of some of its grammatical features such as the HABITUAL verbal {S} suffix. She provides no explanation for the usage of *be* (*bees* in the third person singular) before nonverbal predicates for the same grammatical function. I conjecture that perhaps congruence with a similar, though not necessarily identical, pattern in Gaelic influenced this development in NVE. Although Clarke observes that HABITUAL or periphrastic *do* was already attested in Irish English (presumably that spoken by the elite) in the seventeenth century, ecology-based markedness considerations (chapter 2) should explain why this alternative was not selected in NVE. In the case of Irish and Scots-Irish Englishes, the evidence from research since the 1980s shows that contact with the substratum cannot be denied. Similarities between some (Scots) Irishisms and Gaelic in just those areas that distinguish them from more

Germanic varieties of British English make contact a plausible, if not the only, explanation for these divergent evolutionary paths of English. But then one may raise the question of why these new varieties are characterized as "native," despite the influence of Gaelic.

The main reason is that the communities of those speaking these new varieties as vernaculars consist (almost) entirely of native speakers. To be sure, they must have been indigenizing during some phases of their developments. Given the acknowledged role of contact, one may ask why they are not called creoles, especially their nonstandard varieties. After all, creoles are considered native varieties, at least according to the most traditional and most widely accepted definition of the term *creole* in linguistics. They are also native according to a characterization little noticed in Hall (1966), viz., they are indigenous to the places where they developed. In this respect, they are like Scots and Irish Englishes, as well as like indigenized Englishes. To be equally subversive, why are creoles called separate languages for that matter? Since "creolization" is not a structural process (Mufwene 1986a, 2000a) and most of the features identified as Irish and Scottish are primarily nonstandard and are due to language contact, it requires some innocence not to consider the race and/or geographical location of the speakers an important tacit factor in the naming tradition. South Africa is an interesting case, where the English spoken by descendants of Europeans (including Afrikaners) is said to be "native," whereas the varieties spoken by other South Africans are said to be indigenized, reflecting the many-tiered colonial sociopolitical ecology of the country.

Perhaps an interesting exception here is South African Indian vernacular English (SAIE, Mesthrie 1992a). The reason for not including it among indigenized Englishes is that it is nonstandard and did not develop through the scholastic medium (chapter 1). It is not typically identified as a creole either, though it developed under conditions which may lead some scholars to characterize it as such. It certainly is not considered "native." One reason why, unlike Irish and Scots vernacular Englishes, it does not count as "native" seems to be the following: it counts no people of European descent among its native speakers, contrary to acrolectal Englishes of the Caribbean, where English creoles are also spoken. Technically, SAIE has "fallen between the cracks," as it fits into none of the ill-conceived categories assumed in accounts of speciation of the English language.

In the same vein, one may want to speculate whether there will ever be a time when, for instance, Indian, Singaporean, and Nigerian Englishes may become native. Shouldn't we rather accept the reality that English is less likely to replace the indigenous lingua francas of these territories than it did in Wales, Ireland, and Scotland, because the socioeconomic and political ecologies are not the same? The case of SAIE is a special one, chiefly because it is an exogenous variety and the appropriation of English among Indians in South Africa enabled both wider communication among themselves and communication with non-Indians, especially the British colonists who brought them there. It is also interesting that the varieties identified as "indigenized" are spoken in former exploitation colonies. South Africa was partly a settlement colony, like the territories where creoles have typically developed, and partly an exploitation colony, especially where the British rule is concerned.

Outside the UK, native Englishes are also spoken in former settlement colonies, in which globalizing economic policies have at least endangered the indigenous languages, starting with the Celtic languages in the British Isles. The development of SAIE is associated to some extent with such ecological factors, although these did not obtain in quite the same ways as in the New World. One may argue that SAIE fits among native Englishes but, to my knowledge, no expert has classified it as such. Note also that English creoles are native vernaculars, but not necessarily native Englishes, based on the literature on both creoles and indigenized Englishes. If one had to slavishly follow this misguided tradition, another category would have to be invented for SAIE!

Some may speculate that native Englishes have well-established norms and are associated with some standard. Ironically, indigenized Englishes are in several structural respects no more distant from standard English varieties than native nonstandard vernaculars are. In a way, the educated varieties of indigenized Englishes represent local standards. The question to address is actually whether indigenized Englishes lack norms. I argue in Mufwene (1997b) that, like expanded pidgins, indigenized Englishes **do** have stable norms, although these have been established and perpetuated by populations of primarily non-native speakers. Such realities show that norms are not necessarily developed by native speakers but by a stable population of speakers who use a variety regularly (Chaudenson 1992). Norms emerge out of communicative habits of individual speakers. What the habits share, including patterns of variation, form the community's **norms**, i.e., manners in which a speaker can expect other members of their community to express things. Thus, the "native"/"non-native" distinction as applied to language varieties, rather than to speakers, seems to serve some social ideology more than it sheds any light on language evolution, especially on the speciation that often ensues from it.

4.4   The development of English in England: when does substrate influence matter?

I argued in chapter 3 that North American English varieties are all by-products of language contact. In chapter 5, I defend the thesis that contact is an important ecological factor in language evolution in general, both in cases where it has produced creoles and in those where it has produced varieties which are identified by other names. Regarding the spread of English around the world, I maintain that native Englishes, indigenized Englishes, and English pidgins and creoles have all developed by the same kinds of natural restructuring processes. Structural differences among them are due to variation in the ecological conditions which assigned different values to the variables of the language-restructuring equation and thus determined varying outcomes from one case to another. We will now re-examine some of those putatively nonexceptional cases of traditional genetic filiation (identified as "ordinary" or "natural") and show how contact-based explanations also apply to them.

I do not wish to reactivate the misguided hypothesis that French developed by the "creolization" of Vulgar Latin or that Middle English developed by "creolization" out of the contact of Old English with French. I support Thomason and Kaufman's (1988) position against the creolization-of-Old-English hypothesis with the following arguments: first, it is French which would have "creolized" in England, not English; second, most English speakers did not shift to French as their vernacular (although a handful of the elite who interacted with the Norman colonizers may have);[8] third, the Normans who shifted to English could certainly acquire English very competently, not any worse than non-native speakers of English living in North America or in the United Kingdom acquire English if they are well integrated in these societies – their children must have spoken English as natively as the English children.

To be sure, something ethnographically similar to the formation of creoles happened in the development of Romance languages, in that the Celts shifted to the then-Gallicizing Vulgar Latin, although they did not leave their motherland. However, I do not wish to talk about "creolization" at all, for the simple reason that it is not a restructuring process. It is just a social phenomenon, which does not alone explain how new varieties developed that are called creoles. And, I reiterate, the processes which produced creoles may be observed in the developments of other languages too, as also noted by Hock and Joseph (1996:15).

Assuming the above, let us compare the spread of Vulgar Latin and that of the languages of the Jutes, Angles, and Saxons. Vulgar Latin, which was exported to the Celtic-speaking countries of continental Europe west of the Alps, is a name for vernacular Latin, as a nonstandard variety distinct from Classical Latin, the counterpart of standard varieties of European languages today. It was, as the adjective *vulgar* (from Latin *vulgaris*) says, the language of the common people, a social classification that certainly also applies well to most of the West Germanics who invaded England in the fifth and sixth centuries and would develop Old English. Interestingly, soldiers were involved in both cases of colonization and language spread. The reason why Vulgar Latin was so influenced by the Celtic substrate and became French, Spanish, and Portuguese (focusing on Western Europe, and depending on where the contact took place) certainly had to do with its appropriation by the colonized Celts.[9]

The above appropriation process and shift to the dominant group's language is not different in kind from what produced creoles and indigenized Englishes. Indeed, Thomason and Kaufman (1988) recognize the importance of language shift in both the case of the development of indigenized varieties and that of creoles. Since at first glance one may perceive similarities in the domination of England, France, Spain, and Portugal by foreign powers, the following question arises: Why did the same thing not happen in England until after the seventeenth century, during the colonization of Wales and Ireland in particular? Recall that England was invaded in the fifth century. Crystal (1995) submits a hypothesis, although he does not discuss the development of Romance languages. The Jutes, Angles, and Saxons settled in England in more or less the same way that the Europeans settled in North America, not mingling with the native populations but pushing them further away from their settlements or killing them – in North America, more by the spread of Old World diseases than in wars (Crosby 1992). As Crystal observes, the Germanic invaders called the native Celts "foreigners," the meaning of the term *Welsh*, and did not mingle with them. The native Celts were surely no more eager to appropriate English in their homeland than the Native Americans wanted to shift to European languages. Changes in socioeconomic conditions led them to do so, several centuries later; and when they did there was substrate influence. The social integration of the Celtic populations in the frontiers of the British Isles, coinciding with the development of potato "plantations" there and the imposition of English as the rulers' language, subsequently produced varieties such as Irish and Scots-Irish Englishes (Filppula 1991; Harris 1991).

Among the reasons why there is no Native American structural influence in North American varieties of English lies the fact that Native Americans were not integrated in mainstream American society until the late nineteenth or early twentieth century, as minorities, and under socioeconomic pressures from the majority. To date, there are still Native Americans who speak English non-natively, while most of their children, who are more fully assimilated to the dominant culture, speak American English natively. Thus the Native American influence on North American English remains lexical (cf. Mithun 1992).

Contrary to what some may think, missionaries' attempt to teach Native American children English in boarding schools and thereby spread English among the indigenous populations was no more successful than similar attempts in Africa and Asia. Outside the boarding school, Native American languages, rather than English, served as the vernacular, especially in intimate settings with relatives and friends. English remained an **auxiliary language** for those who did not have to live in socioeconomic settings where it was useful and proficiency in it enabled them to be competitive. The **globalization** of the American economy and the involvement of Native American populations are the factors that did the trick, affecting even those left on the reservations.

Likewise, as reported by Odlin (forthcoming), migrant labor, rather than schools (which taught English as a dead language), are largely responsible for the spread and vernacularization of English in Ireland. The informal contexts of language appropriation are correlated with the nonstandard nature of the varieties which the learners then targeted. They account in part for the extent of substrate influence on the structure of Irish English. This is very similar to cases of language shift and appropriation which resulted in the development of varieties identified, for specific sociohistorical reasons, as creoles.

4.5   The significance of ethnographic ecology

As I elaborate in chapters 5 and 6, ecology is an important factor that should not be overlooked in accounts of language evolution and speciation. English in some extra-European parts of the world speciated into vernaculars called creoles because it was appropriated by non-Europeans under ethnographic conditions that favored extensive restructuring under substrate influence. As explained in chapter 2, substrate influence was possible especially when those who appropriated the language used it not only to communicate with its original speakers but also, and perhaps mostly, to communicate among themselves. One must remember that creoles are different also because of the nonstandard nature of their lexifiers, in contrast with scholastic English, which lexified indigenized varieties.[10] The extent of their deviation from less restructured varieties, especially from the standard varieties with which they have too often been compared, unjustifiably, is enhanced by the typical heterogeneity of their true lexifiers. The conditions of language acquisition were likely to favor those alternatives that were congruent with patterns in some of the languages previously spoken by the adult learners (subject to competition among substrate patterns too).

Whether or not the dominated populations interacted regularly with the dominating populations is a more important ecological factor than the often-invoked low proportion of native speakers of the target relative to the learners – especially in exploitation colonies, where most Natives were not acquiring the colonizer's language. Let us, however, illustrate this point with AAVE. Its creators were generally minorities relative to the European populations. To make the point clearer, let us highlight some observations from chapter 3. It shares many features with White nonstandard vernaculars in North America, because, despite the social reality of discrimination against them, African Americans shared over two hundred years of regular interaction with speakers of those other vernaculars since the early seventeenth century. With the passage of the **Jim Crow laws** in the late nineteenth century, race segregation was institutionalized in the American hinterlands and this factor favored the divergence of White and Black vernaculars. The extent of divergence between the different ethnolects is thus inversely correlated with the degree of interaction between the ethnic groups and the time when segregation was instituted in their evolution. The post-Civil Rights Movements' perpetuation of *de facto* segregation in American society appears to have favored the preservation of distinct African- and European-American vernaculars, leaving it only to African-American children in integrated residential communities to assimilate White middle class linguistic characteristics.

Segregation as an ethnographic factor undermines claims that AAVE has been converging with white American varieties of English by loss of some "creole basilectal features." The fact that African Americans have developed and preserved a host of other cultural peculiarities supports this counterobservation. For instance, they have different prayer and religious celebration styles, different music and dance styles, different cooking and catering styles, and different dress styles, which all converge to mark a different ethnic identity. This is not to deny that the sources of some of these features may well be shared with some cultural features of white communities. Nonetheless, some African-American linguistic and nonlinguistic characteristics are different enough to consider them as diverging from the White traditions and having autonomized in ways specific to the ethnic group.[11]

A careful examination of settlement patterns in North America also shows that variation in ethnographic–ecological conditions of the founder population accounts for differences among (nonstandard) dialects of white Americans. According to Bailyn (1986) and Fischer (1989), homestead communities of early colonial New England more or less preserved ways of East Anglia, from which the vast majority of them had migrated in conservative and financially self-supporting family units. Interacting primarily among themselves in the farm communities which they developed, they preserved most of their motherland's speech ways, restructuring them only minimally into a new English variety. One may understand why New England English is assumed to be the American variety that is the closest to British English.[12]

On the other hand, colonies of the Chesapeake Bay (Virginia, Delaware, and Pennsylvania) were settled by fewer family units, consisted of a large proportion of indentured labor (50–75 percent according to Kulikoff 1991b), and were dialectally more heterogeneous. Although a large proportion came from the London area (Bailyn 1986), London was itself a contact setting to which jobless peasants and artisans had migrated from different parts of the British Isles, including the frontier regions of Ireland and Scotland. Part of the indentured labor also came from continental Europe, especially Germany. Competition and selection of structural features produced an English variety different from that of New England and even more different from British dialects, although specific features have been traced to different parts of the United Kingdom.

Communities such as in the Appalachian mountains with larger proportions of Scots-Irish founder populations developed varieties of their own (Montgomery 1989). Chambers (1991) and Clarke (1997a, 1997b) report similar things about varieties of English in rural Canada, where an Irish element is identifiable. One may propose similar explanations for the development of Italian English, Jewish English, and the like, assuming a social integration parameter which would favor more divergence from other socially less marked varieties. (As Victor Friedman, p.c., March 1997, observed, much of this sometimes boils down to a question of accent.)

Where segregation was implemented in the strongest form, the strengths of factors bearing on feature selection were shifted more dramatically, even if the lexifying input was more or less the same, so that Celtic, or German, or Dutch influence would be stronger in some communities than in others. This is consistent with the interpretation of influence from outside the lexifier as the role which any such language may have played even only in favoring the selection of a particular structural feature over other alternatives in the lexifier itself. Thus, the selections made in the different varieties would not be identical. Where they are now almost identical, such as between AAVE and white American Southern English, rules do not apply in exactly the same ways, e.g., the rules regulating the usage of invariant *be* and PERFECT *done* plus Past Participle or Past Tense.[13]

Schneider (1989), Poplack and Tagliamonte (1991 and later works), and Tagliamonte (1996 and later works), among others, have shown that there are many more similarities than have been admitted in part of the literature on the subject matter. Such considerations are one more reason for arguing that there are many more similarities in the restructuring processes that produced all these varieties. The distinction between internally and externally motivated changes sheds no significant light on how restructuring itself proceeds. It provides no rationale for some varieties among the new Englishes to be treated as children out of wedlock. Instead, the ecological model advocated in this book makes it possible to account for differences where they exist, even if these are only statistical. Such differences matter to the extent that they reflect various ways in which competing alternatives may be weighted in different communities, favoring one or another variant.

4.6   Mutual intelligibility and the contact history of English

In the end, one must concede that everywhere "the story of English" has been a history of contacts, of mixing and competition of features from diverse varieties, and of selections determined in part by the variants then available in English itself and in part by the systems previously familiar to some of the non-English populations. Variation in the nature of the lexifier is an important factor. We cannot continue to assess restructuring in creoles, AAVE, and indigenized Englishes using the same reference system for comparison. For some varieties, the lexifier was nonstandard, while for some others, it was a scholastic variety. Such variation alone set the stage for different outcomes.

Unfortunately, the vast majority of the literature has disregarded or downplayed this *ecological* conditioning. English is generally expected to have changed relatively little in settings where descendants of its native speakers during the colonial days interacted intimately primarily among themselves and/or with other Europeans, as in North America, Australia, South Africa, and Argentina. Features of the new varieties have been related indiscriminately to British English, regardless of the dialectal diversity of their sources. Contact among the different dialects of English and with European languages other than English has not been considered a factor, as long as the other Europeans shifted to English. In some cases facile explanations have been invoked to account for developments which seem too divergent: for instance, the position that White American Southern English reflects corruption under the influence of the African population during the plantation economy era.

Where English came in contact with non-European languages, especially on the sugar cane plantations and rice fields where creoles developed, or at the trade posts where pidgins emerged, it has been too easy to invoke "unnatural" or "nonordinary" developments (e.g., McMahon 1994; Hock and Joseph 1996) or untypical factors such as children (Bickerton 1981 and later works). The fact that the lexifier was appropriated and restructured by non-Europeans seems to have made it easier to accept such accounts and to disfranchise their new varieties under the pretext that they are not mutually intelligible with other English varieties.

It does not seem to have bothered linguists much that dialects of the same language need not be mutually intelligible. Nor do they seem to have been concerned by the fact that most speakers of such disfranchised varieties say they speak English. Certainly, if mutual intelligibility were such a critical criterion, more important than sharing an identifiable ancestor, there would be more reasons for treating Modern English varieties and English creoles as dialects of the same language than for lumping the former together with Old English while excluding creoles, as the following examples show. It is often easier to make sense of the creole and indigenized English texts than to interpret Old English ones.

(1)   Some Old English constructions cited in Traugott (1972:72–3):

a. Syle me ænne hafoc.
"Give me a hawk."   (*Ælfric's Colloquy* 31.132, *ca* 1000 AD)

b. Gaþ þeawlice þonn ge gehyran cyricean bellan
"Go devoutly when you hear of-church bells."
                               (*Ælfric's Colloquy* 48.310, *ca* 1000 AD)

c. Hwæðer ge nu secan gold on treouwum.
"Do you now seek gold in trees?"
                               (King Alfred, *Boethius* 73.24, 880–90 AD)

d. þa gefengon hie þara þreora scipa tu
"then they captured two of those three ships"
                               (*Anglo-Saxon Chronicle* 90.26, 880–90 AD)

(2)   Some Middle and Early Modern English constructions cited in Traugott (1972:119, 144):

a. Weither seistow this in ernest or in pley?
                               (Chaucer: *Knight's Tale* A.1125)

b. Whether had you rather lead mine eyes, or eye your master's heels?
                               (Shakespeare: *Merry Wives of Windsor* III.ii.3)

c. Sirra, take my word, I charge thee, for this man, or else goodman butterfly, Ile make thee repent it.   (Deloney: *Th. of Reading* 313.18)

d. And in the same manere oure Lord Crist hath woold and suffred that thy three enemys been entred into thyn house . . . and han ywounded thy doghter.   (Chaucer: *Tale of Melibee* B.2615)

(3)   Some Gullah constructions from Mufwene's field records (1980s):[14]

JR You trow way . . . trow way wha? En one day, I gone down deh, en talk bout shrimp bin a bite! I bin on dat flat, en I had me line, I done ketch couple a whiting . . . I say, I ga put up da drop net . . . when I look up, duh look from yah to your car deh, I see sompin on da damn side da shoulder comin, like a damn log. I watch um, en when I see him gone down . . .

EL Hm hm!

JR En dat tide bin a comin in . . . en dat sucker swim close, closer en closer, den I look en I see dat alligator open e damn mouth!

(4)   Some Basilectal Guyanese Creole constructions from Bickerton (1975:42):[15]

a. wel if di ded kom aal awi sa tek ded rait he
"Well if death comes, all of us will die right here"

b. den yu go kaal fu boot an so yu a go a kriik
"Then you will call for [a] boat and that's how you go up [the] creek"

c. hi sa pe di rent tu
"He will pay the rent too"

d. if ani blak man fi kom in awi vilij fi mek eni trobl, dem go nak dis drom
"If any black man should come in[to] our village to make trouble, they would beat this drum."

(5)   Some basilectal Singapore English constructions from Gupta (1994):[16]

a. Whole life tell [people] you not [kiasu], then make so much noise only.
"You are always telling people you are not [obsessed with getting on], and then you make such a fuss."   (p. 8)

b. You put there then how to go up?
"If you put [it] there, then how [can people] go up [the stairs]?"   (p. 11)

c. I sit here talk, can hear also.
"I sit here [and] talk, [it] (the tape recorder) can pick up [my voice] too."   (p. 11)

d. Tomorrow Sunday, lor.
"Tomorrow [is] Sunday."   (p. 72)

(6)   Some Hiberno-English constructions from Odlin (1992) and Filppula (1991):

a. Well, I seen the time you'd buy a farm for . . . five or six hundred . . .
Seen farms selling and I young lad

b. But when the house is quiet and us alone you never heard such talk that's going on there.

c. He fell and him crossing the bridge.
"He fell while crossing the bridge."

d. It was all thatched houses was here one time, you know.

e. Father and mother was givin' him hell. 'Twas in harvest time and the weather bad.

(7)   Some Appalachian and Ozark English constructions from Christian, Wolfram, and Dube (1988):

    a. He just kept a-beggin' and a-cryin- and a-wantin' to come out.

    b. That was the prettiest tree that ever he seen.

    c. Well, I've just been lucky I never been bit.

    d. Kerosene, that's suppose to been the cure for everything.

    e. Seem like everybody knowed where I was from.

    f. One of the lights had went out.

    g. The girls is usually the ones who picks them.

    h. I was scared to death after I done stepped on it.

(8)   The Arumbaya Language, according to Leslie Lonsdale-Cooper and Michael Turner, the translators of Hergé's *The Adventures of Tintin: the Broken Ear* (1975):

    a. Owar ya? Ts goota meecha mai 'tee.
       "How are you? It's good to meet you, matey."

    b. Naluk. Djarem membah dabrah nai dul? Tintin zluk infu rit'h. Kanyah elpim?
       "Now look. Do you remember the brown idol? Tintin's looking for it. Can you help him?"

    c. Dabrah nai dul? Oi, oi! Slaika toljah. Datrai b'gib dabrah nai dul ta'Walker. Ewuz anaisgi. Buttiz'h felaz tukahr presh usdjuel. Enefda Arumbayas ket chimdai lavis gutsfa gahtah'z. Nomess in'h!
       "The brown idol? . . . It's like I told you. The tribe gave the brown idol to Walker. He was a nice guy. But his fellows took our precious jewel. And if the Arumbayas catch him, they'll have his garters. No messing!"

Example (8) is fictional and perhaps the only development which one may consider unnatural in settings where English has been appropriated by a foreign group. At age 8, my daughter gave up on trying to interpret it, despite her ability to read eye dialect, because she could not recognize any English words. This is indeed where the primary problem arises in trying to interpret this text, because the creators of this restructured English cleverly segmented the graphic strings in ways that make it difficult to recognize English word boundaries. It is interesting that no English pidgin or creole displays this kind of restructuring at the phonological level.[17]

    A problem with **mutual intelligibility** as a criterion that would help determine whether or not English has changed into a new language is that it depends on which native English is being compared with a creole, AAVE, or an indigenized variety. As stated above, AAVE and creoles developed from the contact of nonstandard English dialects with other languages. Actually, once things are put in the right sociohistorical perspective, one must include in the structure of the lexifier features of non-native varieties spoken by the Scots-Irish who worked as indentured labor in the colonies and interacted on a regular basis with the slaves or other non-European indentured labor. After all, there is growing evidence of similarities between features of AAVE and of Scots-Irish English, starting with Rickford (1986), although this is not the position he defends. Intelligibility of AAVE and creole vernaculars must be determined not from the point of view of the educated English varieties typically spoken by linguists but from the point of view of nonstandard English varieties that developed among descendants of Europeans under similar conditions. Thus AAVE is more appropriately compared with nonstandard varieties of White American Southern English (e.g., Wolfram 1974; Schneider 1989 and earlier work), as African Nova Scotian English is compared with that of the local White communities (Poplack and Tagliamonte 1991 and later works by those authors). It is when speakers of such related varieties say they do not understand each other that we may establish with certainty that these vernaculars are not mutually intelligible. After all, English varieties spoken by descendants of Europeans are not a homogeneous lot, nor can we guarantee that any variety of, for instance, Australian English is mutually intelligible with any variety of American English.

As noted above, an important difference between English creoles and indigenized Englishes is that the latter have been lexified by standard-like, nonvernacular varieties taught or spoken in school. It is not surprising that they are largely intelligible to educated speakers from outside the communities where they are spoken. However, speakers of indigenized varieties who have interacted with native speakers of nonstandard vernaculars can attest to experiences in which they and their interlocutors failed to understand each other. And there are also cases of such incidents between speakers of standard and nonstandard varieties of native Englishes. It has too often been forgotten that mutual intelligibility is determined not only by structural similarities of the relevant systems but also by familiarity with speakers and their systems. (Larry Smith 1992 is quite informative on the subject matter.) Familiarity applies even to cases where speakers of different languages understand each other. Another critical factor worth mentioning here is willingness to understand one's interlocutor, which much of the literature subsumes under "attitude toward the speaker."

4.7   The cost of capitalizing on mutual intelligibility

While mutual intelligibility has been a powerful tool in disfranchising some new varieties of English, it unfortunately has also had some negative effects on research on the development of some other varieties. Today we can claim to know more about the development of pidgins and creoles, although a little less about the development of AAVE and indigenized Englishes, than we do about the development of native Englishes. As interested as we have been in the development of new native dialects, we have generally shown little interest in the ethnographic ecologies that produced them, except in a handful of studies. For instance, did British dialects come to coexist in the same ways in the colonies as they did in the British Isles before the colonization of territories outside Europe? Did the new settlements favor the preservation of the dialects brought over from the British Isles, or did they rather favor the development of new ones out of novel patterns of contacts among speakers of varieties who were less likely to interact regularly with each other in the motherland? Which social and regional dialects were represented in the founder populations and to what extent did this factor influence the fate of English in the colonies? Did the new social structures favor or disfavor the spread of features from particular social classes and/or places? To what extent did the different waves of immigration influence the development of these new varieties? How indeed did koinéization take place? Would this be a different process from the feature-competition and selection model advocated in chapter 2 for creoles? Did the other European languages with which English came in contact, such as Dutch in New Netherland, or German in Virginia, or French in Louisiana, (not) influence the structures of the new native Englishes; how; and under what particular conditions?

Had the experts on new Englishes been asking such ecologically relevant questions, they could have asked in what ways and to what extent the diachronic processes that produced new native Englishes were different from those that resulted in indigenized Englishes, for instance whether there is sub- and/or adstrate influence in new native Englishes. I surmise that feature-competition and selection were involved in the development of all new varieties, subject to ecological constraints peculiar to specific settings, but this must be verified. There is little doubt in my mind that all new varieties of English are adaptive responses to new ethnographic and other cultural ecologies, but more work must be done to verify this conjecture.

4.8   In conclusion

Positing English in the British Isles as the original heterogeneous species, we may claim that creoles are the most conspicuous manifestations of blending inheritance and increased diversity, as they represent more obvious deviations from the original typical range of variation. The ecologies of their respective developments also enabled them to emerge most obviously as new subspecies, because they developed their own norms and became socially more autonomous (Chaudenson 1992). Creoles reached these norms as their predominantly non-European speakers accommodated each other, selecting structural features in and out of their respective idiolects and moving closer and closer to each other's systems. Still, the communal system never became monolithic. (This is evidenced by the literature on creole continua, on which see especially Singler 1997 and Winford 1997a.)

Many of the same processes took place among speakers of the other, noncreole colonial English varieties (Trudgill 1986). This explains why new native Englishes differ from varieties spoken then and now in the United Kingdom. Surely, English in the then British Isles (up to the seventeenth century) has undergone its own share of changes too, which were probably inevitable, given the important population movements and contacts which took place there during the same colonial period. However, such restructuring underscores the fact that dialectal and idiolectal features were engaged in new competitions which yielded different outcomes in different ecologies. The challenge lies in explaining the development of all these new varieties, especially in figuring out the selection principles followed by those who produced them.

Variation remains an important language-internal ecological factor. It may direct the structure of a language (variety) into a new direction if its external ecological conditions change. Under new conditions, a new variety may emerge, as in the case of English pidgins and creoles, indigenized Englishes, and new native Englishes. As explained briefly in chapter 1, one of the external ecological factors is the set of structural options available in the other languages that English came in contact with. Such contacts could not only allow foreign elements into the changing system but also determine which variants in the overlapping idiolects and dialects from the motherland would be selected into the new variety. Even without the non-European factor, new contact patterns in the colonies among metropolitan varieties and the competition of features that ensued are two ecological factors that may be considered internal to the evolving language. An important difference in the developments of new native Englishes and the other new varieties lies thus in the nature and size of the pool of structural features that came to compete with each other, and in whether or not there was a foreign element that could determine differentially which of the competing features of the lexifier itself were selected into the new variety. These are but a few examples of what there is in the ecology of a language that influences its development.

It is pernicious to continue suggesting in our scholarship that some new Englishes are legitimate offspring of an earlier stage of English and that some others are illegitimate ones. The processes that produced them all are of the same kind, although the changes that apply are not the same in all cases. All new Englishes are natural developments and legitimate offspring, although some look more like their ancestors or their present-day British kin than others do. In fact, so do descendants of the same ancestor vary among themselves in a species.

Contact within a language community and between a language and some others seems to have played a more important role in language change and speciation than genetic linguistics has traditionally taken into account. In both cases of contact within and contact with others, variation has been an important system-internal ecological factor, just like in biological evolution. Insofar as variation is recognized, the role of individual speakers as agents of change cannot be overstated. They bring their idiolects in contact and restructure them through their mutual accommodations. It is hard to imagine that native Englishes did not develop by the same principles as indigenized Englishes and creoles.

5   What research on development of creoles can contribute to genetic linguistics

Identifying genetically related language varieties as dialects of the same language or as separate languages is somewhat reminiscent of assigning populations to the same or different races. It is underlain by some social biases that are seldom discussed explicitly or openly. These are often denied when brought up, and all sorts of nonoperational scientific criteria have been invoked to support distinctions that should at least be re-examined. Genetic linguistics has been influenced more by the cladograms of evolutionary biology than by several interesting research questions behind them.

For instance, **blending inheritance**, which has to do with social interaction and accounts for offspring inheriting traits from combined parental gene pools, has been accepted as a normal and typical phenomenon in theories of evolution. For some reason, genetic linguists remain committed to the assumption that language is transmitted on an asexual model, *in toto* rather than piecemeal and reconstructed by every new speaker. Language-mixing has been considered not as a default aspect of language transmission but as an acceptable deviation. A certain expectation for a pure form of a language has led linguists since the nineteenth century to treat creoles and pidgins as seemingly less normal, less regular, less natural, and as not genetically related to their lexifiers. These working assumptions are related to a few others, including the following: a language is an organism and a social institution into which individual speakers are born; it is changed by the latter presumably because something goes wrong. Together these mistaken premises have prevented good use of the facts submitted in chapter 1 about a communal language, viz., it is an ensemble of idiolects and develops a certain amount of homogeneity because individual speakers accommodate each other in their attempts to communicate successfully. Such accommodations are among the factors that bring about change. Language transmission is more horizontal than vertical and there is no particular reason to expect it to proceed under the kinds of constraints that are typical of the animal species. Even in the latter case, blending inheritance is considered a default phenomenon in biology.

Biologists actually recognize more than the animal kind of species. They have long acknowledged that while in some species genes are transmitted from parent to offspring, which is typical of the animal kind, in some others, they are transmitted (also) horizontally, involving a multitude of contributors to the genetic makeup of each of the individuals that form the species through time. Heterogeneity and **hybridity** are thus normal characteristics of a natural species.

It is not completely true that genetic linguists have not acknowledged external influence on the evolutionary trajectory of a particular language. Terms such as *substrate/substratum* and *superstrate/superstratum* are clear evidence that such influence is accepted as part of history, albeit as part of deviations from regular and normal developments. Unfortunately, there are no cases of language evolution that have involved no external influence at all. Nor is it clear where one must draw the line between, on the one hand, those cases that involve external influence but still yield regular and normal language evolution, and, on the other, those cases that do not. As suggested in chapter 4, it is not certain that the distinction between creole and noncreole vernaculars is a valid one on structural grounds. It does not help us gain any particular insights about language evolution in general. Below, I explain why.

5.1   Preliminaries

Hugo Schuchardt disputed a few assumptions of linguistics in the late nineteenth century, including the following two: (i) creoles are aberrations that deserve no serious attention of genetic linguists; and (ii) because they have resulted from language contact, they do not fit the Stammbaum model of one parent per language or language family, hence they should not be included in genetic classifications of languages.

To date only the first assumption has been somewhat rejected. For instance, many of us agree that creoles are natural languages. Since the 1970s, these vernaculars have emerged as a domain where one may verify hypotheses on, for instance, markedness (Mufwene 1991a), or second language acquisition (Andersen 1983), or child language (DeGraff 1999b).

Genetic linguistics has embraced research on the development of creoles with some ambivalence. For instance, like Hagège (1993), Hock and Joseph (1996:15) have no problem identifying in the formation of creoles "principles commonly observable elsewhere." Yet, they also suggest that these vernaculars are not such ordinary dialects of their lexifiers (p. 444). The main reason they invoke is their "special historical origins [in language contact] and [their] formidable structural differences" compared to their lexifiers (p. 442).

These statements are of course consistent with the typical disfranchising of creoles as separate languages (chapter 4). An important reason for this ambivalence is a pervasive commitment to the genetic linguistics *Stammbaum* model, in which contact has played no important role in the normal speciation of languages into their dialects and daughter languages. Thus Appalachian English is a dialect of English, presumably because contact played no significant role in its development, whereas Gullah is a separate language, because it developed out of the contact of English with African languages.

If the origins of creoles are so special, we would indeed like to know how special they are. However, as I show below, our position should not be based on the typically simplistic hypotheses which pervade the literature, in particular: **baby talk, foreigner talk**, exclusive or dominant substrate influence, language bioprogram, imperfect second-language learning, or exclusive or dominant superstrate influence. To be sure, there are differences between the ecologies in which creoles developed and those in which non-creole languages have changed "normally." On the other hand, some studies have highlighted similarities between the two kinds of evolution (e.g., Fisiak 1995; Posner 1996), suggesting that creoles have probably not developed in such "nonordinary," "untypical," or "unnatural" ways. We must thus ask ourselves the following questions: (i) Does language contact make the resulting language change less natural than internally motivated change? (ii) Where does the boundary lie between external and internal motivations in language change (Labov 1994)? I argue below, along with James Milroy (1992), that one cannot do adequate historical linguistics without factoring into one's explanations the social ecology of the changes discussed.

As for Schuchardt's second concern, linguistics does not seem to have changed much on the subject matter. For instance, although they argue for the existence of "mixed languages," Thomason and Kaufman (1988) maintain that these "cannot be classified genetically at all" (p. 3). They state that "it is usually possible (except in relatively borderline cases) to distinguish mixed languages, whose origins are not genetic, from languages whose development has followed the much more common genetic line" (p. 3). Arguing indirectly against Hjelmslev's (1938) observation that all languages are mixed to a certain extent and that traditionally genetic classifications have been based more on shared lexicon than on shared grammar,[1] they reject Weinreich's (1953) position that creoles should be grouped genetically with their lexifiers. They argue that "a claim of genetic relationship entails systematic correspondences in all parts of the language because that is what results from normal transmission: what is transmitted is an entire language" (p. 11). Concurrently, "a language cannot have multiple ancestors in the course of normal transmission" (p. 11). One problem is the reason that they give to defend their position: roughly, this is the way it has been done in genetic linguistics.

The tradition that Thomason and Kaufman espouse is disputable. There is no obvious yardstick for determining the point at which influence from other languages makes the resulting variety nonclassifiable genetically. Thomason (1997) invokes the fact that the model works well for prototypical cases, but she does not address the question of the size of the set represented by prototypical cases, nor that of what the justification is for treating the traditional cases as prototypical. Thomason and Kaufman could very well have used the evidence of language-mixing to dispute the established *Stammbaum* tradition. For instance, the evidence in the case of Romance languages (see below) is still in favor of language contact as a critical factor in their speciation.

One might want to make allowance for **language shift**, which Thomason and Kaufman present as an important factor in the development of creoles. Unfortunately "shift" is an ethnographic concept, which means changing to a communicative system other than the usual one. It is not a structural change within one's language, although it often leads to such a change, due to language contact. Many speakers of European languages outside Europe today, such as the majority of them in North America, have descended from people who shifted from other languages. If we took "shift" and language contact as legitimate criteria for questioning the genetic connection of some language varieties to others, then we would be equally justified in treating North American English varieties as nongenetic developments, unless some measure can be provided of the extent of contact-induced restructuring that does not affect genetic affiliation. I argue below that such criteria are not operational.

One might also want to argue that genetic classifications are based on the comparative method. Unfortunately, the comparative method itself has not been applied to creoles and their nonstandard colonial lexifiers. Thomason and Kaufman's position is based on the usual casual comparisons of creole structures against those of the standard varieties of their lexifiers. Yet, lexical evidence points nowhere else but to the colonial nonstandard lexifiers of creoles. As for grammatical evidence, unless one inequitably expects perfect replication from parent to daughter varieties in the case of creoles, their connections to their lexifiers can hardly be denied. The only issue one may raise regards the multiplicity of dialects of the lexifier to which each creole is partially related. However, the question that arises is whether creoles represent unusual cases or whether the genetic linguistics tradition is flawed by the kind of corpora on which the methodology has been developed, viz., written texts from highly restricted and "conventionalized" varieties which may not represent the normal speech of the average populations of speakers. Creoles may simply be an opportunity for genetic linguists to re-examine accounts of facts about which they cannot continue to be too certain.

5.2   Some noteworthy facts on the development of creoles

Below, I discuss some of the most commonly held assumptions about the development of creoles which may not be clear yet from the preceding chapters. Simply summarizing some of them here should be helpful for this chapter.

5.2.1   Creoles did not develop more rapidly than other languages

The literature claims or suggests that creoles developed rapidly compared to "non-mixed" languages. Such a position can hardly be sustained if one takes into account the development of varieties such as vernacular Irish English (with reference to especially Northern and rural Ireland). According to Hickey (1995), it developed between the seventeenth and nineteenth centuries, just like most Atlantic creoles. If one focuses on North America, the rapid-development criterion would mislead us to wonder whether North American English and French vernaculars should not also be identified as creoles. They too developed over the same periods of time it took related creoles to develop, for instance, Gullah and Louisiana French Creole. All of them developed gradually, concurrently, and out of language and/or dialect contact.

Central to the above position has been a recurrent claim that, for instance, it took the Romance languages over a millennium to develop into what they are today. One would have to wait for another seven hundred years to determine what the structures of present-day creoles will "look like" if they are used under ethnographic conditions similar to the Romance languages over the past millennium. Otherwise, Vulgar Latin turned into Old Romance varieties within more or less the same amount of time it took nonstandard English, French, and Portuguese to turn into their respective creoles and other extra-European vernaculars. The later structural changes in Romance languages are normal evolutionary developments due to changing ethnographic ecologies, including contacts with Frankish (in the case of French) and Arabic (in the case of Spanish), notwithstanding substrate influence in the protracted shift of the Celts to the evolving Romance languages. We may speculate that, given the same kind of histories, creoles may have similar protracted evolutions over a millennium. Otherwise, the relevant comparisons in terms of duration of development should be limited to how long it took Vulgar Latin to develop into Old

Romance varieties versus how long it took a European language to develop into a related creole. Creoles did not develop more rapidly.

5.2.2   Creoles were not created by children

The myth that creoles were developed by children, who nativized and thereby expanded their parents' impoverished pidgins, persists. As shown in chapter 2, creoles could not possibly have been invented by children. Structurally, they would be systems in an arrested developmental stage if they had been formed by children (Mufwene 1999a). Attestations of transfers from substrate languages in several creoles are among convincing evidence against the central role of children in their developments. Besides, the socioeconomic histories of the territories where creoles developed argues against the nativization hypothesis. Rather, the agents of the restructuring of the colonial nonstandard varieties of European languages into creoles seem to have been adult speakers (Chaudenson 1979 and later works; Sankoff 1979; Thomason 1980; Lefebvre 1986; Mufwene 1986b; Holm 1988; and Singler 1992). One wonders whether this ecological factor is different from what was typical of the development of, for instance, Romance languages (Posner 1996) and standard English in England (Lüdtke 1995). In all such cases, the rulers interacted primarily with adult populations, who saw advantages in appropriating the new languages and in the process restructured them under the influence of languages they had been speaking before.

5.2.3   Creoles were not lexified by standard varieties

In order to show how much creoles have diverged from the European languages that have lexified them and should therefore be considered separate languages, linguists have typically compared them with the standard varieties of these languages. Unfortunately, according to the socioeconomic histories of the relevant territories, creoles' lexifiers were nonstandard colonial vernaculars (chapter 2). The settlement histories of the territories also suggest that the lexifiers were not yet completely focused or stabilized (in the sense of Le Page and Tabouret-Keller 1985), since they too were then still emerging as new vernaculars. Such diffuseness did not, however, entail absence of a target (cf. Baker 1997; Thomason 1997). The socioeconomic histories suggest that we should factor in a non-native element on the part of indentured servants who came from parts of Europe other than the metropoles of the different colonies. For instance, some features of AAVE and Gullah have been related to Irish English, which suggests Gaelic influence (since the relevant, nonstandard variety of Irish English was itself evolving then). As in recent European exploitation colonies, whether or not the Europeans with whom the non-Europeans communicated in the European lexifier were native speakers must have made no difference. The new vernaculars evolved by accident from attempts to communicate.

This scenario suggests that the creative role of those speakers who developed creoles does not differ in kind from that of children acquiring a language under exposure to sometimes-conflicting inputs and having to make choices. Children too acquire language imperfectly, subject to different ecological constraints. They have several advantages over adults, including the following: (i) they do not already command another language, which would interfere with structures of the target language; (ii) language development in their case proceeds concurrently with their cognitive maturation, so that aspects of the target language that retain their attention are limited in number and only some are acquired at a particular stage; (iii) they are therefore not under the same magnitude of pressure to develop structural strategies to communicate all sorts of ideas – some of which are very complex – as adults who must do this within a short period of time. Using Hagège's (1993) terminology, such discrepancies tip the scale in favor of re-creations, rather than inheritance, in the case of adults endeavoring to speak another language.

5.2.4   Some features of creoles and the like originated in the substrate languages

Assuming that expanded pidgins are not different in kind from creoles (Todd 1984; Mühlhäusler 1986; Romaine 1988; Féral 1991; Mufwene 1997a), there are clear cases where creoles' structural features are traceable to some of their substrates' systems. The clearest examples come from Melanesian pidgins, per Sankoff and Brown (1976), Faraclas (1988b), Keesing (1988), Sankoff (1993), and Siegel (1998). For instance, these pidgins have developed a DUAL category in their nominal number system, an oversimplified numeral-classifying system with the free marker *pela* (< English *fellow*), an INCLUSIVE/EXCLUSIVE distinction in the pronominal system, a transitive verb postposed marker *im* (< English *him*), and an alternative of bracketing relative clauses with a form derived from the demonstrative *here*. Unlike Atlantic English creoles, they have also selected, on the model of most of their substrate languages, different focusing strategies and different periphrastic markers for time reference, e.g., *stop* for PROGRESSIVE and *pinis* for PERFECT. These Melanesian mixed varieties also illustrate that creoles' structural features have seldom been preserved in the same forms as in the languages they were selected from, e.g., the numeral-classifying subsystem. Boretzky (1993) shows that this is a normal pattern even in the evolution of noncreole languages.

Among Atlantic creoles, Berbice Dutch, which developed primarily from the contact of Eastern Ijo with Dutch and had a relatively homogeneous substratum, shows perhaps the highest proportion of substrate influence, up to grammatical morphemes such as **postpositions** (Robertson 1993; Kouwenberg 1994). Perhaps next comes Saramaccan, with phrases such as *taánga yési* "stubbornness" (lit. "strong ears") and *háti boónu* "anger" (lit. "heart burn"; Alleyne 1980). None of these examples shows a development that is unlike what has been observed in the evolutions of noncreole languages, although items and structures selected in these cases from the substratum have traditionally been described as borrowings in the case of noncreole languages.

5.2.5 The important, though nonexclusive, role of the lexifier in the selection of creoles' structural features

Like their vocabularies, the vast majority of the structural features of especially the Atlantic and Indian Ocean creoles can be traced back to their lexifiers, as shown in much of the debate against substratists. The markers of time reference, of noun delimitation, and of relativization, among other things, can generally be traced back to one or another nonstandard variety of the lexifier.

So a question that should concern us is not where those specific features came from but what ecological factors favored their selection and to what extent they were modified to suit the emerging systems. We may also ask whether those specific forms would have been selected if they did not satisfy some structural conditions in the lexifier. For instance, would *dos* in Guyanese Creole ([dɔz] in Gullah) have been selected as a HABITUAL marker if *does* did not play a similar function in some English dialects? Would *go* ([gə] in Gullah) have been selected as a FUTURE marker in several English creoles if *going to*, or *gonna*, did not play a similar role in the lexifier? As instances of restructuring, what distinguishes these selections into the creoles' systems from those in the Melanesian pidgins whose functions were induced by the substrate languages? Are there really *ex nihilo* innovations in the structures of creoles or are the above examples instances of normal system adaptation, hence normal language change, under specific ecological conditions? Likewise, isn't there a good ecological reason – having to do with the lexifier – why, unlike their English counterparts, French Atlantic creoles didn't develop a complementizer from the French verb *dire* (Frajzyngier 1984)? Why didn't Sranan develop such a function with *taki* "say/speak" (Plag 1993)? (See Mufwene 1996a on the latter two questions.)

As explained in chapter 2, there is no reason to deny that there was continuity, without a break anywhere, from the nonstandard lexifiers to the creoles. However, restructuring entailed more or less taking the competing systems apart and developing new ones out of the "matériaux de construction" selected from the feature pool that formed in the contact setting. Nobody actually stopped to do things literally in the way described here, but this is what the tacit actions of speakers which resulted in the new vernaculars amounted to over time. Linguistic feature transmission does not guarantee perfect replication, as is evident from the literature on second-language acquisition. Thus, structures selected into the creoles have hardly remained perfect replica of their models. They have usually been adjusted to be compatible with other concurrent developments during the gradual formation of the creoles' systems. Also, as explained in chapter 2, the "matériaux de construction" could originate from any of the languages or dialects in contact. This development scenario is consistent with the fact that linguistic systems are not monolithic (Mufwene 1992a; Labov 1998).

5.2.6   *No nonordinary explanations are needed for the development of creoles*

I assume that markedness values are determined relative to specific ecologies in which a particular language variety is used or targeted. Like other speakers, those who developed creoles selected into the new vernaculars structural options that were unmarked to them. These observations also point to the adequacy of arguing that the lexifiers evolved naturally into creole vernaculars in specific ecologies. No nonordinary explanations need be invoked to account for the development of creoles.

Congruence, or convergence in Thomason's 1983 terminology, has often been invoked in my own accounts of factors that assign markedness values to competing alternatives in the feature pool. In the context of language contact, there is a less utilized interpretation of **convergence** which deserves highlighting here, viz., conspiracy of separate processes which have led to some new structures. A case in point is that of serial verb constructions (SVCs), which have typically been attributed almost exclusively to substrate influence. Let us consider constructions such as *go/come fishing* in English and their translations *aller/venir pêcher* in French. In the context of creole development, loss of verbal inflections alone would have produced SVCs such as *go/come fish* and *va/vin pêche*. This core would be catalytic enough to allow a natural development of other SVCs in which a predicate describing manner would precede a verb of motion, such as "run go/come" (although the order of the constituents is different from *go/come running* (meaning "run to/from") in English and *aller/venir en courant* in French); or SVCs in which "take" functions as the head verb, as in "*take* knife *cut* meat," or others in which "give" is used serially, as in "*buy* hat *give* me."

What becomes significant here, relative to congruence, is the role of ecology. The presence of serializing substrate languages in the contact setting indeed favored the selection of SVCs into creoles' systems. It largely determined what other kinds of SVCs developed in specific creoles. It is thus interesting that not every creole nor every serializing language has dative serial constructions (with serial "give"), nor have all of them grammaticized a serial "say" into a complementizer. We would like to know under what specific ecological conditions such developments were possible and where they were precluded. It remains curious that AAVE, which developed in different ecological conditions from those of Gullah, does not have more serial-like constructions than White American nonstandard English vernaculars.

5.2.7 Creoles developed by the same competition-and-selection process as other vernaculars

The above considerations highlight the role of selection, where there is competition, in language evolution. It seems to operate the same way in the development of creoles as in other cases of language change. Thus, the competition-and-selection account proposed in section 2.2.6 for creole development differs only in details from Trudgill's (1986) explanation of the development of Australian and North American dialects of English. Both invoke markedness in ways which suggest that there are no groups of speakers around the world who would select options which are marked – hence less preferable – to them when they have a choice. Both also show that despite some exaptive innovations, the new systems have made choices from among alternatives that were available to speakers.

5.2.8 The Founder Principle accounts for an important proportion of creoles' structures

Significant in the above scenario is the role of the Founder Principle (chapter 2), according to which the features of creoles' systems were largely determined by the varieties which competed with one another during the **founding period**. By this I mean the earlier stages of the colonies, especially those during which contacts conducive to the restructuring that produced the relevant creoles took place. To understand where creoles' structural features originated, one must not only heed Sylvain's (1936) and Turner's (1949) lead in examining structural options available in the substrate languages, but also follow Bennett (1908, 1909), Krapp (1924), Kurath (1928), Johnson (1930), Sylvain (1936), McDavid and McDavid (1951), Chaudenson (1973 and later works), D'Eloia (1973), Schneider (1983,

1989), Rickford (1986) in paying attention to the nonstandard vernaculars spoken by the European indentured servants and yeomen with whom the non-European laborers interacted regularly in the colonies.

5.3   Ecology and linguistic evolution

Once things are put in perspective, Hock and Joseph's (1996:15) observation that creoles have developed according to "principles commonly observable elsewhere" becomes more compelling. It will also help to re-examine aspects of the development of noncreole varieties, for instance, the fact that European-American vernaculars have evolved as different from their metropolitan kin. A common explanation has been that these New World varieties did not participate in the later waves of changes that affected their European counterparts.

While these explanations are not totally wrong, they have typically exaggerated the conservative role of the extra-European varieties. One cannot help noticing that the features of these vernaculars originated in different metropolitan dialects. There was competition and (nonexclusive) selection of specific alternatives from different sources (Trudgill 1986). Population movements, hence contact, are undoubtedly an important reason for the restructuring of English in the United Kingdom during the colonization of the New World. However, contacts of the same metropolitan dialects in colonial settings under similar circumstances would have produced similar linguistic outcomes. Such contacts have indeed been suggested by historians such as Bailyn (1986), Fischer (1989), Kulikoff (1991a, 1991b), and others. Since the outcomes are different, we may hypothesize that ecological specifics of the contacts varied from one setting to another, thus yielding different outputs to what is basically the same restructuring equation everywhere.

In the sociohistorical context of the development of creoles, ecology includes factors such as the following which are summarized from chapter 2: Which populations were present in the contact setting and in what proportions relative to each other. What language varieties were spoken and what are their structural typological features. How heterogeneous the lexifier was and what specific lexical and structural choices it offered that competed with one another. (These structure-related questions apply to the substrate languages too, for the range of options available among them tend to explain why some structural options were selected into a creole's system.) Relative to ethnicity and/or social class, what intergroup patterns of interaction obtained between their members. How the above factors varied from one stage of colonization to another.

Other relevant factors include cross-colony "differences in initial conditions, stochastic events, time lags, processes operating on different time scales, and spatial subdivisions" (Brown 1995:15–16). Thus, all structural input factors being equal, differences in the latter algebraic variables account for cross-creole differences. For instance, we know that in the territories where large-scale plantation industry started early, basilectal varieties also developed early and they tend to be more drastically different from those of other colonies. The case of scantness of Spanish-based creoles was also discussed in chapter 2, in which it was pointed out that in Cuba, for instance, it took the Spaniards until the nineteenth century to launch into the sugar cane economy, over 150 years of homestead economy during which they had lived closely with their slaves and taught them Castellan Spanish too. The switch to the plantatation economy was also during a time marked by no rapid population replacements nor dramatic labor population increase.

It was also shown in chapter 2 that early European:non-European population disproportions account for cross-colony differences regarding the basilect. This accounts for differences in the development of Creole in, for instance, Jamaica and Barbados. Early removal of the lexifier, or demographic attrition of its speakers, also accounts for differences between, for instance, the English creoles of Suriname and those of the Caribbean. The nature of the plantation industry – tobacco in Virginia, rice in coastal South Carolina, and sugar cane in the Caribbean – as well as the timing of segregation, account for more cross-colony differences.

There are thus numerous ecological factors which explain why every creole differs somewhat from another, although they share many structural features. The ecological factors also explain why creoles are generally different from new extra-European dialects of the same lexifiers spoken by descendants of Europeans, despite some similarities. Several creolists have invoked break in the transmission of the lexifier to account for the development of creoles. However, it was shown in chapter 2 that this argument does not apply even to the plantations of Suriname, where the English left early, during the homestead phase of colonization. The lexifier did not need the presence of Europeans to be spread in its early colonial koiné form. There was hardly a time when language was not transmitted normally in the colonies. There was no time when those who developed creoles did not resort to strategies used by other speakers in natural, nonscholastic contexts of language transmission. Their target was of course not metropolitan, nor necessarily focused. Still it was a target. The ecological factors and selective restructuring which produced creoles are of the same kind as those which produced "normal" language change. Contact at the interidiolectal level is a critical factor in almost any case of language evolution.

5.4   "Creolization" as a social process

I summarize here the gist of the arguments presented in Mufwene (2000a).
In light of the preceding discussions, what is called *creolization* in the linguistics literature does not correspond to any particular structural process
or any combination thereof. One can safely say that it amounts to a social
process by which vernaculars associated with particular social groups, typically descendants of non-Europeans in exogenous colonial settings, were
disfranchised from other colonial varieties that developed around the same
time but are related primarily to descendants of Europeans. The tradition
of this social process has existed in colonial societies, and in those which
succeeded them, since before linguists became interested in "creole
genesis." Creolists simply became trapped in some of the social biases
which influenced their research, and attempts to operationalize not only the
term *creole* and the like, but also the process *creolization* have failed.

The different stages posited by linguists about the development of creoles
– from jargon or pidgin to creole – are not consistent with history
(Mufwene 1997a). As shown in chapter 1, a useful rough generalization is
that pidgins developed in trade colonies but creoles developed in settlement
colonies.[2] The most adequate interpretation of *creolization* – if such a
process must be posited – appears to be the social marking of a particular
colonial vernacular of the seventeenth to nineteenth centuries from other
colonial varieties because of the ethnic/racial affiliation of its primary
speakers. The interpretation of the term as *basilectalization*, a more neutral
term that can apply to any communal variety which diverges maximally
from the local acrolect, is just an attempt to validate the social process with
structural evidence. However, there is no basilect common to all creoles.
Every basilectal variety is identified relative to its acrolect. Having been
restricted historically to (sub)tropical European colonies of the past few
centuries, creoles are far from being a general structural type of language,
although they form a special sociohistorically defined group of vernaculars
and share several features on the **family resemblance model**. To be sure,
similar social and linguistic developments took place elsewhere and at other
times. However, the term *creole* was not used for their outcomes there and
then. Thus, what we have everywhere seems to be simple evolution of languages from one state to another in different ecological conditions.[3]

As observed above, the fact that the (ex-)colonial vernaculars spoken by
descendants of Europeans outside Europe are different from their metropolitan kin suggests that they too are outcomes of restructuring under
contact conditions. Only some ecological conditions were different. In
British North American colonies, for instance, an important proportion of

the indentured servants came from continental Europe, and a large proportion of the indentured servants from the British Isles, especially from Ireland, were also not native speakers of English. Thus, even if the Africans had not been present in the North American colonies, American Southern White vernaculars would still have wound up different from their metropolitan kin. Appalachian and New England English vernaculars, for instance, reflect variable restructuring despite their limited contacts (during the colonies' founding periods) with speakers of African languages. Trudgill (1986) underscores the role of restructuring in the development of English also in Australia and the Falkland Islands.

What we should now do is focus on how much light socioeconomic history can shed onto genetic linguistics. I have tried here to articulate more explicitly the notion of "**sociohistorical linguistics**" presented in Romaine (1982). In the next section, I espouse the "**Uniformatarian Principle**" – adopted critically by Labov (1994) – in the looser sense that basically the same processes have produced creoles that have also produced new varieties of other languages. I then go back in time to highlight the role of contact in the evolution of especially English and French.

5.5   The role of contact in the histories of English and French

Nobody questions the fact that the Romance languages developed from Vulgar Latin, to which continental Celtic populations in the Roman Empire gradually shifted all the way to the twentieth century, according to several Romanists. Surprisingly, although the notion of "substratum" was developed in Romanistics, there has been little explicit reference to the contribution of Celtic languages to the development of Romance languages, not even in the few misguided attempts in the 1980s to treat the **Gallicization** and **Iberianization** of Vulgar Latin as "creolization." Likewise, with the over-reliance on internally motivated change to account for the speciation process, the influences of Frankish and Arabic, which must have borne on the differentiation of French from Portuguese and Spanish, have typically not been invoked. (See, e.g., Green 1988; Harris 1988; and Posner 1996 for refreshing views.)

The relevant social history makes contact a plausible catalyst of the changes that affected the nonstandard Latin vernaculars to which the Celtic populations gradually shifted at the expense of their own indigenous languages. Even in Italy, Latin changed because it was appropriated by non-Roman populations who became the majority of its speakers. Contact emerges again as a catalyst of restructuring, although structural similarities between Latin and other Italic languages seem to have made the process less extensive than outside Italy. Thus Italian is closer to Latin than the Iberian and Gaulish Romance languages are.

The social history of this part of Europe suggests that external motivation did not play a peripheral role in the change of Latin into its offspring. It prompts us to investigate more of the ecology of language change. Thus, we would like to know why the whole of France did not Gallicize at the same time, or why more than one dialect of French developed from Vulgar Latin. Are all these facts just attributable to randomness, or is there more in the social ecology of the shift of the Gaulish people to Latin that deserves attention? It would be absurd to ignore substrate influence, especially if it is interpreted as the role played by the substrate languages in determining the direction of the restructuring of a language?

As argued in section 5.2.1, the Romance languages did not develop from Vulgar Latin in a longer time than creoles did from their lexifiers. Even if they did, would the difference in **speed of development** reflect a difference in the kinds of restructuring involved? Since ecological conditions of the shift to the lexifier were not identical – endogenous in the case of Romance languages and exogenous in the case of creoles[4] – does variation in ecological conditions entail variation in nature of restructuring processes rather than simply variation in outcomes and in the specific processes that applied?

The neglect of the role of ecology, especially that of language and dialect contact, is equally striking in the case of English. History tells us why it has taken up to the seventeenth century for Celtic influence to impose itself in varieties of British English, viz., Irish English (Filppula 1991; John Harris 1991; Odlin 1992; Hickey 1995; Kallen 1997). The Angles, Jutes, and Saxons colonized England more or less in the same style that Europeans colonized North America, driving the Natives away, barely mingling with them, and hardly causing them to shift to English for some centuries. In both parts of the world, it is in the later stages of the anglophone presence in the host setting that the Natives have shifted gradually to the colonizer's language as their vernacular – starting especially in the urban environment – and have brought with them novel structures or favored alternatives that may have been disfavored in other varieties.[5]

What is explained least is why and how Old English became different from the languages brought over by the Angles, Jutes, and Saxons. (See Hogg 1992, especially his Introduction, for interesting discussions.) Is it not plausible to assume that contacts among these languages themselves produced the range of new varieties called "Old English," which differed regionally and socially according to diverse "mixing recipes" in different settings? Was this process different from the restructuring of English brought about primarily by dialect contacts since the seventeenth century not only in the British Isles but also in English colonies such as white North

America, Australia, and New Zealand? Can the influence of Old Norse on Old English be overlooked, at least in the sense of an ecological factor determining the direction of selective restructuring? (See Kroch, Taylor, and Ringe, 2000, in this regard.) Can the role of Norman French be ignored when the Anglo-Norman rulers seem to have been catalytic in shaping up what would emerge as standard English (Lüdtke 1995)? Does the fact that (some of) the same tendencies already obtained in varieties of English entail that contact would not have played a catalytic role in favoring parametric options shared with Old Norse and/or with French? Could we, for instance, be sure that *WH*-relatives and Pied-piping would be so common in standard English without French (and Latin) influence? Why aren't they used in nonstandard vernaculars and in creoles? I return to aspects of these questions below to underscore the role of contact in language evolution.

5.6   Language as a species: whence the significance of variation

The topic of this section is the focus of chapter 6. Suffice it here to recall from chapter 1 that much insight about language evolution is lost in analogizing a language with an organism. A language as a communal property is a construct extrapolated from the existence of similar idiolects, very much like a species is extrapolated from the existence of individuals who are successful in reproducing their kind or at least show such a potential. In accommodating one another and/or in exapting current forms or structures, individual speakers actuate changes. Such changes vary according to, for instance, who interacts with whom. One can argue, as I do in chapter 2, that contact starts at this idiolectal level and is central to any evolutionary process, because it determines whether or not a change initiated by an individual speaker will spread to a community.[6] What is also important here is the significance of blending inheritance, once it is shown that the linguistic species is of the parasitic and **Lamarckian** kind. This is because its feature composition keeps changing throughout its lifetime, the features are transmitted perhaps more horizontally than vertically, and multiple sources of influence are the norm rather than the exception. Blending inheritance leads us to re-examine whether or not (sticking to the tradition of one parent per family of daughter languages) the *Stammbaum* tradition does justice to the complex process of language speciation.

Only part of English, the one that was appropriated by the Normans and their English associates, was directly affected by contact with Norman French (Lüdtke 1995). Other English dialects were influenced indirectly and not to the same extent by this new variety. By the same token, we can also argue that only some English varieties, those that were appropriated by non-Europeans in some colonial settings, were restructured into creoles.

Likewise, only the English varieties exported to settlement colonies changed into such new varieties as American and Australian Englishes. By the same token, only parts of African languages that were exported to the New World died, not those that were left behind in Africa. Such a differentiating perspective on the evolution of a language is an advantage of the language-as-species approach, which the language-as-organism approach cannot provide.

5.7   Some conclusions

The tradition that has excluded contact as an ecological factor from genetic linguistics is at odds with European social history, which has been marked by migrations and conquests, hence by population contact. In the case of the British colonies, extra-European migrations were extensions of what was already taking place in Europe (Bailyn 1986). One would expect that at least some of the same factors which have affected language evolution outside Europe have also affected language change within Europe. Ignoring such similarities, except in the most conspicuous cases such as the Balkans, is subscribing to the principle of "deux poids, deux mesures." It is tantamount to refusing *a priori* to understand the ecology of change, regardless of whether the innovations originate within or outside a specified community. It amounts to lack of interest in the causation of change itself, as if this needed no trigger.

At this point, we must ask ourselves whether we can fully blame those who have claimed that English and French developed by "creolization." I disagree with them because, as noted above, "creolization" is not a structural process – there are no restructuring processes which are specifically creole. Some new vernaculars have been named creoles for sociohistorical reasons which are peculiar to a specific period in our history – especially the seventeenth to nineteenth centuries – and to specific geographical areas, viz., European settlement colonies especially in tropical areas. We really have no reasons for looking for creoles elsewhere.

However, we cannot dismiss offhand the observation that contact of dialects or languages has generally played a catalytic role in favoring specific restructuring paths in the evolution of a language. Thus, we cannot completely fault those who suggest that English and the Romance languages developed in more or less the same ways as creoles did, from the restructuring of a lexifier in a contact setting. That is, they developed in ecologies in which structural features internal and external to the lexifier came to compete with each other through people aiming to speak the same language but modifying it in the process. Those who developed new varieties knew what language they wanted to speak, although they probably were not aware of the deviations they either produced or learned, especially when the target was loosely focused.

Why should creoles not be genetically classifiable at all, if the following ecological conditions show that they cannot be distinguished from other languages? (i) Contact played similar roles in the development of English and Romance languages as of creoles; (ii) there are no restructuring processes that are particularly creole; (iii) creoles have typically selected more than 90 percent of their vocabularies from their lexifiers; (iv) a large proportion of their structural features may be traced to nonstandard varieties of their lexifiers; (v) their native speakers typically think that they speak dialects of their lexifiers; and (vi) the correspondences to which historical linguists subscribe do not hold the same strengths in all families (the case of standard French, according to Posner 1996). Could the problem lie not in how creoles are genetically related to their lexifiers but in how genetic kinship is conceived in genetic linguistics? Is there any particular reason why genetic kinship must be established on the assumption of only one parent per language or language family?

As we focus on language spread and speciation, let us analogize language to a stream flowing down into a delta and splitting into several other streams whose colors and sand contents come to differ from one another. Could one discuss this speciation without taking into account the surfaces on which the water flows? The obviously negative answer to this question suggests that substratum, hence language contact, should not be overlooked in accounts of language change. Let us also think of a stream whose water merges with that of another to form a shared course. Would we be justified in claiming that either of the streams alone produced the merged portion of their courses by itself? Here too, the negative answer underscores the role of contact in language evolution.

Things become of course more complicated with languages conceived as species consisting of individual idiolects, which are produced by speakers whose individual actions affect the species' fate. The new species that emerges out of competition and selection of features in the contact setting is typically a transformed state of one or more species that came in contact with one another. Part of the transformation lies in the inclusion of features that a species did not have in its earlier state, part of it lies in the strengthening of features which may have been marginal in the earlier state, and part of it may lie in the elimination of features it had in the earlier state. So the new species has evidently been affected by its contact with other species, even if the others only helped it enhance features that it had all along or lose features that were not salient in the first place.

The above suggests that we are dealing with a matter of degree of change, subject to specific ecological conditions. Differences among outcomes of the restructuring of the same language in different ecological conditions lie more in the outputs of the equation than in the nature of the equation. So far decisions on whether or not to classify languages genetically seem to have relied on that degree of restructuring, based unfortunately on the wrong comparisons in the first place and without an explicit identification of the structural cutoff line. To be sure, such variation in strengths of genetic links – determined by the proportion of features inherited from a parent language – should not be overlooked. It could be captured by modifying the representation of genetic connections, contrary to the nineteenth-century taxonomic tradition to which genetic linguistics still subscribes. However, things are question-begging when some offspring are simply denied legitimate descendance because they do not look very much like the recognized exclusive parent. In social families, many children would accordingly be disowned because they do not replicate closely enough the phenotypes of their parents!

6 Language contact, evolution, and death: how ecology rolls the dice

In this chapter, I elaborate the population genetics perspective introduced in chapter 1 and adopted in the subsequent chapters. I submit more justification here for the position that there are indeed heuristic advantages in approaching language evolution on the model of population genetics, assuming that a language is a species but not an organism. However, I also argue that the linguistic species need not be a clone of any biological species, despite the fact that it shares several properties with the parasitic species. In fact, the proposed population genetics of language evolution is more than an analog of population genetics, although its heuristics has been very much inspired by the latter.

A linguistic species must be defined on its own independent terms and its evolutionary properties hypothesized according to its own combination of ontological characteristics. These account for both the similarities and differences which it displays with its closest kin in biological evolution. The basic assumption is that there are general evolutionary principles which apply similarly to the linguistic and biological species. However, there are species-specific principles which distinguish them from each other, based in part on whether a species is of the Darwinian or Lamarckian kind, on whether traits are transmitted sexually or asexually, horizontally and/or vertically, on whether the default quality of copying in trait inheritance is with or without modification, etc. One cluster of factors that plays an important role in any theory of evolution is "ecology." An important part of this chapter is devoted this notion, articulating how it causes and/or determines language evolution.

6.1 Introduction

The notion of "**evolution**" is used here in the same sense as introduced in chapter 1, viz., "the long-term changes undergone by a language (variety) over a period of time." From the point of view of structure, they consist in different ways of producing sounds, of expressing things (morphosyntactically, lexically), or of encoding meanings. They can amount to more, or less,

145

structural complexity. The evolution can also be pragmatic, regarding, for instance, sociological constraints regulating usage of expressions. All the preceding may result in diversification into other varieties, regardless of whether these are identified as dialects or separate languages. From an ethnographic perspective, changes can consist in the erosion of the vitality of a language variety, and/or in confusion of its identity, or in its *death*. Not all language varieties have had a life marked by all such changes, nor have they all followed identical evolutionary paths if they underwent combinations of such changes. To account for both differences and similarities in these diverse evolutions, it will be necessary to understand the respective *ecologies* of the developments.

Johanna Nichols (1994:276–7) distinguishes between different senses of *evolution*, including "progressive change toward increasing complexity" and "Darwinian evolution, that is, change brought about by natural selection of existing variation." She says that "no evidence has been uncovered to indicate that morphosyntactic structure has been subject to progressive evolution," which, among other things, involves "increasing complexity, rationalization of structures and functions, and increasing independence from the environment." She argues that

There are very few instances of natural selection in human language . . . The only instance of natural selection encountered here is the approximation to a standard profile in residual zone. Residual zones by definition involve language contact and multilingualism, and such features of the standard profile as greater morphological complexity, cliticization or other increase in head-marking patterns, and propensity for accusative alignment and SOV word order evidently arise as speakers select from the inventory of grammatical patterns made available to them by multilingualism. This kind of evolution yields a standard statistical profile for certain features in each individual residual zone, but there is no reason to think it affects language generally.

A subtype of Darwinian evolution is speciation, whereby one population comes to differ from another, eventually giving rise to a new species. No evidence of anything like speciation has been found in this or any other typological work. Although linguistics has no analog to the biological notion of species, it is safe to say, informally speaking, that languages and linguistic lineages are related to each other as individuals or kin groups of a biological species are, not as species in a genus. (276–7)

As I show below, linguistics clearly has an analog to a biological species, though this is not of the animal kind. Linguistic evolution proceeds by **natural selection** from among the competing alternatives made available by the idiolects of individual speakers, which vary among them (however slightly in most cases). Contact is everywhere, starting at the level of idiolects; the coexistence of these encourages the natural selection approach. There is plenty of evidence of speciation in language evolution, evidenced by the development of new varieties, as discussed in chapters 2–5.

I should reiterate that evolution has no purpose or defined goals. It should not be interpreted as progress (Gould 1993:323), although it is often characterized in terms of adaptations to changing ecology. Linguistic systems may evolve as much toward more structural complexity as toward more simplicity, just as they may be *restructured* without becoming more complex or simpler. Why they change is not well understood, but it seems clear that systems are not passed on intact from speaker to speaker. Speakers accommodate each other (a practice which need not produce changes in the communal system) and innovate by exaptation to meet different communicative needs. Such adaptations do not necessarily improve the system and they are not necessarily conscious in the first place. Linguistic evolution is therefore not planned, at least not in the most natural form of the process.

Natural selection (out of competing alternatives) plays an important role in language evolution, at the mercy of ecology. This is a complex of factors that normally sustain variation (a central factor in any evolutionary process), but sometimes they favor some variants over others, often also prompting the advantageous ones to adapt to other changes. The evolution of a language proceeds through individual speakers, through their individual speech acts and their idiolects, with ecology working on variation, as entailed by the coexistence of idiolects. These, as we must recall, are more similar than they are identical. An important question which I undoubtedly do not answer in this chapter, but to which I want to draw attention, regards the coexistence of **individual** versus **group selections**. Although the relation is germane to that between idiolect and communal language, the question of the coexistence does not arise in quite the same way, viz., when and how do individual selections amount to group selections? In other words, when and how do changes in idiolects amount to changes in a language variety?

Conceiving of a language as a species makes it important to distinguish between the two kinds of selection. The approach makes its easier to realize that there is no group selection that takes place without individual selections. Yet the two kinds are not always convergent. This state of affairs highlights the reality of competition in a living language, the continuous **negotiations** that take place as individuals communicate with one another, and the relevance of both structural and nonstructural factors to the selections that speakers make, as well as how accumulations of the selections determine the evolutionary trajectory of a language. Before we can make more sense of evolution and the question formulated above, it will help simply to explain more explicitly than in chapter 1 why a language must be thought of as a species, what its ecology consists of, and why its evolution is better understood on a competition-and-selection model, just like biological evolution.

6.2   Languages as a species

Since the nineteenth century, languages have been claimed to have life. Not only is it accepted tradition in linguistics to speak of dead languages – in contrast to the living ones – it is also commonplace to identify some languages as in decay or dying, often in tacit opposition to those which are still thriving. The biological analog to support this vivid language has been that of *organism*. Surprisingly the rising variationist sociolinguistics has not questioned this working assumption, perhaps because its main emphasis has been on comparisons of varieties (such as AAVE, creoles, nonstandard dialects, and standard dialects) rather than comparisons of idiolects. In any language variety, the latter have been treated as generally the same, rather than similar. The closest justification for this working assumption would be that members of a language or speech community communicate with one another because they share the system that underlies the variety which they speak.

We should question a number of these ideas. To begin with, it is not necessary for speakers to share a system in order to communicate with each other. All they need is familiarity with, and some ability to interpret expressions generated by, each other's system, more or less like the algorithms of our computers and word processors. Then one may ask whether the assumption of a system underlying a communal language should also be altogether rejected. No, it need not, although **systematicity** is not a communal requirement. With all the variation that is typical of communal languages, it may turn out that there is more systematicity in idiolects than in communal languages. Systems are needed by individuals, and in idiolects, for consistency in individual behaviors. It is all right when they translate into the communal system, but it is not necessary that they do.

If idiolects are not identical and if communal systems may be less systematic than idiolectal systems, how do members of the same community communicate so successfully? Linguistics has swept under the rug the following related question: Why is it that on some occasions independent of performance factors, members of the same community (or even of the same family or network) fail to communicate successfully? These observations and the justifications provided below advocate thinking of a language as a species rather than as an organism. There are several good reasons for this proposition.

First of all, the language-as-organism metaphor does not capture variation within a language. This state of affairs makes it more difficult to think of language-internal variation as what makes internally motivated change possible. If there were no variation in the production of sounds, in the expression of concepts, in the encoding of meanings, etc., then the only reasons for change would have to be external, quite contrary to what genetic linguistics has advocated. As a matter of fact, it is curious that in a subfield which has been influenced by cladistics, language-internal variation is not as central to accounts of language speciation as species-internal variation is in evolutionary biology. Much of the substance of the latter presupposes variation.[1]

Second, the language-as-organism metaphor also makes it difficult to account for partial or differential change in a language where some speakers may participate in a change while others may not, or may do so in a different way. This phenomenon can be illustrated by the fact that English has undergone divergent kinds of changes in England and in North America since the seventeenth century and is spoken differently in the two territories. A notion of organism that accounts for such a differential evolution would be tantamount to that of species.

Third, the organism trope cannot account for the variable speeds at which long-term changes proceed in a language, not only faster among some speakers than among others but also faster in some dialects than in others. Such a condition, similar to **differential reproduction** in biology, may be illustrated with statistical variation in the usage of *aller* in French and *(be) going to* > *(be*$_{contracted}$*) gon(na)* in English as FUTURE auxiliary verbs.[2] A notion of organism that captures such facts would not in essence be different from that of species.

Fourth, the same language may thrive in one territory and yet fall into attrition or die in another (Hoeningswald 1989). This was the case for several immigrant languages in the New World which continue to be spoken in their homelands. Only a notion of organism which is tantamount to that of species can capture such differential processes in the life of a language.

Fifth, language and dialect boundaries are fuzzy; there is no question of fuzziness in the boundaries of organisms as individuals (Jerry Sadock, p.c., May 1998). The closest analog to an organism may be an idiolect. Just as one needs more than one organism to speak of a species, a language is an extrapolation from idiolects which are governed by similar structural and pragmatic principles or which may be traced to the same ancestor.

I submit that a species, not an organism, is a more adequate analog for a language.[3] Consistent with Hagège (1993), with Keller (1994), and with practitioners of accommodation theory (e.g. Giles and Smith 1979) and of network theory (Milroy and Milroy 1985; James Milroy 1992), I also submit that the agents of language evolution are individual speakers. The variation that matters to evolution really begins at that interidiolectal level, before reaching the next higher level of cross-dialect and/or cross-language differences. Contact, which has been dealt with primarily at the level of dialects or languages, really begins at this level of idiolects. Since the locus of dialect or language contact is the mind of the individual speaker, the difference between idiolect contact and language or dialect contact is more quantitative than qualitative. I assume perhaps gratuitously that idiolects of the same dialect are likely to show more similarities than dialects of the same language. In any case, as in population genetics, changes start taking place by selection at the level of individuals who, while interacting with each other, cause their varying features to compete with each other.[4] If Labov (1998) is correct in observing that there is not as much interidiolectal variation as I suggest is possible, this state of affairs would be the result of the kinds and extents of accommodations that speakers make to each other in particular communicative networks or speech communities.

One important caveat is in order here regarding how fast changes spread in a speech community: typically faster than in a species in which change is effected through vertical transmission of genes from one generation to another and with little modification in the process. However, linguistic features are passed on primarily horizontally, more or less on the pattern of features of parasites, through speakers' interactions with members of the same communicative network or of the same speech community. The default condition of linguistic transmission is with modification, however slight this may be. Horizontal and polyploidic transmission independent of generations makes it possible for a new feature to spread fairly rapidly. If some restructuring follows from such unfaithful feature transmission, such as the vowel shifts in North American White varieties of English (Labov 1994, Bailey and Thomas 1998), the process need not wait for generations to become evident. Still, there is generational variation in the way the process takes place in different idiolects.[5]

Like a species, a language is an aggregating construct, an extrapolation from individual idiolects assumed to share common ancestry and several structural features. Like a biological species defined by the potential of its members to interbreed and procreate offspring of the same kind, a language can be defined as "a population of idiolects that enable their hosts to communicate with and understand one another" (Robert Perlman, p.c., November 1999). This position assumes communication to be the counterpart of **interbreeding** in biology and the activity through which a language is passed on. Membership in a linguistic species is predicated on a family resemblance model. There is, however, a range within which variation is considered normal and outside which one is considered as not speaking a particular language natively or fluently. From this perspective, evolution consists of changes within the structure of the acceptable range of variation within a species.[6]

The following questions arise from the approach outlined here: (i) Why are language boundaries not more random? (ii) Why isn't there more variation among speakers of the same language? The answer to the latter question lies in the role of the contact of idiolects, at which level different speakers accommodate each other and make their systems more and more similar. As argued in chapters 1 and 2, there is one basic form of contact, that between idiolects of individuals who communicate with one another. This is a basic factor that accounts for what Le Page and Tabouret-Keller (1985) identify as *focusing*, a process whereby members of the same speech community communicate more like one another than like nonmembers.[7] Through accommodations, some features gain selective advantage over other competitors which are selected out.[8] In some cases, a network begins using a feature which is more typical of a different network even when most of the members of the two networks do not interact with each other. Individuals commuting between such networks, the counterparts of "dispersing individuals between habitat patches" in ecology (Hanski 1996), are the agents of transmission. They are the initial agents of the change, as they propagate linguistic features – like they would germs – from one community to another.

Nothing by way of focusing or change would take place without individuals interacting with one another, setting their respective features in competition and having to accommodate one another by dropping some features, or accepting some new ones, or even by modifying their respective individual systems. Little by little, linguistic features spread in a community, affecting a whole language or most of it, and often leading to a minor or serious reorganization of its system. Speciation into separate subspecies (identified as dialects or separate languages) obtains when networks of communication have little contact with each other and make different selections even out of similar feature pools.[9]

In some cases, it is not evident that different features have been selected into, or out of, a linguistic system. Differences between two varieties may lie in the weights accorded to the competing variants and/or to their conditioning factors. The distinctiveness of, for instance, AAVE from other nonstandard American English vernaculars is sometimes interpreted this way. Also, differences that have developed among new "native Englishes" (chapter 3) are consequences of differential feature selections. A similar explanation applies to the development of different regional and social dialects, based on which individuals interact with which other individuals the most and what features have competed with each other within their communication networks.

I submit that a language is more of the parasitic, symbiotic kind of species than of the animal kind. Parasitic species are a fairly adequate analog chiefly because a language does not exist without speakers, just like parasites do not exist without **hosts**. The life of a language is, to borrow from Brown (1995:191), "closely tied to the distribution of [its] hosts, which provide many of the essential environmental conditions necessary to [its] survival and reproduction." Many of the ecological factors that affect a language are not physical features of its speakers but features of other parasitic systems that are hosted by the same individuals, such as culture – which brings along notions such as status, gender, and power – and other language varieties.

There are other justifications for analogizing a language with parasitic species. They include the following:

(i) a language vanishes if the population of its speakers is decimated;

(ii) a language falls into attrition and/or dies if things are done to its hosts which do not enable it to thrive, for instance, if its speakers are relocated to an environment where another language must be spoken as a vernacular;

(iii) whether or not a language thrives or falls into attrition depends very much on social habits of its speakers, e.g., whether, in a multilingual community, knowledge of a particular language provides some socioeconomic advantages or disadvantages (in ways similar to avoiding hosts of a particular parasite or to selecting individuals more resistant to it in interbreeding patterns);

(iv) parasites affect the behaviors of their hosts and adapt themselves to the hosts' behavioral responses (Thompson 1994:123);

(v) different life histories of both parasites and hosts favor different patterns of specialization geographically and otherwise; and

(vi) parasitic populations are more likely to specialize, hence to diversify into related subspecies, than their hosts (Thompson 1994:132), as well illustrated by dialectal speciation. In such a case, the development of separate dialects is not necessarily correlated to the development of different ethnic or biological groups.

On account of the above considerations, a speaker's knowledge of more than one language makes one linguistic system part of the ecology for the other, just as much as knowledge of competing structural features of the same language used by other speakers makes them part of the ecology for the speaker's own features. (The competing features may be phonological, morphological, syntactic, semantic, or pragmatic.) One speaker's features may affect another speaker's way of speaking, thereby setting conditions for long-term change in the overall structure of a language qua species. All this leads to two important questions regarding language evolution: (i)

How can feature competition be articulated in an approach in which one feature becomes part of the ecology for another, assuming ecology to be both external and internal to the species? (ii) How different is internally motivated change from externally motivated change? It will help to explain *ecology* more explicitly.

6.3   The ecology of language

Ecology has been invoked to account for language evolution for quite some time now, although less frequently than might be expected, despite progress in the ethnography of communication. Among the earliest instances are Voegelin, Voegelin, and Schutz (1967) and Haugen (1971), who use it in basically the sense of the social environment in which a language is spoken, for instance, in reference to whether socioeconomic conditions in a particular polity favor or disfavor usage of a particular language. This is also the sense in which Mühlhäusler (1996) uses it, as he puts in perspective the coexistence of Melanesian languages among themselves and with the invading European languages.[10] Like them, I am interested in how the ethnographic environment affects a language; in this particular case, how it may trigger or influence its restructuring. However, I am also influenced by the usage of the term in **macroecology**, a branch of biology in which *ecology* is treated as a cover term for diverse factors which are both external and internal to a species and bear on its evolution. Such factors include "population size, habitat requirements, and genetic variation" (Brown 1995:5), as well as "differences in initial conditions, stochastic events, time lags, processes operating on different time scales, and spatial subdivisions" (Brown 1995:15–16).[11]

A practical way to approach this subject matter without making it too abstract is to discuss specific cases and show how they justify invoking ecology to explain language evolution. I will select them from the experience of colonization and the fates of various languages in North America. I will often go beyond these geographical and linguistic delineations to compare language evolution in North America with changes elsewhere. I use the term *colonization* to characterize any case where a population migrates of its free will from a territory and settles in another in which it controls much of its fate. This justifies my observations on the earliest stages of the development of the English language from settlements of the Angles, Jutes, and Saxons in England. As I discuss colonial phenomena, I also cover all sorts of structural and ethnographic developments in a colonized territory which affect languages that are indigenous to it or were brought to it by third-party populations.

6.3.1   A species-external interpretation of ecology: an ethnographic perspective

The language contact literature of the New World has focused mostly on what European colonial languages have become after being appropriated by descendants of Africans and the extent to which they have been influenced by African languages. More has been written on the survival of African cultures than on the survival of African languages. Warner-Lewis' (1996) discussion of Trinidadian Yoruba is an exception, compared to the vast literature on Haitian Voodoo, on Shango cults in several parts of the New World, and on Brazilian Orisa rites. To be sure, there have been some publications on African-based secret languages, but not on the survival of African languages as vernaculars. The main reason may be that evidence of surviving African languages from the plantation industry is rare.

The American colonial socioeconomic settings were not hospitable ecologies to the survival of African languages, in part because the plantation populations were so ethnolinguistically mixed that a lot of Africans could not speak their native vernaculars with anybody else. So, knowledge of these must have gradually fallen into attrition, an experience common among some Africans living in North America today. Even on plantations where a few Africans shared an African language, be it a vernacular or a lingua franca, the language had to compete on every plantation or polity with the local European-lexicon vernacular. Typically this colonial variety gained selective advantage from being associated with the dominant political and/or socioeconomic system, which everybody had to accommodate. It prevailed not only over African languages but also over other languages brought by Europeans of various nationalities.

Species and ecology become useful tropes here in several ways. One such way is that only the parts of those languages which came to the New World were negatively affected by the competition with the local vernaculars. Those languages died in the relevant colonies but not in their homelands. The case of European languages is doubly interesting. They died in parts of the New World but not in Europe, and only in some colonies but not others. For instance, French died in Maine but not in Quebec, and it has been belatedly **endangered** in Louisiana. Dutch survived in a new, colonial, but not extensively restructured, form in New Netherland (New Jersey and New York) until the early twentieth century (Buccini 1995), but it was significantly restructured into Negerhollands in the Virgin Islands and into Berbice Dutch in Guyana, where it was appropriated as a vernacular by (descendants of) Africans. It has apparently thrived (identified also as Dutch) in Suriname, where it has been spoken by the Dutch rulers and the non-Dutch elite as the official language but not as a vernacular.

These examples also illustrate how selection operates on and through individuals. The loss of both African and European languages did not take place concurrently in all its speakers. Some speakers used them longer than others. The fact that some African languages survived as ritual or secret languages in some communities likewise suggests that for a while these languages were also passed from one generation to another. However, in population genetics terms, there were fewer and fewer individuals who could successfully contribute as agents or as hosts to the reproduction of the relevant species, and little by little the relevant languages died in the relevant territories.

Yoruba in Trinidad and French in Louisiana highlight an important aspect of ecology which determines whether or not a language may thrive in a new setting. The Yoruba language which survived in Trinidad up to the mid-twentieth century was brought over by post-Abolition indentured servants, virtually all of whom originated in the same part of Nigeria and lived in communities marginalized from the creole ones. Its gradual death was an inverse reflection of the relative integration of its speakers in the larger, creole community. In the case of French in the United States, the Louisiana Purchase in 1803 was resented by the French settlers (who were in turn being colonized). The integration of the francophone and anglophone populations of European descent has been a gradual process. The present **endangerment** of French in Louisiana is likewise an inverse reflection of the integration process. In this cultural globalization era, the more a population is integrated into another that controls its socioeconomic system, the more likely it is to lose its language variety.

The socioeconomic history of settlements in the New World suggests that integration was a critical factor in the general disappearance of African languages and the regionalized loss of European languages in the Americas. The plantation industry did not develop overnight and was generally preceded by small farming industry in which slaves were generally well integrated – although discriminated against – in homestead settlements. (Besides, the plantation industry never replaced the farming economy, although it often grew out of it.) Reasons of practicality led the Africans to speak the local colonial languages as their vernaculars. Their children acquired these local colonial languages as their native and only vernaculars.[12]

By the time segregation was instituted in the colonies, the creole, and, later, seasoned slaves became the agents of enculturation and of linguistic transmission. Every new installment of slaves targeted the local vernacular spoken by these local members of the populations, with whom they interacted. Its appropriation as their primary means of communication also led to the attrition of the African languages in the New World, whose traces lie in whatever substrate influence can be identified. The explanation for the loss of African languages lies thus in a simple effort on the part of African captives to survive in the new ecology by being practical and shifting to the vernaculars that would enable them to function as adequately as they could.

Colonial history also suggests that Native American languages must have been endangered in two ways and at different periods. In the earlier stages of colonization, Native Americans were driven away and not integrated in the colonial populations, despite some trade and various negotiations with them. Because Native Americans maintained typically sporadic trade contacts with the European colonists, and more often than not in restructured varieties of their own indigenous languages, these latter were endangered mostly by the decreasing numbers of their speakers. The decrease was due to wars with the immigrants, to diseases brought over from the Old World (Crosby 1992), and to their relocations (Patricia Nichols 1993) to new physical environments which were sometimes inhospitable. This trend actually continues to date in Latin America, where the physical ecology qua habitat of Native Americans who have remained marginal to the ever-changing world around them is being destroyed by modern industry (e.g., deforestation). In all this history, we are reminded of the parasitic nature of language, whose fate depends very much on that of its hosts.

The second kind of endangerment is concurrent with the absorption of Native Americans into the larger American populations that have already adopted English or French as their vernaculars or lingua francas. Since the late nineteenth century, there has been more pressure on them to shift to the same European languages in order to compete with the dominant populations for jobs. Reservations, on which Native American languages could have thrived, have lacked the socioeconomic vitality necessary to sustain their communities as autonomous and to keep them free from the lure of life in mainstream North American society or from the pressures to acquire English or French. Socioeconomic integration has benefited the capitalist socioeconomic system at the expense of Native American traditional ways of life in particular. No human intervention will stop the endangerment of the Native languages unless it recreates socioeconomic ecologies that may either grant them selective advantage or make them equally competitive with the European languages. A favorable ecology involves fundamentally the use that a speaker can make of such heritage to survive and thrive in the new way of life.

In Latin America, where the integration of Native Americans started earlier, as reflected by what may be identified as the Hispanicization of races, the lopsided restructuring of socioeconomic systems has favored the

European cultural and linguistic elements. The only chance for the indigenous languages to survive and possibly thrive has lain in those Native Americans who did not participate in the physical **hybridization** of the people, which was concurrent with the cultural assimilation of non-Europeans. Thus, from the beginning of colonization, the Native American languages suffered from a numerical erosion of speakers, which was in inverse proportion to the people who shifted to Spanish or Portuguese, chose to acquire them as native languages, and found few rewards in their ancestral languages.[13] There is indeed an ethnographic aspect of the transmission and retention of languages that must be articulated in terms of costs and benefits to speakers.

6.3.2   A species-internal interpretation of ecology

This section presupposes that languages are *complex adaptive systems* (CASs). They share with CASs in macroecology the following properties articulated by Brown (1995:14):

(i)   They consist of numerous components of many different kinds which interface with each other – some linguists will argue that such systems are modular.

(ii)   The components interact nonlinearly and on different temporal and spatial scales – thus, the phonological component, for instance, may undergo some changes while the syntactic component does not, or while the semantic component may be more extensively influenced by another language than the syntactic component is.

(iii)   They organize themselves to produce complex structures and behaviors – this is precisely the case even if one considered only, from a simple mechanical perspective, the complexities of the phonological, morphological, and syntactic subsystems and tried to explain how they interface to produce speech.

(iv)   Some inherent features of the smaller units allow the systems to respond adaptively to environmental change – this captures the traditional concern of historical linguistics, which should also include the development of new varieties such as creoles.

(v)   Because the direction and magnitude of change are affected by pre-existing conditions, there is always a legacy of history in the current system (chapter 2). For instance, American English varieties reflect to a large extent the kinds of language varieties that the earliest colonists spoke, including nautical and non-English influence in the original proletarian colonial communities (Dillard 1985).

From a structural point of view, language evolution is marked by *restructuring* (chapter 2). This may consist of the redistribution of phonemic contrasts in a language if some phonemes are lost, such as /æ, ə, ʌ, θ, ð/ in several new English varieties, or when a new sound is introduced, such as the flap (the word-medial [D] in *writer* and *rider*) in American English. It may consist of new ways of introducing subordinate clauses, such as with the use of *sɛ* < *say*, instead of *that*, to introduce object clauses but not relative clauses in Atlantic English creoles. The change may also consist in differing ways of weighting alternative markers of the same grammatical function, for instance, whether *going to/gonna/gon/ga* (pronounced [gə] in Gullah), or *will* functions as the primary marker of FUTURE in a particular English variety.

When several such changes co-occur, a language may be restructured into a new variety that some speakers may doubt belongs in their language. This has typically been the case for creoles, which linguists like to disfranchise as separate languages. Part of the ecology that determines such system reorganization lies within the affected language itself. Below, as in the previous section, I will invoke some specific examples of new varieties that developed by restructuring, which reflect an important role of language-internal ecology.

It appears from Trudgill (1986) that even without the presence of Africans and continental Europeans in the New World, North American English varieties would have wound up different from British English varieties. Important indirect evidence validating this conclusion comes from the fact that Australian, New Zealand, and Falkland Islands Englishes all sound different, reflecting in part differences in the specific compositions of the pools of features that competed with each other in these colonies. Even if the same features were taken to all these territories, their preference strengths relative to their competitors sometimes varied from one pool to another, which led to the selection and/or dominance of different variants from one new variety to another.

It also happens that English in the British Isles was undergoing changes during the colonization of the Americas, Africa, and Asia by western European nations. Since English was never regionally homogeneous before the seventeenth century, the metropolitan population reshuffling was producing various new local and regional varieties independent of what was developing in the colonies. As a matter of fact, this gradual process seems to continue to date. Thus, differences in the timing of migrations to different colonies accounts for part of the territorial variation, for instance, between Australian and American Englishes. They partly reflect differences among the varieties that were taken to the colonies, regardless of influence from the other languages that English came in contact with. The fact that Australia was colonized over 150 years later than North America is significant and must be considered as one of the species-internal ecological factors that bore on the evolution of English in these territories.

However, regional and social variation in the metropole influenced language evolution in the colonies in yet another way. Different mixes in the colonies would also yield different outputs to restructuring. This is part of what we seem to observe as we correlate the regional English origins of settlers in parts of North America with the relevant regional dialects. Settlement patterns in the original North American English colonies were not identical (Bailyn 1986, Fischer 1989). Most of the colonists in New England, for instance, were Puritan farmers who migrated in family units from East Anglia. They engaged in family-run subsistence farms that used limited indentured or slave labor. They continued to interact among themselves in much the same way as they had in the metropole. Despite influence from speakers of other languages (e.g. French) and dialects (e.g. maritime English) that they came in contact with, New England's English is often claimed to have remained the closest to British English. This is a situation where English's internal ecology in the colony varied little from that in the metropole. Therefore the colonial variety diverged less significantly than others.

On the other hand, the Chesapeake colonies (Virginia and Maryland in particular) were settled from more diverse places and socioeconomic classes in the British Isles. There were the plantocrats, who descended largely from English aristocratic families and came in family units, mostly from the cities of southern England, notably the London area (Fischer 1989). Up to 75 percent of the colonists by the mid-seventeenth century (Kulikoff 1986) came as singles, not only from southern England (London and Bristol) but also from northern England (including Liverpool), and many others came from Ireland and Scotland (Fischer 1989). Most of those who came from Ireland did not speak English natively, as English in Ireland was used pretty much the way it is used today in former British exploitation colonies of Africa and Asia (chapters 1 and 4).

Such internal diversity among the English-speaking colonists set things up for restructuring. Several variants came to compete with each other in novel ways and the selections that were made were not always consistent with those made in metropolitan cities – those important initial contact settings. Nor were the selections identical to those made in New England, where the population mix was relatively conservative, with a majority of **founder colonists** who spoke alike already.

The Appalachian Mountains received larger proportions of Scots-Irish, who also came in family units and brought with them some Gaelic influence. Their English has been claimed to share some features with non-educated Irish English, which also developed concurrently with English in North America (chapter 4). All these facts show that variation in the internal ecology of the colonial language bore significantly on how it would be restructured during its adaptation to its new external ecology.

6.3.3   Another species-external interpretation of ecology: a structural perspective

As suggested above, part of the external ecology of colonial languages consisted of the other languages they came in contact with. While they were being appropriated by adult non-Europeans and Europeans who did not speak them, the latter's languages availed their structures as alternatives to those of the target. Among the Africans, such restructuring typically under partial systemic congruence seems to have been the case with, for instance, the introduction of an object clause with *say* or in the omission of the copula before a nonverbal predicate (chapters 1, 2, 5). In the case of *say*, the fact that it is often used in colloquial English to report speech quotatively is another important ecological factor. The copula was apparently not identified as significant where it is contracted, as in *he's shy/gone* (just like the possessive marker in NP*'s* + Noun constructions and the third person singular marker on the verb in the simple present tense). The fact that the copula is semantically empty, although it carries tense in finite clauses, may have been a more significant factor, as several languages around the world do without a copula in similar constructions.

Languages previously spoken by such new speakers of the colonial languages favored patterns they shared with the lexifier. Such patterns need not have been statistically significant in either the substratum or the lexifier, as long as they represented a viable alternative in the cumulative feature pool of the contact situation. In communities where the second-language speakers were either the majority or marginalized from the more integrated populations, the languages they spoke previously favored variants that were sometimes at variance with selections made in the other communities. It is such differing ecologies that initiated divergences in varieties spoken by descendants of Europeans and non-Europeans, especially in North America.

As already explained in chapter 2, such selections were accompanied by some modifications. Regarding the case of complementation with *say*, note that although nonstandard English offers the alternative of quotative object clauses introduced by the verb *say*, its use as a subordinator in AAVE and Atlantic English creoles is much more extensive. Moreover, in Atlantic creoles, it is also used for indirect reported speech and in combination with verbs other than *verba dicendi*, for instance, in *Uh hear say Robert gone* "I heard that Robert is gone/has left" in Gullah. In AAVE, *say* also functions as a discourse marker used by the narrator to remind the listener that the speaker is still the same in a chunk of quotatively reported speech (Mufwene 1996a). These extensions of the original patterns in the lexifier are evidence of substrate influence on the selected material. This is part of the restructuring process.

The ethnographic ecology as discussed above definitely affected the role of the external structural ecology toward more, or less, influence, as it determined the particular conditions under which it was possible for a language to influence the restructuring of the target language. One more example will suffice here to illustrate how all this works. The point is that when English came in contact with other languages, no particular restructuring process took place that was different in kind from what took place in situations in which mostly dialects of English came in contact with each other. In the vast majority of cases, English as a vernacular among descendants of Africans was restructured with parametric options that were available in the lexifier but were not equally weighted.

For instance, English has more than one kind of POSSESSIVE construction, as in *the cover of the book* vs. *the book cover* vs. *the book's cover*. There is a semantic difference between the last two alternatives, but this may not have been so obvious to non-native speakers in colonial settings. Since several West African languages mark POSSESSIVE by word order only, on the pattern of *book cover*, it is not surprising that this pattern is the dominant one among Atlantic English creoles. In AAVE, which developed in sociohistorical conditions where segregation was institutionalized only toward the end of the nineteenth century and its speakers generally constituted a minority, the NP + Noun possessive construction alternates freely with the **Saxon-genitive** construction, as in *the book's cover*. The fact that in the relevant substrate languages the same POSSESSIVE construction applies both to nominal and to pronominal possessor nouns accounts for constructions such as *me/we book* "my/our book" in several of these creoles. Incidentally, there are nonstandard dialects of English in which *me book* is normal. Hence, part of what happens in creoles is generalization, although there is no convincing reason for preferring this single explanation to the multicausal one, which acknowledges the convergent influences of several factors and thus seems ecologically more plausible.

Thus, at least in some cases, the respects in which English creoles differ structurally from other English varieties today are developments from English itself. The differentiating selections were made in contact settings where the external structural ecology favored options not selected by the others. In some cases, these options were, of course, generalized to some novel uses or adjusted to be consistent with other aspects of the emergent grammatical systems. These are processes which are not so unusual in language change.

There is evidence of such external ecological structural influence in the development of noncreole varieties of English in North America too, for instance, the *bring/take/come/go with* construction, as in *Mary bought a card to bring/take with*, which seems to have developed under German (Goodman 1993) and Scandinavian influence. Another example comes from Trudgill's (1986) discussion of the alternation between infinitival and gerund object clauses in English, as in *(It was) nice to see/seeing you.* Trudgill observes that the infinitival construction is used more commonly in North America than in the UK. According to him, this change, compared to England, may reflect influence of continental European languages: most of them do not have a gerund and use an infinitival construction in similar syntactic environments. The explanation is bolstered by the fact that since the founding of the North American colonies many European colonists came from continental Europe. Such immigrants became the majority after the American Revolution.

In North America, the additional effect of settlement/residential segregation on the new vernacular of non-native speakers has not been unique to descendants of Africans. The (late) nineteenth and early twentieth centuries produced interesting ethnic varieties among European Americans, e.g., Yiddish and Italian Englishes. Recently, the movie *Fargo* illustrated such a development among Scandinavian immigrants in the midwestern USA.

In the competition-and-selection approach proposed in chapter 2, the language that prevails actually wins a pyrrhic victory, as it adapts itself to its new speakers and contexts of communication, i.e., to part of its changing ecology. This validates again approaching languages as parasitic species and seeing their evolutions in terms of how they adapt to the responses of their new hosts while affecting, or eliminating, other linguistic species that they come in contact with. How individual selections turn into group selections is part of what linguistics is expected to explain. We must take into account processes such as accommodation, which leads to focusing in Le Page and Tabouret-Keller's (1985) sense, and ethnographic notions such as communication networks.

The strong version of my approach to language evolution is that the competition-and-selection process has been typical of language change in any community and at any time. Languages are generally osmotic and the traditional distinction between language-internal and language-external causes of change seems irrelevant. The main cause lies in the imperfect replications which are observable in the communicative acts of individual speakers. When the accumulation of their effects produces changes in the communal system, especially after a period of no remarkable change, we can perhaps say that its equilibrium has been punctuated, though in reality the evolution has been gradual.[14] Regarding restructuring, there seems to be no obvious processual difference in whether the features which compete with each other are inherent in the same language variety or in more than one, and whether the varieties in contact and in competition are assumed to be the same language or separate ones (chapter 5).

6.4 In conclusion, how history repeats itself

The history of English in North America is largely reminiscent of what happened over one thousand years ago in England, and much of the same explanation proposed above applies to language evolution in different parts of the world. In the early Middle Ages, the Angles, Jutes, and Saxons, who spoke related Germanic language varieties but probably not the same language, migrated to England. Their descendants have ruled it ever since. First they drove away or killed some of the indigenous Celts. Eventually they assimilated the survivors through government and economic systems that led to the attrition or extinction of the Celtic languages, of which Welsh and Gaelic are apparently the best known cases.

Until the seventeenth century, very few Irish – generally in urban centers – appropriated English as a vernacular. It remained a colonial language, used very much in the same ethnographic way it is spoken today in former English exploitation colonies, such as Nigeria, Kenya, and India. Although the integration process started earlier in Wales, the development of Old English, then confined as a vernacular to England, must be interpreted largely, though not exclusively, on account of contacts among the invaders/settlers themselves as they accommodated each other. Explanations of subsequent changes all the way to Early Modern English must factor in contacts of English with Old Norse (Kroch, Taylor, and Ringe 2000), Latin, and Norman French (Lüdtke 1995). One must remember that external influence may consist simply in determining which options from those available in the evolving language will be preferred to others. Explanations of why indigenous languages and the exogenous languages that followed English died in England, or why they did not lead English to extinction but only influenced its structures, must be sought in English's external ecology. A relevant question is: What kind of ethnographic **symbiosis** obtained between English and these other languages that it came in contact with?[15] On the other hand, English's internal ecology should explain why the influence of French is more significant in its educated varieties than in its nonstandard vernaculars.

The fact that English endangered the Celtic languages is actually quite informative, as we learn from its ethnographic history that political power is not as critical an explanation as it sometimes looks regarding language endangerment. These languages survived as long as their speakers were not assimilated to the Germanic rulers, just like the Native Americans who were not killed in the colonial invasion were able to preserve several of their languages up to the early twentieth century. In both cases, the indigenous populations were marginalized and continued to interact mostly among themselves and in their own languages. Gradual socioeconomic integration since the seventeenth century led the Irish to interact more and more, and in less subservient terms, with the rulers. In the process, more and more of them have shifted to English – just like the gradual socioeconomic **demarginalization** of Native Americans has been a catalyst in the endangerment of the indigenous languages. There are, of course, differences in the ecological structures of these integration processes, but we need not delve into them here.

One important thing to remember about Native Americans' varieties of English (Mithun 1992) is that they do not seem to have developed during the same time, at the same pace, or in the same ecological conditions as, AAVE or English creoles in the Caribbean. The integration process which absorbed the African slaves in the globalizing economic system – albeit not in the same way as it did the European immigrants – did not affect Native Americans until much later in North American history.

While marginalized and yet integrated to some extent (until the Jim Crow laws were passed in the late nineteenth century), the Africans in North American English (ex-)colonies needed English to communicate among themselves, because the setting was exogenous to them. Thus, their usage of it as a vernacular among themselves, in segregated communities, made more allowance for distinctive patterns of their own to develop.[16] Similar developments have taken place among immigrants who aggregated in communities of their own, more recently the Hispanic immigrants.[17]

On the other hand, at least during the colonial period, the Native Americans needed English less to communicate among themselves than with the colonists and other immigrants. The endangerment of their languages in the twentieth century is largely the result of their relative integration into, or dependence on, the mainstream American socioeconomic ecology, which has eroded their language transmission from one generation to another. As with other ethnic groups, the restructuring of English among them has been inversely correlated to their relative integration in the dominant culture.

Integration also inversely accounts for why AAVE and Gullah are still thriving as distinct varieties and will probably continue to do so for several generations to come: in the main, European and African-American communities form their own separate mega-networks of communication whose members do not have to accommodate each other across the mega-networks but must learn the other's variety if they want to participate in their social or economic activities. This trend has typically been in the direction of white middle-class English, with African Americans having to learn it. At the same time, they are also under pressure of ethnic loyalty to preserve African-American features within "the community." "To talk proper," or "sound White," is often derided among African Americans, especially in the lower class.

It should help to clarify that no ecological factor alone accounts for everything. Lack of, or less, integration alone does not explain why AAVE is closer to white nonstandard varieties of English in North America than Gullah is. To repeat some of what was presented in chapter 2, Gullah developed in colonial settings where the Africans were the majority, in the rice fields of coastal South Carolina and Georgia, i.e., in settings similar to the sugar cane plantations of the Caribbean, where similar English creoles have also developed. Rigid segregation was institutionalized within fifty years of the founding of South Carolina, thus enabling early divergence of African-American and European-American speech habits. On the other hand, AAVE developed on the tobacco and cotton plantations of the hinterlands, as well as on smaller farms, where the Africans were the minority. Although there has always been discrimination against them, they were not rigidly segregated until the last quarter of the nineteenth century. Although this fostered the divergence of African-American and European-American vernaculars, the preceding 250 years of common socioeconomic history, marked by regular interactions between the two groups, account for the large amount of similarities among them, which are due to more than sharing the lexifier (Mufwene 1999b, 1999c).

We should note in the development of AAVE and Gullah a phenomenon that is inversely reminiscent of the appropriation of English by the Celts in the British Isles and by Native Americans. At first, such populations were marginalized by the English. Subsequent, gradual integration led them to shift to English and develop new varieties. The Africans were integrated early but were marginalized after appropriating the language. In the case of Gullah, its greater divergence is due largely to later massive importations of servile labor under conditions of rapid population replacement in which fewer and fewer native speakers of the colonial English varieties served as models among the slaves. These conditions favored the basilectalization of the vernacular.

The indigenized varieties of English spoken by Native Americans could not thrive as long as their speakers were being absorbed by the general American populations outside the reservations. Irish and Scots Englishes thrive because they are spoken in their homelands, in which the speakers are the majority and use it to communicate among themselves. Although Native Americans are in their homelands, the socioeconomic ecology has changed to the extent that external pressures seem to have disempowered them linguistically.

Getting back to the development of European-American English varieties, the process also has more concomitants in the United Kingdom itself. According to Bailyn (1986), British emigrations to extra-European colonies in the seventeenth and eighteenth centuries were an extension of population movements that were taking place in the British Isles. People in search of jobs moved to different parts of the British Isles, which led to the restructuring of English, especially in urban centers such as London, Liverpool, and Bristol, to which the more northerly populations migrated and from where a large proportion of the colonists also emigrated.

The fact is that population movements in England in the seventeenth and eighteenth centuries also account for why English developed into diverse contemporary dialects. It is evidence that English would have changed even if it did not come into contact with other languages. That more than one particular dialect emerged in England since then, some of them probably more conservative than others, is also evidence that extra-European varieties of English would still be different from British varieties. Neither the actual English variants in contact and competing with each other nor their strengths were identical from one contact setting to another. More recent evidence for my position may be found in the development of recent British dialects out of recent population movements such as reported by Kerswill and Williams (1994) and Britain (1997).

Overall, answers to diverse questions about language evolution, such as why a particular language was restructured and in what specific ways, or why a particular language was/is endangered, are to be found in its ecology, both internal and external, and both structural and nonstructural. Such considerations undermine the significance of the distinction between internally and externally motivated linguistic change, except for sociological reasons. Linguistic systems are osmotic; no differences in kind of structural processes may be clearly and exclusively associated with external or internal ecological factors. Approaching languages as species makes it possible to capitalize on variation within a population, to highlight factors that govern the competition and selection processes when equilibrium is punctuated in a speech community, and to pay particular attention to the linguistic behaviors of individual speakers, on whom selection operates. We can thereby understand language evolution better as we can make more explanatory uses of notions such as accommodation, networks of communication, and focusing.

7   Past and recent population movements in Africa: their impact on its linguistic landscape

The following two themes are among the most central to this book: (i) language evolution involves not only the structural changes undergone by a language, possibly also its speciation into offspring varieties, but also matters having to do with its vitality, viz., whether it thrives, dies, or is endangered; (ii) some of the external ecological conditions which determine evolutionary trajectory also affect the vitality of a language in any of the senses stated above. In this chapter, focusing on Africa, I discuss the differential role of external ecology in determining the dispersal and speciation of some languages and the direction of their vitality. In the latter respect, I return to the distinction between exploitation and settlement colonization styles explained in chapter 1, and I highlight how differently they bear on social dynamics of languages. I show that in some polities such as South Africa, where the styles overlapped, their respective linguistic consequences can also be identified.

Chronologically, I approach the subject matter retrogressively, starting with the most recent and better understood events and moving step by step back to the distant past, arguing that basically the same evolutionary processes have been repeated over time. We can learn from the present to make sense of the past.

7.1   Preliminaries

7.1.1   Diverse consequences of language contact

African geolinguistics has been marked by quite a spectrum of contact phenomena. Most obvious are perhaps cases where some languages more indigenous to a region, such as those of the Pygmies and the Khoisans, have been driven to extinction by the Bantu dispersal into their territories. Very few of these languages of central and southern Africa have survived, and perhaps they too have been structurally eroded by their present Bantu neighbors.

On the other hand, some Bantu languages have clearly been influenced

167

by these substrate languages. The evidence lies in the clicks attested in the phonemic systems of those spoken in the southern tip of Africa (e.g., Xhosa and Zulu). Although not in exactly the same way, the European colonial languages, which are undeniable additions to the African **repertoire**, have also been affected by contacts with indigenous languages. In some cases, they have developed into pidgins and creoles; in some others, they have been indigenized into *African French*, *African English*, and the like. Such developments are yet in contrast with those of Arabic vernaculars in North Africa, where most of the more indigenous non-Semitic languages have been ousted or led to attrition.

There are also a few cases where the invaders lost their languages. Examples include the Tutsis, who migrated to Rwanda and Burundi about four to seven hundred years ago and now speak Kirundi and Kinyarwanda, rather than their ancestral Nilotic languages, as their vernaculars. This experience was not shared by another Nilotic population, the Maasai in East Africa, who have preserved their language. In this chapter, I sketch a macroecological background against which such diverse directions of language evolution can be interpreted.

7.1.2   What this chapter adds to the extant literature

A great deal of the literature on language contact in Africa has focused on the development and structural characteristics of pidgins and creoles, viz., Nigerian and Cameroon Pidgin Englishes, Krio, Casamançais, Guinea Bissau Kryol, Cape Verdian Crioulo, São Tomense, Principense, Angolar, and Indian Ocean French creoles. Much has also been published on contact varieties such as Lingala, (Kikongo-)Kituba, Sango, and Fanakalo, which were lexified by more indigenous languages, as well as Kinubi, which was lexified by Arabic. Other literature has addressed the status of urban varieties of some less restructured, more indigenous languages, e.g., Town Bemba, Shaba Swahili, Songhay, and Wolof.

No less impressive are publications on Afrikaans, especially regarding whether it is a creole, and whether or not contact of Dutch with African languages accounts at least partially for how it diverges from European Dutch. A lot has also been published on code-mixing and code-switching, typically when speakers purport to speak traditional African languages. And now there is growing research on language competition and endangerment, an interesting recent contribution to which is Mazrui and Mazrui (1998).

In this chapter, I attempt to show how the present linguistic landscape of Africa came about. An interesting commonality of the scholarship on the phenomena mentioned above lies in the focus on both the **colonial** and **post-**

colonial periods, in contrast with an apparent neglect of the **precolonial** period. The handful of exceptions include Nurse (1997), Nurse and Spear (1985), Nurse and Hinnebusch (1993), and Mazrui and Mazrui (1998). Going back to the ninth century AD, the first three studies argue that coastal Swahili is neither Arabic-based nor a creole. The Mazruis compare the penetration of Arabic and European languages into Africa and conclude that Arabic may be considered an indigenous language, because it has been part of Africa's linguistic landscape for much longer and because it is spoken as a vernacular or lingua franca by a larger proportion of non-Semitic Africans. European languages continue to have a foreign status. They have typically been associated with a small non-European elite and their appropriation by the latter has not granted the speakers a European identity. In North Africa, however, **Arabic ethnicity** has depended more on **assimilation** to Islam and usage of Arabic as a vernacular than on race.

It is difficult to propose a "unified" explanation for all these phenomena. I submit that an ecological approach offers the potential to develop a more adequate understanding of, and a natural account for, these diverse evolutions. They are not random developments.

7.1.3   Adding time depth to the ecological approach

I wish to approach the subject matter of population movements and their effects on the African linguistic landscape from a *sociohistorical* perspective, covering more or less 2,500 years of African history. I intend to show that phenomena similar to what we know of the present or the recent past took place much earlier in African history. The continent offers us enough information to conjecture a typology of macro effects of language contact, enough to explore (i) when a new language may be appropriated by a dominated population and when it will barely have an impact on it, (ii) when its spread may endanger other languages and when it may not, (iii) when addition is literally additive but not replacive, and (iv) whether prestige and the spread of a language go hand in hand or whether factors other than prestige are relevant to its appropriation by another group.

7.1.4   A creole-inspired approach

While comparing different languages and language groups, I make no distinction between, on the one hand, pidgins and creoles and, on the other, other kinds of languages. To reiterate one of the observations in chapter 5, the distinction as traditionally stated in the literature is rather inhibitive, as it prevents general linguistics from benefiting from aspects of research on the development of creoles that shed light on language evolution. One of those benefits is the relevance of socioecological factors, such as whether or not the populations in contact are integrated, and what patterns of interaction they maintain.

I begin with recent contacts and proceed back to the past, to the early stages of Bantu dispersal. I invoke evidence from archaeological and sociohistorical literature, especially McEvedy (1980) and Newman (1995), to reconstruct aspects of the relevant ecologies.

7.2   The linguistic impact of European colonization

7.2.1   Pidgins and creoles in Africa

The linguistic effects of European contacts with Africa have not been uniform. Phenomena still to be explained vary, depending, among other things, on the time of contact, the kinds of language varieties involved, the kind of language that was imposed and/or targeted as the lingua franca, and the modes of interaction that took place. Also worth considering in this case is the style of colonization, viz., trade, settlement, or exploitation (chapter 1).

Settlement colonies such as São Tomé, Cape Verde, Réunion, and Mauritius produced creole varieties similar to those of the Caribbean. These vernaculars have replaced the languages previously spoken by the enslaved populations brought over from diverse linguistic backgrounds.[1] In the historical sense of the term *creole* adopted in chapter 1, exploitation colonies produced no such vernaculars. The evolutions that are the closest to them are varieties such as Nigerian and Cameroon Pidgin Englishes, which have been identified as *expanded pidgins*, because they are structurally as complex as creoles, and they also function as vernaculars for some of their speakers. They are primarily lingua francas which developed in the trade colonies that preceded the exploitation colonies that Nigeria, Cameroon, and other African countries became in the late nineteenth century.

The European exploitation colonization produced two kinds of new language varieties which diverge structurally from their lexifiers: (i) those lexified by European languages (the indigenized varieties), and (ii) those lexified by languages indigenous to Africa (e.g., Sango, Kituba, and Lingala). In both cases, the agents of their developments were Africans. However, variation in ethnographic ecological conditions accounts for the emergence of the one kind or the other, including the choice of the lexifier itself. Both cases involved movements of African laborers. I return to them below. Here, I focus on pidgins and creoles.

An important reason for the above distinction between pidgins and creoles, based on colonization styles, lies in the kinds of interactions that the European colonists had with the Africans. Settlement colonies started with intimate interactions between the two parties. Segregation was subsequent to the increase in the sizes of the European populations and the larger proportions of non-Europeans. Multilingualism led the Africans to adopt the languages of the groups in power as their vernaculars. These were restructured during the appropriation process.[2] Trade colonies were characterized by random contacts between the European traders and their African counterparts. The adoption of European languages under these conditions of limited, occasional exposure to them allowed the development of what have also been identified as "broken languages," a reflection of the minimal uses to which elements of their lexifiers were put.

As explained in chapter 2, degrees of divergence of both creoles and pidgins from the standard varieties of their lexifiers were determined in part by the nonstandard nature of their lexifiers and by the kinds of social interaction that their native and/or European speakers had with the Africans. During the critical periods of their developments, the greatest proportions of verbal interactions were among the Africans and in settings where native or fluent speakers were increasingly minorities. Creoles and pidgins are also typical of the time when Europeans made little effort to learn African languages in these contacts, and the onus was left on the Africans to accommodate them and accept the European languages as lingua francas. Language was typically transmitted without an across-the-board constant model, with some model speakers speaking close approximations of the European varieties and some others producing varieties that deviated in various ways and to differing extents. Such ethnographic settings favored the restructuring of the lexifier.

7.2.2   New "native" European vernaculars

As outside Africa, contact among European varieties themselves produced new, restructured colonial varieties. The most conspicuous of these is Afrikaans, which has added to linguistic diversity in South Africa. Another noteworthy case is South African English (SAE), the so-called "native" variety spoken by descendants of Europeans, as opposed to the indigenized variety spoken by Black South Africans, and to South African Indian English.[3] As in the Americas and Australia, Afrikaans and SAE have developed where European settlers have not given up their languages. They are largely by-products of the emergence of new communities next to more indigenous populations (which have also reorganized themselves into new communities) in the same geographic space. The role of the more indigenous African languages in the restructuring process that produced Afrikaans and the like is inversely proportionate to the nature of the integration of their speakers with the more indigenous African populations.

We need to better understand the history of **pre-apartheid** Dutch settlements in South Africa before we can fully assess what role African languages (not necessarily Bantu) played in the development of Afrikaans. The relevant literature is controversial on the subject matter (Roberge 1994). Likewise, we must seek to understand from a linguistic point of view the sociohistorical ecology of British settlements in South Africa, taking into account the diversity of English at that time, the patterns of interaction between the English-speakers and the Dutch colonists, and the interactions of these populations of European descent with the more indigenous Africans. It is informative that by end of the nineteenth century the Dutch settlers decided to identify themselves as **Afrikaners**, distinguishing themselves from the British colonists, while also distancing themselves from the more indigenous Africans. Whatever we may learn about their developments, these new vernaculars are consequences of population movements from Europe into Africa and new patterns of contact in the colony. There is also a sense in which these new varieties and their speakers are African, except that they are not integrative, "**communalist**" in the language of Mazrui and Mazrui (1998), as explained below.

7.2.3   Indigenized European language varieties

Related to the emergence of the above varieties are developments from scholastic varieties of European languages. These are outcomes of the kind of contact that has affected only small parts of the more indigenous African populations, viz., the few that are well schooled and have had opportunities to use the colonial languages as lingua francas and often as tools of status and power. Originally, the languages were introduced to train **auxiliaries** of the colonial systems, in part to ensure the success of their roles as intermediaries between the Natives and the Europeans. To date, only a tiny proportion of speakers of these varieties use them as vernaculars! The vast majority speak them as lingua francas, in functions and communicative settings that are novel to traditional Africa, e.g., school and white collar jobs. In either the vernacular or the lingua-franca status, these varieties of European languages have been indigenized – or Africanized – and they have become the focus of a growing literature on the indigenization of European languages. (Limiting myself to books, see, e.g., Schmied 1991; Kachru 1992; Manessy 1994; Bambgose et al. 1995; Klerk 1996; Calvet 1992.) In the African industrial ecologies, they have become part of the linguistic repertoires of only a few, and they have not displaced the more indigenous African languages in their traditional functions.

In other words, the position of the indigenized European lingua francas in Africa has been **additive**, not **replacive**. They fulfill new communicative functions and are not in competition with the more indigenous African languages. If anything, they compete with each other (Mazrui and Mazrui 1998). For instance, in some francophone countries, such as Rwanda, the role of French is being encroached and threatened by English. In some polities, such as Tanzania, the position of English may be endangered by Swahili, as it is being adapted to meet the communicative functions formerly reserved for the former colonizer's language. However, in this case the threat consists more realistically in sharing some functions with English, rather than in replacing it. English is still very prestigious and holds the status of international language, despite the fact that Swahili is also spoken in countries bordering on Tanzania.

Thus, when we discuss language endangerment in Africa, these European lingua francas, unlike their creole/pidgin vernacular kin, are not part of the arena where some languages grow at the expense of others. These lingua francas of the elite are simply additions which colonization brought along with some additional ethnographic functions that they serve. It is also from the perspective of these functions that we can interpret the division of Africa into primarily Anglophone, Francophone, and Lusophone areas (see Map 2). First, the divisions have tended to overlook the manifold position of Arabic as both a vernacular and a lingua franca in North Africa and as a religious language in many parts of West and East Africa. Second, they disregard the fact that Francophone Africa, for instance, is subdivided into subregions in which Swahili, Lingala, Kituba, Sango, Mandingo, and Wolof, among other languages, function as nonelite lingua francas. They are indeed used by many more people than the few who speak the European colonial languages. Third, they overlook the fact that Swahili, like a number of other major indigenous languages, is also spoken internationally, in this case, in Tanzania, Kenya, Uganda, Rwanda, Burundi, and the Democratic Republic of the Congo, serving communicative needs of larger proportions of the populations than are served by French and English in these countries. In other words, reflecting the effects of colonial domination more than anything, the distinctions based on European languages are simply superposed on other linguistic groupings based on the vernaculars and lingua francas spoken by the majority of the more indigenous African populations. What emerges is thus a more complex linguistic landscape of Africa, with overlapping geographical groupings.

7.2.4   Indigenous lingua francas at the service of the masses and of the colonizers

The Europeans colonized the masses of the African populations in African languages and depended significantly on mobilizing laborers sometimes

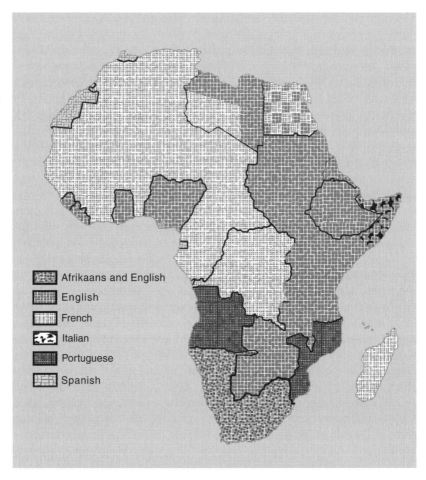

Map 2 European colonial languages in Africa in the 1950s

from long distances (see Map 3). From a linguistic perspective, these population movements and contacts left marks that date from the late nineteenth
century. We are beginning to understand these linguistic developments,
although perhaps not differentially enough yet to tell why Kituba is apparently more restructured than Lingala (Mufwene 1989d), or why Shaba
Swahili apparently complexified rather than simplifying (Kapanga 1991) –
if we ignore the second-language varieties on which Polomé (1971, 1985)
focused to develop his pidginization-qua-simplification thesis. Likewise,
Town Bemba and other major languages have developed, which are apparently not restructured enough to be called anything like pidgin or creole.

    We cannot deny that European colonists played an important role in pro-
viding the ethnographic settings in which these new varieties of African

Map 3 Labour migrations in colonial Africa

languages emerged. However, they can hardly be considered the agents of the restructuring process. The agents were the African colonial laborers and auxiliaries who spoke the targeted more indigenous languages non-natively while they were not (fully) integrated by the native speakers. In the case of Belgian and French colonies in Central Africa, colonial auxiliaries and colonial administrations' militia were originally recruited from non-Bantu areas in West Africa (Samarin 1982, 1990). Although the Europeans typically adopted as a lingua franca a variety that already served as a trade language (Kikongo-Kimanyanga in the case of Kituba, Bobangi in the case of Lingala, Yakoma in the case of Sango, and Zulu in the case of Fanakalo), they did not encourage the integration of their nonlocal auxiliaries and laborers in the local populations. Instead, they developed special labor camps or sections of towns for them, in which they communicated among themselves either in their own ancestral languages or in the new lingua francas. In the latter case, communication and language evolution proceeded on more or less the kind of pattern which produced creole vernaculars on the plantations of the New World and the Indian Ocean.[4]

Little by little, new language varieties emerged which were associated with colonization, as evidenced by names such as the following in the case of Kituba: *Kikongo ya leta* "Kikongo of the state" and *Kikongo ya bula-matari* "Kikongo of the rock/stone-breaker" (Mufwene 1997d). The best known cases of such evolutions are in the Bantu area, with the exception of Sango. It is not yet clear what the role of the Bantu populations was, as opposed to that of the non-Bantu populations, in their developments (e.g., Samarin 1982, 1990; Mufwene 1989b, 1997d; Mesthrie 1992b). After all, those which developed from Bantu lexifiers remain structurally Bantu in some important respects (for instance regarding verbal "extensions"), despite Owens' (1998) observation that their morphologies are very much simplified.

As the Europeans developed the infrastructure for the colonial industry, they recruited labor not only locally but also from places very distant from where the manpower was needed.[5] For instance, the Belgian colonial administration recruited labor to build the railroad between the Atlantic coast and Kinshasa from as far east as Zanzibar. They recruited labor to work in Shaba mines from as far as South Africa. Likewise, the British recruited the labor for their South African mines from Namibia, Botswana, and Mozambique, and even from as far away as India, a fact that has apparently contributed to the vitality of Fanakalo (Mesthrie 1992b). The expansion of the industry took the new lingua francas to places quite distant from their birth places, a factor which also facilitated more restructuring away from the lexifier.

The early twentieth century in Africa was also marked by the emergence of new, urban and multiethnic communities, some of which developed to become cities. These cities became linguistic arenas where the new lingua francas prevailed over the more indigenous languages even outside the labor camps and the sections reserved for the militia and the administrative auxiliaries. In the vast majority of cases, it seems like the native speakers of the lexifiers themselves went along with the restructuring cum simplification process, except in the case of Shaba Swahili (Kapanga 1991) and Town Bemba (Spitulnik 1999). The reasons for such differing developments are yet to be understood. In any case, the evolutionary processes remained as natural and spontaneous as elsewhere.

The African linguistic landscape evidently became more complex with the emergence of these new language varieties, whose communicative functions have grown rapidly from those of lingua francas to additionally those of urban vernaculars. We can now list among African languages Kituba, Lingala, Sango, Shaba Swahili, Town Bemba, Fanakalo, and others in southern Africa. Their genetic classifications are of course no more straightforward than the question of whether or not they should be considered dialects of their lexifiers; they are typically not included in genetic lists of African languages. The reasons are apparently not different from those discussed in chapter 5.

7.2.5   Other, perhaps less indigenous, contact languages

On cannot ignore the introduction of Indic languages with the Indian indentured labor into especially South Africa. Of particular interest here is how Bhojpuri came to function as an important lingua franca among the South African Indians, as among East Indians in Guyana and Trinidad. This was a consequence of speakers of different Indic languages coming to coexist intimately in new settings. Although as a contact variety Bhojpuri began in India, South Africa has favored it ecologically over other Indic languages.

More significant in terms of language contact is the fact that Arab domination in Africa also led to the emergence of new, restructured varieties of Arabic (identified in the literature as "pidgins/creoles") in southern Sudan, Chad, Uganda, and Kenya. According to Owens (1997), the cradle of these varieties of Arabic lies in southern Sudan, where the protovariety developed in the early nineteenth century. Only northern Sudan had been Arabized by this time. Northern Sudanese traders and militia men, Arabic speakers, not only married local women but also engaged themselves in slavery in southern Sudan. These local populations were integrated in the trading and military camps, and they became the majority.[6] During the third quarter of the nineteenth century, after the Egyptian government was expelled from southern Sudan and after trade between the north and the south became less controlled, Sudan Arabic underwent restructuring among the non-Arabs, apparently along with the concurrent emancipation of the former slaves. Later some of these former slaves and militia men served European colonists in, or simply migrated to, neighboring Chad, Uganda, and Kenya, and they took the new language variety with them. Juba Arabic has since become a lingua franca of all of southern Sudan, and it is the vernacular of 40 percent of the town of Juba (Miller 1985, cited by Owens 1997). In Kenya and Uganda, it has become an ethnic language, spoken as a mother tongue in urban settings by (descendants of) those who migrated there from the Sudan.

7.2.6   A brief transition

Among the consequences of nineteenth- and early twentieth-century population movements and contacts are the fact that the African linguistic landscape and local linguistic repertoires have become more complex. The
communicative functions of different languages have been reassigned, as
interethnic communication has come to depend more and more on the new
lingua francas, just as much as nontraditional administrative transactions
even in rural areas, which are otherwise linguistically conservative, have
also been conducted largely in the same lingua francas.

Based on Samarin's (1982, 1990) hypothesis that Kituba, Lingala, and
Sango did not develop before the late nineteenth century, the use of these
restructured varieties is a new phenomenon in Africa. Traditionally, travelers just used the languages of the people that they visited, which explains
why precolonial trade in Africa left no evidence of such restructured lingua
francas. The colonists just selected the ethnic languages that other groups
tended to speak during those precolonial transactions.

I show below that neither Arabs' infiltration of East Africa nor their
domination of North Africa led to such linguistic developments. Nor did
the settlement of the Tutsis in Rwanda and Burundi, nor that of the Maasai
in East Africa. Large precolonial African kingdoms and empires were geographically multilingual and they too failed to produce such contact-based
restructured lingua francas. From an ethnographic–ecological perspective,
the European colonization of Africa produced some drastic changes in patterns of interethnic contacts in Africa, which produced the new kinds of
lingua francas.

7.2.7   European colonization: a linguistic assessment

Eventually these new, restructured language varieties based on more indigenous African languages increased in importance among the masses,
through association with city life, through popular music, through military
rule, and through the lower levels of school systems. Consequently, more
and more of the younger generation have doubted the importance of con-
tinuing to speak their ethnic languages. This state of affairs has led to the
demographic attrition of some languages, marked by a decrease in the
number of speakers, typically caused by the functional erosion of the relevant languages. In some cases, the lower ethnographic status assigned to the
more indigenous languages has led to their structural erosion through
code-mixing with the more prestigious lingua francas. To the ears of some
elders, more and more children acquire their ethnic languages inadequately,

although there is little evidence of across-the-board structural changes in the languages.

In any case, in urban environments, where the lingua francas have also acquired vernacular functions, fewer and fewer children acquire any active competence at all in the ethnic languages. What we want to remember is that the ethnic languages are losing ground not to European languages but to African-based lingua francas and to pidgins/creoles, which have increased their vitality and have been gaining more and more speakers at a proportion higher than those of the European lingua francas.

Competition and selection have been operating naturally in this case, favoring some languages and disfavoring others. Although colonization is an important ecological factor and played an undeniable trigger role in the endangerment of some indigenous languages, the agency is that of the masses of African speakers themselves. It is also noteworthy that much of this effect is postcolonial. We should investigate what interactional or other ethnographic differences have obtained between the colonial and postcolonial periods to understand why African-based lingua francas have such a destructive impact on ethnic or traditional African languages.

There are some reasons why, as Africanized as they are, European languages are not the explanation of why several indigenous languages are endangered in Africa. To begin with, languages such as Afrikaans and SAE are used by communities that are not traditionally African. Their speakers have not integrated themselves into the more indigenous African populations. As much as languages are analogs of parasitic species, languages and linguistic features do not spread like cold germs. Regular interaction with a particular community is a critical factor in the potential for a language to influence another. Thus, taking into account the masses of African populations, Afrikaans and SAE are not part of the competition in any of the arenas where ethnic languages are endangered. They have undoubtedly claimed geographical and societal positions, but they have not become vernaculars outside their communities of European descent. *Mutatis mutandis* the same may be said of Asian communities which speak Asian languages. Social integration is an important factor in the coexistence that endangers some languages. There is thus no chance for the Asian languages to spread now among the more indigenous African populations. They are actually disfavored by the economic ecology, in which they are not associated with lucrative industry.

The indigenized varieties spoken by Black Africans have not really endangered the African languages either, because they are seldom used as home varieties or for socialization with the masses. Those who speak them do not expect other Black Africans to learn them. They fit in the repertoires of the vast majority of their Black African speakers additively, to meet non-traditional communicative functions not met by the ethnic languages. If anything, they receive competition from African-based lingua francas whose communicative functions are now encroaching on theirs, such as Swahili in Tanzania. In Kinshasa too, French has had to face the competing appeal of Lingala in urban life. Thus in many offices, white collar workers conduct "small talk" and discuss their social activities in Lingala rather than in French, unlike in other major cities. The late President Mobutu found it natural to give his public addresses in Lingala, although it does not have an official language status, because it enabled him to reach the urban masses. Overall, from the point of view of language endangerment, it is the African lingua francas, not the European languages, which are a threat to the traditional ethnic languages. This phenomenon is mostly postcolonial, which underscores the need to better understand the social dynamics of language usage in Africa during this period.

7.3   Population movements and language contacts in precolonial Africa

The term *precolonial* is used here in reference to the period before the Europeans started trading with Sub-Saharan Africa and later decided to colonize the continent officially by dividing it among themselves at the Berlin Treaty in 1885. Below, I discuss the Nilotic migrations southwards (7.3.1) and the Arab colonization of the continent (7.3.2), highlighting their linguistic consequences and explaining what they teach us about conditions under which a language new to a region may thrive without endangering its new neighbors, may displace them, or may simply not survive in the new ecology. I proceed retrogressively, starting with the more recent cases.

7.3.1   Nilotic migrations southwards

Nilotic migrations southward (Map 4) about four to seven hundred years ago are an interesting starting point. The Maasai and Tutsi migrated south, the former to the Kenya–Tanzania area and the latter to Rwanda and Burundi. Although they have remained pastoralist, the Tutsi have to some extent assimilated Bantu ways, participating in the local economic structure in which possession of cattle was highly valued. They became sedentary and used the value of their cattle to rule over their Bantu hosts, the Hutu. Somehow they lost their Nilotic language in the process and now speak their subordinates' languages: Kirundi and Kinyarwanda.

On the other hand, the Maasai have remained largely nomadic, although some of them became agriculturalists and developed good relations with

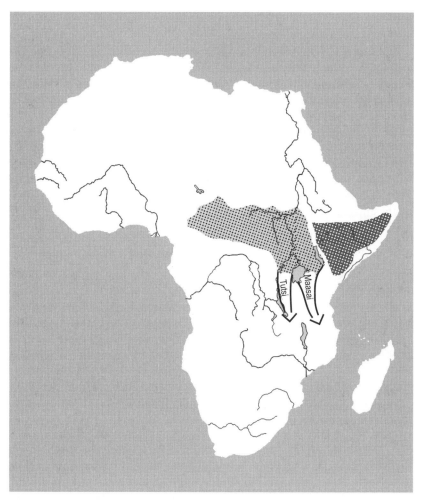

Map 4 Nilotic migrations by 1750

their Bantu neighbors, such as the Gikuyu and Chaga. According to Newman (1995), the Maasai speak Maa, the relation of which to Mbugu in Tanzania is not clear. Thomason (1997) says they speak Maasai, thus a Nilotic language, and she suggests that they have resisted cultural assimilation. Whether or not the Maasai preserved their language or retained the Mbugu's language after driving them off to Tanzania is not clear. Newman (1995) suggests that the Maa are a branch of the same Nilotic group as the Maasai.[7] Pasch (1997) reports that populations such as the Aasáx and the Yaaku in Tanzania have recently lost their languages to the Maasai, having been assimilated to them, which suggests that the Maasai did not lose their language, at least not everywhere.

In a nutshell, population movement and contact have produced confusing effects in the interlacustrine area. There are certainly differences in the way the Tutsi and the Maasai settled in the region. On the one hand, an apparently peaceful coexistence with their new neighbors led to the loss of at least one Nilotic language in Rwanda and Burundi. On the other, relations of domination or dissimilation with the Bantu and Cushitic hosts introduced and preserved Nilotic languages in the region. They may even have caused the loss or restructuring of some of the Bantu and Cushitic languages. The nature of socioeconomic ecological differences between the Tutsi and the Maasai cases are not yet clear. Future research will shed light on these aspects of language contact.

7.3.2   The Arabian colonization of Africa

Further back in time, the importation of Arabic into Africa from the Arabian Peninsula since the seventh century is noteworthy. There are two kinds of migrations and settlements associated with it, and both are different from the European style of colonization. These style differences seem to account for why one may want to support Mazrui and Mazrui's (1998) claim that Arabic is an African language whereas even Africanized European lingua francas are probably marginally so. It is not only because Arabic has been spoken longer in Africa than the European languages have, but also because the strategies of its introduction to Africa and spread there have been quite different.

7.3.2.1 One interesting pattern is that of the contact of Arabic with Swahili on the eastern coast of Africa by the thirteenth century. Arab traders came and settled on the African coast and married African women. They learned to speak Swahili for interethnic communication but maintained Islam as their religion and Arabian economic values in their transactions with their hosts. Arabic was thus retained as an ethnic and religious language in the region, hence a marker of ethnic identity. In addition, it was selected as the medium of education, whereas Swahili was adopted as the trade language, consistent with the extant communicative practice in the region before the Arabs moved in. Arabo-African children and those other Africans who converted to the Arabian values were assimilated, consistent with an Arab notion of ethnicity defined more by culture than by race (Mazrui and Mazrui 1998). This mode of coexistence of Arabic and Swahili in the region explains in part why the former's influence on the latter is confined to specific domains (Nurse and Spear 1985), despite myths that Swahili is an Arabic-based creole (Ohly 1982).

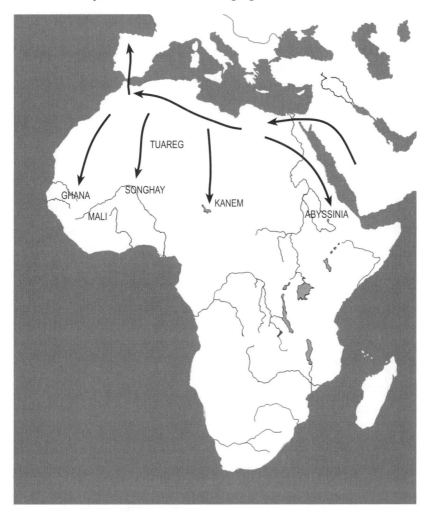

Map 5 The spread of Arabic in Africa since the seventh century

7.3.2.2 The greater impact of the Arabs' settlements in Africa is from their earlier conquest of Egypt in AD 639 . From there, the Arabs occupied the rest of the North African Byzantine colonies and incorporated the Maghreb into the Arab world by the eighth century (Map 5). Then they started expanding their settlements southwards through trade routes. By the tenth century, they had already reached the southern border of the Sahara desert, having established trade posts in Ghana, Songhay, Mali, Kanem, and Abyssinia. Arabic spread with these population movements, less by military and/or administrative imposition than by an interesting absorptionist approach. The Arabs formed alliances with the conquered populations and often married them too (Newman 1995). They allowed them to Arabize and share their status by becoming Muslims. Arabic became an important lingua franca through religion and trade, and it gradually became the vernacular of the Maghreb, encroaching on, or displacing, indigenous languages in the process. Today, Berber language varieties, which preceded Arabic in North Africa, have become minority vernaculars.

As is often the case in such situations, the language that prevails wins a pyrrhic victory, because it is influenced by substrate languages and undergoes restructuring. Owing also to variation when it was brought from the Arabian Peninsula, Arabic has developed into new African varieties which, according to some, are separate languages today. Any account of its speciation which would not take into account contact both among the varieties that came from the Arabian Peninsula and with the languages of the populations that shifted to it would be questionable.

7.4   The linguistic consequences of Black populations' precolonial dispersal

The focus of the present section is the spread and speciation of Niger-Kordofanian languages, more specifically the Bantu dispersal from about two thousand years ago. I ask more questions than I can answer conclusively, hoping simply to arouse more interest in the ecological approach developed in this book and its application to the subject matter.

7.4.1   Background

The tradition in African genetic linguistics has been to discuss the dispersal of Bantu languages as if some liquid that was originally homogeneous had been poured on an uneven slope and split into several streams which became miraculously different from each other, independent of the nature of the surfaces on which the liquid flowed. Assuming that the streams do not crisscross, the approach has ruled out by fiat not only the influence of the beds on which the metaphorical liquid has flowed but also the possibility that the different streams might meet again and produce something new. An examination of demographic maps of Africa over the past two thousand years suggests a different kind of story. So does oral history in some parts of Bantu-speaking Africa, such as the Bandundu area of the Democratic Republic of the Congo, where I came from.

There are oral narratives among the Yansi (my ethnolinguistic group) and the Mbala (a neighboring group) which suggest that the Bantu dispersal did not proceed in straight lines from a homeland in the

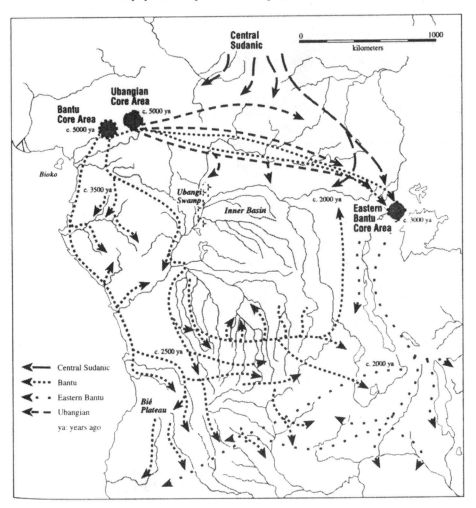

Map 6 Bantu dispersal

Nigeria–Cameroon area to the east and to the south. The narratives suggest
that sometimes people who had reached the south migrated back north, as
shown in Map 6 taken (from Newman 1995). As they proceeded northward
from the south, they often came in contact with other Bantu speakers who
had migrated there before them. It is not clear to what extent such contacts
have influenced the ways in which different Bantu languages came to differ
from, or be more closely related to, each other.

As the map also shows, Bantu speakers came in contact with speakers of
non-Bantu languages too, such as the Sudanic and Cushitic languages

(section 7.3.1). Later, the Nilotic languages came in contact with some of the Bantu languages. What kinds of interactions did the Bantu-speakers maintain with the non-Bantu-speakers, and to what extent was the speciation of Bantu languages influenced by these contacts? These are questions that deserve further investigation in African genetic linguistics. See also Vansina (1990).

7.4.2   The Bantu colonization of Central and Southern Africa

It is informative to travel even further back in time, to the period before the Bantu dispersal started, and see what the African linguistic map looked like in the areas where Bantu-speakers now live. We cannot help concluding that as the Bantu speakers moved southward and eastward, they came in contact with the Pygmy and Khoisan people (Map 7), who occupied much larger territories than they do now. The Bantu invasion produced serious demographic and linguistic attritions among these people, hitherto the only natives to the region.[8]

One is reminded of the spread of Arabic in North Africa. In the absence of written diachronic evidence, one must wonder whether the Bantu speakers interacted with the populations which they colonized on the same pattern as the Arabs did with the Natives in North Africa – absorbing them linguistically and culturally – and whether substrate influence played no role, or just a limited one, in the speciation of the Bantu family into its present subgroups. Could the split of the Bantu family into the present subgroups have happened at all without the contribution of the Pygmy and Khoisan languages? What can we make of the fact that some Bantu languages in the southern tip of Africa have clicks and the languages of the northern border of the Bantu family have labiovelar consonants?

The above considerations all boil down to the question of whether language contact should continue to be overlooked in genetic-comparative linguistics (chapter 5). I may have been trapped in a vicious circle in the cartographic evidence presented here, since some of the dispersal routes on which I have based my discussion have been suggested by genetic linguistic conclusions, aside from topographical and archaeological considerations. Nonetheless, it remains that the Bantu populations did not migrate into territories that had been uninhabited before them. Since we can infer from the Bantu migrations that the Pygmies' and Khoisans' languages have been disfavored by the changing social ecologies, we must ask what Bantu speakers' adaptive responses were to the same contact conditions.

The maps examined so far clearly suggest that what concerns us today about language endangerment and language death has recurred several times before, as populations moved around and came in contact with each

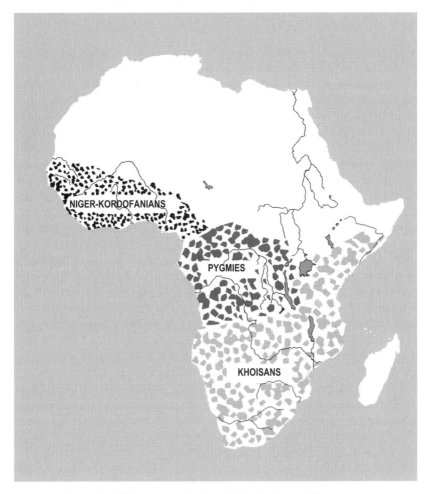

Map 7 Sub-Saharan populations before the Bantu dispersal

other over the past two thousand years and even before that. What lessons
can we learn from the present or recent past for a better understanding of
the remote past? One thing that cannot be overlooked is the relevance of
sociohistorical ecology, especially the significance of patterns of interaction among the populations in contact at specific points in time. Although
not everything can be explained at this point, quite a number of interesting
questions arise that deserve attention. This way we can determine how
some languages are favored over others and which ones become part of the
current repertoires of speakers.

7.4.3   The relevance of communalism to language evolution

Mazrui and Mazrui (1998) make a distinction between languages that are "communalist" (like Arabic) and foster a sense of group identity, versus those which are not (like the indigenized European languages). The former have promoted a unifying sense of Arab or Arabized identity, which depends on culture rather than race, whereas the latter have contributed to more social stratification, supporting social gradation not only between European colonists and the Natives but also among the Natives themselves. **Communalism** has thus been an important factor in the spread of Arabic both as a vernacular or lingua franca even among the less educated in North Africa, and it accounts for the extent to which the number of (speakers of) the more indigenous African languages decreased in the region. Although more and more Natives have been exposed to European languages through schooling, few have appropriated them as lingua francas, least of all as vernaculars, because the languages are not part of their daily cultural activities. The fact that African economic systems are not global and that the lower tiers of the continent's populations – the largest part, consisting of manual labor – does not operate in the indigenized European languages has not helped these languages that are still considered foreign. There are obviously **cost-and-benefit** considerations among the ethnographic aspects of language evolution: speakers have something to gain in the languages they choose to speak (the most). The gain may mean access to jobs, greater geographic or social mobility, greater sense of social membership, etc. Speakers certainly do not decide to abandon those languages which they do not use as often, but increased practice of some languages in some communicative domains strengthens them at the expense of those languages that are less put in practice.

Mazrui and Mazrui also distinguish between languages, such as Swahili and Lingala, which enable "**horizontal integration**" of their speakers, from the colonial European languages, which have putatively established "**vertical integration**," i.e., more social stratification, and even some dissociation from the masses of the populations. It appears that the less integrative a language is, the less likely it is to pose a threat to host or neighboring languages, even if it is not associated with power. That is why, excluding pidgins and creoles – which are more obviously mixed in linguistic heritage and have been integrative – European languages have typically not constituted threats to the more indigenous African languages. Rather, it is the African lingua francas, increasing in vitality and becoming urban vernaculars, which have been the big threats. They are the ones targeted by the nonelite segments of the populations. Colonial and postcolonial socioeconomic structures are implicated primarily to the extent that they have provided occasions for the development and expansion of these new languages.

Interesting in this case is Afrikaans. As indigenous to Africa as it is, it has not enabled the kind of cultural assimilation or integration that North African Arabic has. Its failure to acquire more speakers from other ethnic groups (except among the colored people) and to assimilate or integrate such speakers culturally makes it nonthreatening to languages of the region. It is certainly a lesser threat than SAE, if the latter may be considered a threat at all to Black ancestral languages.

By the same token, even the additive development of mixed language varieties such as Isicamtho, intended to distinguish its speakers from the other speakers of Nguni (Childs 1997), constitutes no threat to the Nguni languages. Although their speakers are the more indigenous Africans, such new varieties are not communalist either. As an Indubil-like variety based on mixing Nguni and Afrikaans and spoken almost exclusively by some male urban Black workers, Isicamtho's ethnographic function is nonintegrative in relation to the Nguni and larger Black South African population. Isicamtho is spoken non-natively and as a secret lingua franca. What deprives it of the potential to affect negatively the vitality of other languages is that it does not share communicative functions with them. Only languages that overlap in communicative functions with others can be said to be in competition and therefore to have the potential to endanger them.

7.5   Conclusions: the differentiating role of ecology

There remains just one phenomenon that I must highlight before venturing some general conclusions from this discussion of language evolution in Africa: the same language may be affected differently under varying ecological conditions. For instance, European languages were affected in diverse ways by their contacts with African languages. Under some contact conditions, they became pidgins or creoles, and under some others they simply indigenized into local educated varieties for the elite. Here the ecology has had to do with different factors:

(i)   the kinds of varieties brought in contact: diverse nonstandard vernaculars in the case of pidgins and creoles versus scholastic varieties in the case of the indigenized lingua francas;

(ii)   the nature of contact: assimilating or integrative versus nonintegrative; and

(iii)   the medium of transmission: spoken/oral versus written.

Each different value on each of these factors yielded a different output, notwithstanding the role of substrate languages in the contacts.

In a somewhat different vein, but still having to do with the variable role of ecology in language evolution, the development of Kikongo-Kimanyanga, Bobangi, and Sango-Yakoma into, respectively, Kituba, Lingala, and Sango is informative. The emergence of the new varieties has not necessarily inhibited the continuation of their lexifiers, not any more than the development of European-based pidgins and creoles has inhibited the continuation – into less restructured varieties – of European languages in Europe and elsewhere.

The above observations favor thinking of languages not only as complex adaptive systems (having life) but also as species rather than as organisms. The analogy makes sense in discussions of language evolution because there are so many processes that affect languages partially and differently, through responses of interactive speakers to variable ethnographic ecologies. Thus a language may thrive in one territory but be endangered in another, just as it may undergo changes variably in the same community, behaviors which are more typical of a population than of an organism (chapter 6).

Although languages evolve gradually through the communicative acts of their speakers (chapter 1), some changes can be associated with the **punctuation** of the current ecological **equilibrium**. Languages can mix their structural and pragmatic systems. From an ethnographic point of view, they may gain or lose vitality, they may acquire more speakers or lose some, they may thrive or die, etc., just like species do, at the mercy of changing ecological conditions. The population-movement-and-contact approach adopted here, a concomitant if not a requisite of the competition-and-selection approach advocated in this book, should help us better understand what factors have affected language evolution in Africa, and how its present geolinguistic map came to be what it is now. We are still not able to answer many questions conclusively but at least we can articulate them for future research.

In the end, and in light of the above considerations, we can still ask ourselves questions such as the following: What specifically happened in the evolution of Bantu or Niger-Kordofanian languages? Why did they split into so many different subgroups? Was Proto-Niger-Kordofanian or Proto-Bantu more homogeneous than any other species, or did internal variation within itself contribute to its many-pronged speciation into so many different languages (and subgroupings)? Was migration in different directions a sufficient reason for language speciation? In light of the macrolinguistic history of Africa outlined in this chapter, can contact really be factored out of African genetic linguistics and its models of language speciation? How much substrate influence did the Pygmy and Khoisan languages exert on the speciation of Bantu? I think all these questions, and undoubtedly many others, deserve more attention in future research on language evolution in Africa.

The literature on language endangerment is growing rapidly. The phenomenon itself is a concomitant of ongoing ecological changes. As languages compete in communicative functions some thrive and prevail at the expense of others. The case of Africa also shows that the most prestigious ones often do not thrive better than the less or nonprestigious ones, and in some cases the latter are the ones that should be considered endangered. Like other aspects of language evolution, language endangerment is a consequence of ecological changes. We should definitely work harder at understanding the causes of this phenomenon. Genetic linguistics will be very much enriched by new findings in this research area.

8   Conclusions: the big picture

The main working assumptions and primary themes of this book regarding language evolution, as they apply to creole and noncreole languages, were detailed in chapter 1. Each of the other chapters articulates its own conclusions, which need not be repeated here. Below, I focus on the big picture that emerges from these discussions.

8.1   From the development of creoles to language evolution from a population genetics perspective

Creole vernaculars are not outcomes of abnormal, unusual, or unnatural developments in language evolution. Rather, they make more evident restructuring processes that must have taken place in the evolutions of other languages. In this book, I have advocated approaching language evolution from combined ecological and population genetics perspectives. Among the working assumptions of this approach is that a language is like a parasitic, Lamarckian species, although it has some structural properties that are distinctively linguistic. These peculiarities bear on its evolutionary patterns and account for the respects in which linguistic evolution differs from some established principles in biological evolution.

I have shown, nonetheless, that some principles of biological evolution are applicable to linguistic evolution. The language-as-species analogy maintains that languages as complex adaptive systems have lives; some die while others come into existence, as a consequence of what their speakers qua hosts do. The analogy is more adequate than the language-as-organism trope inherited from the nineteenth century. For instance, we can factor language-internal variation in our accounts of linguistic evolution and thereby make better use of external and internal ecological factors that trigger or influence evolutionary processes. External ecology causes changes but the nature of these is determined in part by structural characteristics (i.e., internal ecology) of the evolving system. We can also address more adequately the actuation question, taking into account the communicative acts of individual speakers.

A respect in which a language is not fully like a parasitic species is that speakers are not only a language's hosts but are also its creators. Still, the fact that the analogy between a language and a parasitic species is not perfect need not detract from the approach proposed in this book. It would in fact be counterproductive to try to clone everything about language evolution on biological evolution. It is more rewarding to assume initially that a linguistic species has its own ontological properties. Only informed comparisons should reveal how many structural and evolutionary properties the linguistic species shares with biological species, in what respects it differs, and to what extent evolutionary patterns generally are consequences of structural peculiarities of a species.

We must also bear in mind that several different kinds of species are acknowledged in biology. The linguistic species need not be similar to just one of them. From the point of view of structural and evolutionary principles, the different (kinds of) species are alike and yet different in diverse ways, on the family resemblance model. It is significant that the following italicized requisite conditions for evolution articulated by Lewontin (1970) are also met by the linguistic species: (i) it has intrapopulation *variation*; (ii) its mode of transmission from speaker to speaker is similar to *heredity* in epidemiology, though it is partly indirect inheritance from the E-language to which an individual has been exposed and partly recreation by that individual as an active language-acquirer;[1] and (iii) it meets the condition of *differential reproduction*, since every speaker acquires a language in a somewhat different idiolectal version. The latter property is an important anchor of the argument that one cannot insist on imperfect replication as a feature that distinguishes creole from noncreole vernaculars. Unlike in biology, where imperfect replication is a deviation from the norm, in the linguistic species imperfect replication is the rule. Every new speaker replicates their target communal language imperfectly, starting with the trivial fact that they couldn't possibly replicate all the idiolects of which it is an ensemble and no idiolect replicates another. The rest is a matter of degree, depending on the learning skills of each particular individual speaker, the extent of heterogeneity in the target, and the extent of influence of prior linguistic knowledge on the language acquisition process. Why do all cases of imperfect replication not result in language evolution? That is another matter to which I return below.

Languages have been overly reified and have been attributed lives that seem to be autonomous of their speakers, even though it is the latter's speech acts that fashion them. The reality of languages lies in speech, which has physical properties. The action lies there, while the abstract system, the I-language which the theoretical linguist endeavors to explain, is really the interpretation that an individual makes of speech. At the communal level, an I-language is like a species, an abstract ensemble of individual idiolects. This relation is very important, because a communal language is a reflection of properties of its idiolects, and nothing affects it that has not affected at least some of those idiolects from which it is extrapolated.

It is also useful to note that the principles of a language as inferred by the linguist do not shape speech. Just the opposite is true. Principles are hypothesized to account for regularities in the ways speakers communicate. If speakers knew the principles in the way they are hypothesized in linguistics, languages would hardly evolve. Speakers would be correcting their deviations according to the principles they have internalized. Consistent with Noam Chomsky's *competence/performance* distinction, everybody would be coming back to their community's established conventions. Yet, speech patterns in all the modules of a language vary with every speaker, to differing extents of course, and some modules show less variation and more crossidiolectal stability than others. For instance, phonetics shows more interidiolectal variation overall than syntax.

However, extant variation guarantees stability, as new deviations produced by a speaker are likely to converge with some other speaker's variants, rather than diverging completely from them. Evolution in a language occurs when the extant variation ends or when it changes qualitatively and/or quantitatively (Fracchia and Lewontin 1999:61). In their own words,

the evolution of the ensemble occurs because the different individual elements [of the variation] are eliminated from the ensemble or increase their numbers in the population at different rates. Thus, the statistical distribution of properties changes as some types become more common and others die out. Individual elements may indeed change during their lifetime, but if they do, these changes are in directions unrelated to the dynamic of the collection as a whole and on a time scale much shorter than the evolutionary history of the group.

As in biology, we should then be prompted to check what in the ecology of a language accounts for its evolution, for instance, when time reference in a language comes to be expressed exclusively through periphrastic delimitations and no longer by inflections or by a combination of this strategy with inflections. Many of the evolutionary processes associated with creoles are of this kind.

As noted above, part of the ecology of a language lies in its nature as an extrapolation from its idiolects, which are not identical. Its evolution is in fact a by-product of the contacts which these idiolects have with each other and how they influence each other through the mutual accommodations of speakers. The interactions of these speakers determine the overall system of a communal language in ways not too different from Fracchia and Lewontin's observations above, although the relevant details are much more complex. Because languages as either idiolectal or communal systems are multimodular, complex adaptive systems, one subsystem may be stabilizing while another may be evolving to another state. The phonology of a language may remain relatively stable while its morphosyntax undergoes substantial restructuring. Several creoles differ from other offspring of their lexifiers more by their morphosyntactic systems than by their segmental phonologies. (Such observations depend of course on comparing the right varieties!) Gullah's segmental phonology is less different from those of other nonstandard varieties of American English than is its morphosyntax.

One subsystem may also cause another to develop in a particular direction. For instance, when the relevant semantic distinctions are preserved, loss of inflections not only encourages more periphrastic delimitation of the noun and verb but also different ways of forming complex sentences. It is not just because of substrate influence that creoles tend to exhibit more serial predicate constructions. As noted in chapters 2 and 5, loss of subordination with a gerund in English creoles or with an infinitive in Romance ones just made more room for serialization to prevail. Likewise, the option of having predicative copula-less prepositions made it easier for the preposition *for* in English creoles and *pour* in French ones to develop a modal function. Convergence of loss of inflections with the development of a system of predication in which a verb is not required to head a predicate phrase in the syntax made it much easier to delimit any predicate with a semantically compatible free tense–aspect marker.

In all these developments, speakers remain the ever-present external ecologies of their idiolects and languages. Anything external to a particular language variety acts on it through its speakers, who are equally hosts to other linguistic and cultural systems. Because principles and subsystems are inter-related and affect each other, components of a language form part of the ecology to itself. This is another facet of the internal ecology, which goes all the way to the coexistence of individual units, individual rules, and individual constraints within a language. It may be analogized to the coexistence of different pieces of a complex architecture. A better understanding of it should thus shed light on structural factors that bear on language evolution.

Another important factor that accounts for linguistic evolution is that a language is not transmitted wholesale. It is, rather, deconstructed and gradually recreated to meet the ever-increasing communicative needs of every speaker. Its transmission can be said to proceed piecemeal and no speaker perfectly recreates one particular idiolect nor the ensemble of idiolects they targeted. Also, at least in naturalistic language acquisition, neither the deconstruction nor the recreation are conscious activities. Changes occur in spite of what speakers intend to produce.

Children have typically been claimed to be capable of replicating the language of their social environment. In reality, they only come close to replicating selectively much of the system spoken around them. This success is guaranteed by a few factors, including the following: (i) Not counting the role of Universal Grammar, children start *tabula rasa* and often do not have other systems that compete with those they are targeting. (ii) Because their cognitive capacities grow gradually, they are under no pressure to acquire the whole linguistic system concurrently. Rather, they start with more essential components and enrich their emergent systems gradually with distinctions that are less essential and with more complex strategies. For instance, simplex sentences are produced before more complex ones, and the acquisition of basic main verbs starts before that of auxiliary ones (although the latter is rapid and complete in a short time, while the former does not end until a speaker dies or loses their capacity to communicate verbally). Overall, children's linguistic systems do not develop any faster than their cognitive capacities, hence not faster than their communicative needs for more detailed semantic and formal distinctions and for more complex structures.

On the other hand, with fully developed cognitive capacities, adults face enormous pressures to learn different components of a language concurrently and in a shorter time than it takes a child to acquire such components natively. This ecological peculiarity of adult language acquisition leaves a lot of room for confusion and for influence from languages or dialects acquired previously. It is apparently because of this role of adults in the development of creoles that this specific form of language evolution has been claimed to be abrupt. Yet history suggests that the process was as gradual as in other cases of language speciation. Gullah developed within the same period of time that other American English vernaculars emerged as distinct from each other and from their British kin.

The main reason for the seemingly abrupt developments of new varieties in the colonies is that these places were settled by adults from diverse ethnolinguistic backgrounds. Adults have more communicative needs than children to satisfy, and they proceed faster. Children before the **critical period** of language development should thus be considered a stabilizing factor in the evolutionary processes that produced creoles. They were not the creators of these vernaculars, not any more than they would initiate significant changes in any other population where the majority of speakers are non-native, regardless of the extent of variation in the linguistic community.

Aside from the fact that nothing in the socioeconomic histories of the former plantation colonies supports the hypothesis of abrupt development of creoles, evidence for the noninitiator role of children lies in former

European exploitation colonies where indigenized varieties of colonial languages are spoken. Their norms are set by the adults who speak them as second-language varieties, not by children. The latter target their teachers or parents as models (Mufwene 1997b). There is nothing that suggests that the Romance languages, for instance, would have developed under ecological conditions drastically different from the above – except that, unlike today's indigenized varieties, they became vernaculars and ousted the Celtic languages of the region. I return to this aspect of language evolution below.

All internal and external ecological factors considered, there is no particular reason for assuming that creoles developed by any restructuring processes that distinguish them from other languages. Only the ecologies of their developments, including the makeup of the local koinés that functioned as the lexifiers, were different. These koinés varied from one place to another, which partly accounts for structural differences even among creoles lexified by the same language.

There are no documented cases of break in language transmission, and those that are claimed to have obtained in Suriname or Jamaica are highly disputable. Unless command of the lexifier is misguidedly associated with nationality or ethnicity, there was always contact between speakers of the local vernacular and the newcomers who had to learn the lexifier as one of the conditions for their survival in the new setting. Noteworthy about plantations while creoles were developing is that the speakers who served as model speakers were no longer necessarily fluent nor native. Thus things proceeded from close to more remote approximations of the system originally targeted by non-natives in the founder population. The scenario is complicated in this particular case by the amplified heterogeneity of the targeted colonial koiné, which was still in gestation, due to competing inputs, first from diverse metropolitan dialects brought to the same settings, and second from non-native speakers among the Europeans who interacted regularly with the non-Europeans.

These considerations say nothing about the actual restructuring processes involved in language transmission from one group of speakers to another. Rather, they highlight ecological factors that bear on the outcome of the process. The mechanisms leading to such outcomes boil down to competition and selection from a common feature pool. They are of the same kind as the processes that produced new noncreole varieties of the same European languages in the same colonies, except that where creoles developed the feature pools also contained elements from non-European languages. The role of these substrate languages in the restructuring of the lexifier still needs a more adequate account. An important question here is whether the linguistic features in such a larger pool are mutually exclusive. A similar question arises in regard to gene pools in biology, quite conspicuous in island populations where and when race segregation was not rigid, viz., to what extent are genes from different sources mutually exclusive, if at all? In language evolution, nothing precludes the "Cafeteria Principle." It is the "principle" part of the phrase that deserves more attention.

In a way, creoles' structures are a precious opportunity for linguists to think more about the nature of mixed and nonmonolithic systems (Mufwene 1992a; Labov 1998), and about the nature of osmosis in a language (Chaudenson 1992) in terms of questions such as the following: If there are any structural constraints about when and/or how features from different sources can combine together into new systems, what are they? Is language-mixing more natural when done by native than by non-native speakers? Or have linguists applied double standards that should be dispensed with? Other interesting questions arise, such as: How and/or when do norms emerge? Is there any evidence that the emergence of norms depends on the presence of native speakers in a community? Or is it simply a question of what regular speakers agree to do in their communicative networks, regardless of whether they are native or non-native?

Blending inheritance accounts for mixedness both in a language and in a biological species. This happens not because languages or species coexist in the same space but because members of the biological species, or individual hosts of the linguistic species, interact with one another. It is through the interactions of individuals – idiolects in the case of a language – that blending of genes/features occurs. Through competition and selection within the same feature pool, some variants are eliminated or their distributions are statistically affected, and some species-wide changes can occur. The feature pool itself may be affected by contact, which can introduce new variants, but this changes nothing of the nature of the basic competition and selection mechanisms that determine the evolutionary trajectory of a particular species. The fact that variants for the same function may coexist in the same idiolect is significant. It is probably a respect in which a linguistic species differs from a biological species. Still, variation is central to any theory of evolution, and these factors are no less significant for language. Competition, selection, and differential reproduction are consequences of variation in a population of interacting individuals. Articulated as part of language ecology, all these factors should help us better understand both how and why languages evolve, with or without speciation. They help us better understand restructuring qua system reorganization both at the idiolectal and at the communal level.

8.2 Language vitality and endangerment as aspects of language evolution

Another important point made in this book is that the same external ecologies that bring about structural changes also account for changes in the vitality of a language. Languages do not die suddenly nor on their own; they typically die because their speakers choose to speak other languages. The effect of such shifts is that those languages which are spoken less often fall into attrition and/or are no longer transmitted to other potential speakers, especially the younger generation. That is, the population of speakers is no longer self-reproductive and is comparable to a biological population with a high rate of infertility (Sadock, p.c., January 2000). As time goes by, the current generation of speakers becomes smaller and smaller, and eventually there may be no more speakers of some languages. This accounts for the loss of African languages in the contact societies of the New World and the Indian Ocean, in which some European languages were deemed more advantageous.

Note that in the same settings European languages that did not prevail economically experienced the same kinds of attrition and loss, although they survived a little longer. An important factor in this case is that in places like the USA there were European communities that were still clearly German, Italian, Irish, etc. The African slaves did not have the privilege of being grouped according to their ancestral ethnolinguistic groups. However, socioeconomic pressures eventually affected those initial social organization patterns, favoring English as the most advantageous vernacular, and making the other European languages less and less necessary, especially as the White communities became less and less ethnically segregated. Like the African slaves, who had been integrated in the economic system – as mechanical components – although not socially, White Americans from continental Europe also lost their ancestral languages as vernaculars through socioeconomic integration.

This form of integration emerges as an important factor in the competition among languages. It brought about a rapid loss of African languages in slave plantation colonies. The few cases where such languages survived long enough involve post-Abolition importations of indentured labor, such as the Yoruba in Trinidad or Indians in Mauritius and the Caribbean. The significance of social and/or regional integration as an ecological factor in language evolution is underscored by the following: segregation generally made allowance for more substrate influence on the colonial varieties that developed among those who were marginalized from the economically dominant groups. When non-native speakers of the lexifier were integrated, second-language acquisition features generally disappeared with the deaths of the non-native speakers, while their children acquired features which became native to the colonies. Indeed, socioeconomic history suggests that the children of African slaves born in the preplantation communities spoke the colonial koiné varieties of the European adults and children around whom they grew up.

Regarding language endangerment, languages other than the lexifier survived longer when speakers of the same language were not absorbed by the speakers of the lexifier. In the United States, several European immigrants continued to speak their ancestral languages as long as they continued to live in their own segregated communities, but it was all a matter of time. The Africans did not have that chance, although they were not absorbed socially by the English-speaking populations. The multiplicity of ancestral languages they brought along and the way they were mixed on the plantations (not necessarily by design) disfavored the survival of African languages more effectively than in African cities today.

Socioeconomic integration also accounts for the endangerment of Native American languages. The more the Native Americans are integrated in the mainstream global economies and cultures of the present American polities, the more pressure they experience from the dominant languages of these territories and the less motivation they feel to speak their ancestral languages even in domains that are private to them. It is not a question of losing pride in one's heritage; it is a matter of wanting to be like everybody else. This is a costly price that integration in the dominant socioeconomic system and assimilation to its culture have had everybody else pay – from the African slaves to European colonists and later immigrants.

8.3   Integration and segregation as key ecological factors in language evolution

The integration/segregation hypothesis accounts for the development not only of creoles and AAE but also of Appalachian, Amish, and Cajun vernacular Englishes, as well as of perhaps-moribund varieties such as Yiddish English. Overall, communities that developed in isolation from mainstream groups developed their own distinctive varieties, through the same competition-and-selection formula. The varieties cited here have been made more conspicuous by the language contact literature that simply assumed that some special, unusual, abnormal, if not unnatural, processes were involved in the evolutionary processes which produced them. As noted in section 8.1, substrate features generally participated in the colonial feature pool in which the same competition-and-selection processes as elsewhere took place.

Ecology bore on the selection and would in some cases favor structural options in the lexifier that were congruent with those of some substrate languages. As a matter of fact, much of the same account applies to the development of all varieties of languages that came into contact with others. Congruent options were among the advantageous selections. A great deal can be learned about language evolution in North America and other former colonies by approaching the subject matter from an ecological perspective.

This approach also leads us to pay attention more to the global sociohistorical situation of some populations than to ethnicity alone or first. Even in places such as South Africa, ethnicity can more adequately be subordinated to the more general socioeconomic factors that influence language evolution. For instance, it would be tempting to equate the situation of Black South Africans with that of African Americans, taking into account how oppression and segregation have been exercised against both groups. Yet the socioeconomic histories of South Africa and the United States suggest that Black South Africans are more like Native Americans in being more indigenous to South Africa, though they are different in having remained the majority. They are also like Native Americans in having generally been kept very long on the margins of the global economic development and being involved belatedly in the global economic system. Thus, Black South Africans and Native Americans are alike in feeling later the global pressure to develop fluency in English for success in the new economic system. There the similarities end and one must interpret the evolution of English among South Africans differently from its evolution among both African Americans and Native Americans.

The cases of Black South Africans and Native Americans would be more comparable if the former did not remain the majority and if relative to them colonization had been in the settlement style. However, the colonization of Black South Africans has been on a largely exploitation style which happens to have coexisted with a settlement colonization style involving populations nonindigenous to Africa. It is not to vernacular English that Black South Africans, unlike Native Americans, have been exposed. Rather, it is to a scholastic English similar to those introduced in Nigeria and India during the colonial period. As in these former exploitation colonies, this scholastic variety is now being indigenized by Black South Africans. (It was also introduced later to them than into the other colonies.)

Neither the English variety to which Black South Africans were exposed nor the means by which they were exposed to it makes the evolution of English among Black South Africans comparable to its evolution among African Americans. The closest South African counterpart of African-American English or of English creoles in former slave plantation colonies is South African Indian English, a by-product of importation of a multilingual indentured labor. Clearly, socioeconomic explanations should be considered before those that privilege ethnicity.

Regarding the significance of segregation as a factor in the development of creoles and the like, it is also noteworthy that a demographic majority of the relevant populations, such as was the case on sugar cane plantations and rice fields, is not the primary reason why such vernaculars developed to be so different structurally from other colonial offspring of their lexifiers. According to the socioeconomic histories of the territories where creoles developed, transmission of the lexifier was definitely continuous and did not depend on the presence of a European population among the non-Europeans. When the European languages started basilectalizing into creoles, there were already enough locally born non-Europeans (the creole people, who spoke the local lexifier but not Creole) to propagate models similar to those spoken by White creole colonists. The following two factors, among others, bore on language evolution: (i) social isolation made more allowance for substrate influence, and (ii) rapid population replacement offset the founder effect of the earlier non-European creole populations on language evolution in later generations of imported labor.

If it were all a matter of numbers, AAVE, Old Amish, Cajun, Yiddish, Appalachian Englishes, and the like would not have developed. They are spoken by minority populations relative to speakers of English varieties considered mainstream. On the other hand, note that AAVE has remained structurally close to White American Southern English simply because their respective speakers had shared over two hundred years of intimate socioeconomic history before segregation was institutionalized through the Jim Crow laws in the late nineteenth century. Differences between them reflect independent evolutions which they have undergone since that institutionalization of segregation. This is consistent with Guy Bailey's (1997) thesis that the divergence of White and African-American varieties of English dates from the early twentieth century. Such developments underscore the importance of understanding more adequately the nature of socioeconomic interactions in different settings in order to make better sense of their linguistic evolutions.

The same ecological approach also sheds light on why White American English vernaculars differ more conspicuously from each other regionally than AAVE varieties do. It is easier for a non-White American to tell a White New Englander from a White Southerner or from a White Midwesterner than it is for a non-African American to tell a New Yorker AAVE-speaker from an Atlantan or Chicagoan AAVE-speaker. One must first consider the fact that AAVE's cradle lies in the American southeastern tobacco and cotton plantations (Bailey and Thomas 1998, Rickford 1998);

the vernacular spread throughout the USA since the late nineteenth century, with the Black Exodus, after it had already developed into something close to what it is today. On the other hand, White American varieties developed locally, in the regions in which they are spoken.

Second, African Americans spread throughout the USA only to find themselves segregated again in ghettoes of the cities to which they migrated, although they remain minorities. Thus they have not socialized regularly with White Americans, at least not in ways that would lead them either to influence structures of White American English varieties or to restructure their own vernaculars under the latter's influence. There have of course been lexical transfers across these ethnic varieties; but there has been little motivation from outside for AAVE-speakers to speak differently, despite its stigmatization.

Third, contacts with other Americans have been limited to the workplace. Matters of ethnolinguistic identity left alone, blue-collar jobs have brought AAVE speakers into contact with speakers of other vernaculars that already shared several features with theirs. There has been no more pressure on African Americans than on speakers of these other varieties to restructure their vernaculars in the direction of standard English. For white-collar jobs, the main pressure on African Americans, as on other Americans, has been to learn standard English as a second-language variety and therefore to alternate between the standard and their vernacular. Pressure in the community not to sound White has guaranteed the retention of African-American ways thought of as a continuum from acrolect-like to basilectal varieties. In sum, segregated living conditions have prevented African Americans from participating in those changes occurring in White communities, consistent with the divergence hypothesis of the development of AAVE (Labov and Harris 1986, Bailey and Maynor 1989). African and European Americans' vernaculars have thus followed different evolutionary paths that reflect patterns of socialization, rather than numerical proportions, of their speakers.

The above considerations are supported indirectly by Caribbean societies, where social dialects are socioeconomically, rather than ethnically, based. Blacks and Whites of the same socioeconomic classes speak alike. Although Whites are minorities in these territories, this linguistic integration is a consequence of post-Abolition socioeconomic integration. Blacks and Whites of the same socioeconomic classes live in the same neighborhoods, a phenomenon that is far from being universal even among the most affluent in the United States.

If our scholarship had not made ethnicity more central in American historical dialectology than patterns of social interaction, one would easily realize that minority White nonstandard vernaculars have had fates very similar to AAVE and Gullah. Only one important difference must be highlighted here, leaving other questions for future research: the endangerment of Ocracoke Brogue because of the influx of mainlanders to the barrier islands of the Carolinas is not matched by a similar fate of Gullah. The primary reason is integration/segregation. Although affluent White Americans have constituted the majority of the in-migrants overall, the residential settlement practices have been different on the islands with originally White majority and those with originally Black majority. On the former, the in-migrants have mixed with the locals and have been assimilating them to their mainland cultures, whereas on the latter they have formed their own separate neighborhoods. Consequently, assimilation on Ocracoke has endangered its local brogue, whereas segregation on the Sea Islands of South Carolina has not played a role in the endangerment of Gullah, where Gullah is in attrition. On islands such as Daufuskie, Gullah has suffered serious demographic attrition caused by the continuous exodus of its speakers for the city. It has suffered no debasilectalization. In places like Hilton Head, ethnic identity and resentment of the takeover of the Island by land developers have encouraged the African-American islanders to hold on to their linguistic heritage. This reaction is similar to the loyalty of nonassimilationists to the local nonstandard vernaculars on Ocracoke (Wolfram and Schilling Estes 1995) and on Martha's Vineyard (Labov 1963). In the cases of the Ocracoke brogue and Gullah, ethnicity bears on socialization. The differential fates of the two vernaculars regarding endangerment reflect whether or not the groups in contact are integrated. The similarities between Gullah on Hilton Head and Martha's Vineyard's vernacular reflect similar attitudes of the locals to the economically powerful newcomers. In this case, one can also argue that ethnicity takes second position to other socioeconomic forces that bear on language evolution, although, to be sure, it cannot entirely be denied.

8.4   Colonization styles and language evolution

Differences in colonization style were also identified in especially chapters 1, 4, and 7 as relevant to language evolution. This variation is also related to integration/segregation of the coexistent populations. Trade colonization entailed sporadic contacts; these are restricted to a specific socioeconomic function, like exchange of commodities. Such contacts restricted regular access to the full lexifier and led to the development of pidgins. If any of these lingua francas have endangered some of the more indigenous vernaculars, it is for reasons that no longer have to do with the particular sociohistorical conditions under which they developed. Such an effect on other languages would occur after the pidgins have developed into full-fledged languages that can serve all sorts of social functions. They are then called expanded pidgins and have structures similar to creoles. Their structures reflect both the nonstandard nature of their lexifiers and the role of adult second-language learners whose communicative needs they had to satisfy as the contexts of their usage expanded.

Settlement colonies are associated with differential patterns of interaction. Under conditions of socioeconomic integration without significant contributions from languages other than the lexifier, restructured varieties developed that are not treated as creoles, such as Québécois French and most mainstream varieties of American English. Much of what has happened in such developments reflects the structural kinship of the systems in contact.

Under conditions of social and/or regional segregation, several nonstandard restructured varieties have developed, some of which are treated as creoles apparently because their speakers are (partially) of non-European descent. The more divergent restructuring observed in such cases reflects the role of non-European languages in determining structural selections that are different from those made in other communities where the same lexifier prevailed as the vernacular. In more or less the same category as creoles fall several stigmatized varieties such as Appalachian and Ozark Englishes, Amish and Cajun vernacular Englishes, and AAVE, which apparently display less restructuring. The structural peculiarities of the lexifier, the influence of other languages, and social and/or geographical isolation from mainstream communities are ecological factors that account (partially) for the divergence of their structures. One common genetic feature of the varieties that developed in settlement colonies is the adoption of the lexifier by the coexistent populations as their vernacular. Their different evolutions are consequences of this ethnographic act.

Exploitation colonization is also associated with segregation straightforwardly combined with power stratification. Access to a scholastic variety of the lexifier is provided through formal education, designed for the formation of a local elite sandwiched originally between the colonizers and the colonized, and later between the outside world and the indigenous culture. The appropriation of this new lingua franca to the service of the elite has resulted in its indigenization. This colonization style introduced the foreign lexifier in a more sustained, though artificial, form. Its communicative functions were also supposed to be limited, because it was not expected to function as a vernacular. Part of the indigenization process is associated with the expansion of its communicative function, under less and less influence of native speakers.

Even in terms of causation or contributing factors from languages other than the lexifier, one would be hard pressed to argue that different restructuring processes are involved in the development of all the above (ex-)colonial varieties. What makes the distinction between colonization styles particularly informative is the influence of the varying ecologies, including the nature of the lexifier, on language evolution. In places where different forms of colonization came to coexist, such as in South Africa, the landscape of outcomes calls for more careful analysis. Since things fit in such categories typically in degrees, a family-resemblance model may in the final analysis be much more informative, as long as one recognizes that variation in any of the ecological parameters amounts more or less to changing the value of a variable in an algebraic formula and yielding a different language variety as output.

As shown in chapters 6 and 7, another advantage of approaching population movements and language contacts from the point of view of colonization style is the light it sheds on language endangerment. In Africa, Europe, and the Americas it is assimilationist settlement colonization that has led to the attrition and/or loss of the more indigenous African, Celtic, and Native American languages. In exploitation colonies, the colonial languages adopted as elite lingua francas have not endangered the indigenous languages. Rather, it is indigenous lingua francas like Swahili, Lingala, and Hausa which have gained more and more speakers at the expense of ethnic vernaculars. An important reason for this is that these lingua francas are ethnographically **integrative**, whereas the European colonial languages have been **segregative**. Although they have enabled crossnational communication, as among the anglophone or francophone countries of Africa, such bridging has been only at the level of the elite and has excluded the majorities of the populations of those regions. For the masses of the populations in this part of the world, where economy is not yet on the Western global model, access to jobs, regional mobility, and crossethnic integration continue to depend partly on the indigenous lingua francas. These are the same factors that have led to language attrition and loss in former settlement colonies of Europe and the Americas, if we do not mind assuming this perspective for as far back in time as the colonization of the now Romance countries by the Romans and the invasion of England by Germanic populations. Why the Norman rule of England did not Romanize this colony linguistically deserves investigating, as much as the case of the Nilotic invasion of the Bantu population in Rwanda and Burundi, where more indigenous languages – Kinyarwanda and Kirundi – have prevailed. From an ecological perspective, it should be informative to re-examine language evolution in Europe and elsewhere from the point of view of colonization. Genetic linguistics stands to benefit from such an approach.

8.5   Overall...

What was really needed in order to articulate questions about language evolution in informative ways was a set of alternative assumptions about a language. These should enable linguistics not only to benefit from what has already been learned about evolution but also to make whatever contributions it can that will enrich and advance the relevant theories. Time will tell how much the proposed ecological approach to language evolution will contribute to theories of evolution, for instance in cases where elements external to a target language are added to extant variants but do not replace them. I now wish to summarize some benefits for linguistics.

A language is more like a bacterial, Lamarckian species than like an organism. A subset of innovations/deviations in the communicative acts of individual speakers cumulate into the "invisible ecological hand" that produces evolution. Central to this position are also the mutual accommodations of speakers, a consequence of variation in the species and the contact needed to transmit linguistic features. This contact of idiolects is the only basic one needed to account for language evolution, including both the cases that have traditionally concerned genetic linguists and those that have been the focus of genetic creolistics and of the literature on the indigenization of European languages. The structural processes involved in the contacts of idiolects, dialects, and languages are the same, with the contact arena situated in the mind of the speaker. The same rules posited in historical linguistics to represent change apply to all cases where the structure of a language has changed. Ecological factors remain relevant to account for all such changes, but they cannot be confused with the restructuring processes themselves. There are internal and external factors that bear on language evolution, but they apply concurrently in all cases of language evolution. They play complementary roles in determining the evolutionary trajectories of a language under different ecological conditions, including its own structural properties, those of other languages it came in contact with when this is relevant, and the ethnographic conditions of its use.

Notes

1 I will generally refrain from using this established term, because it is misleading. Although the origins of features of creoles have received a lot of attention, the debate of especially the past decade has been increasingly on their development, which has proceeded beyond the mere selection of features from the languages in contact and has also been about the integration of the features into the new systems.

1 INTRODUCTION

1 The term *transmission* is used here neutrally to subsume the passage of a language from its current speakers to others. Normally, the speakers do not actively teach it to those who target it; nor do the learners passively wait for its system to be passed on wholesale to them. According to Hagège (1993), language acquisition involves both inheritance and recreation. Likewise, Lass (1997) observes that language is imperfectly replicated. These observations suggest why languages evolve from one state to another. I argue in chapter 6 that the best transmission analog in population genetics is epidemiological.

2 DeGraff (1999:9) may have had this kind of question in mind in positing a distinction between *I-creole* and *E-creole*. I will thus misinterpret his "E-creole" as a communal language, an ensemble of I-creoles qua idiolectal systems. Hence, we can deal with interspeaker variation in creoles and address the following questions among others: When and how do properties of individual I-creoles amount to properties of communal creoles? How did I-creoles and communal creoles develop from the I-systems of their lexifiers?

3 The distinction between "exploitation" and "settlement colonies" is useful, because each kind of colonization largely determined the kinds of interactions which obtained between Europeans and non-Europeans. In **exploitation colonies**, Europeans had no, or little, interest in developing local roots. They worked for their governments or some companies on fixed terms, hoping to make some money and eventually return home for retirement, after serving in some other colonies. **Settlement colonies** were intended as new, permanent and better, homes than what was left behind in Europe (Crosby 1986).

   Here, Europeans had more commitment to seeing their languages prevail as vernaculars, rather than simply as lingua francas, despite the institution of segregation. Therefore they used them also in communicating with the dominated populations. In exploitation colonies, they kept their languages almost to themselves and their colonial auxiliaries, including the local elite to whom they taught scholastic varieties. As a matter of fact, the development of pidgins is also tied partly with usage of native auxiliaries called "grumettos" (see Hancock 1986a), although it is not true that the only varieties that developed among the grumettos were pidgins.

4 I speak of "heuristic [creole] prototypes" (Mufwene 1996a) in a different way from Thomason's (1997) and McWhorter's (1998) invocations of "prototype." We know of no creole prototypes either in the sense of first specimen or in the sense of best exemplar (Mufwene 2000a). I use the term to identify classic creoles as those which first caught the attention of linguists and have informed our assumptions about their structures to date. They are heuristic prototypes because it is from what is known about them that the term *creole* has been extended almost perniciously to many other contact-based language varieties around the world.

5 The meaning of the term *creole* applied to people varies almost from one colony to another, as becomes obvious in the discussion below. For the latest informative discussion of the term, see Ira Berlin's article in *Encarta Africana 2000*. Domínguez (1986) is a detailed sociohistorical discussion of its usage in Louisiana.

6 Literally, *basilectalization* means the development of a *basilect*, the nonstandard variety that is the most different structurally from the *acrolect*, or local standard variety. In the context of this book, in which the development of creoles is treated as a subject matter of both historical and genetic linguistics, the term denotes the process by which a language variety diverges structurally toward a pole at an extreme from that of its lexifier. This process contributes to language speciation as discussed below and in chapter 2. The structural properties of a basilect reflect the extent of its divergence from the lexifier or the local acrolect. There is no uniform basilect that is common for all creoles lexified by the same European language.

7 Lightfoot (1999:82, 88f) argues that an I-language changes abruptly. This is plausible if one considers only transitions from one state of an I-language to the next. However, when a new rule is adopted or a current one is modified (Harris and Campbell 1995:48–9), not all the relevant items are affected at the same time. For instance, those English speakers who associate words such as *criteria, phenomena, data*, and *desiderata* with a Greek or Latin plural did not acquire a general rule for the whole class at once. They made the associations only on those occasions when they could hear the words used in this fashion. It is not unusual to hear *data* and *phenomena* also as singulars (on the pattern of *agenda*), while the others are used strictly as plurals. The gradual expansion of the class of items to which a speaker applies the *-um/-a* and *-on/-a* alternations suggests that an I-language does not change abruptly. With regard to a communal language, it definitely takes time before such patterns or changes spread across a population of speakers. This is what makes language evolution gradual.

8 To be sure, one must deal with the case of South African Indian English, which developed in contact conditions similar to those involving Africans in the New World and the Indian Ocean. To my knowledge the term *creole* has not been applied to this vernacular. Sierra Leone Krio also deserves mention here, since

the term *Krio* itself is derived from *creole*. Part of its development has a lot to do with the "repatriation" of former slaves from the New World. See also note 2 to chapter 7.

9 Owens (1998) advocates just the opposite of my proposal and argues against characterizations such as "restructured Kimanyanga" or "restructured Arabic," because "restructured X" does not seem operational. He would prefer to use the term *creole*, despite the absence of a yardstick for measuring the extent of structural divergence from the lexifier which would help us determine when a "contact-based" language variety is a creole. His position is based on the fact that varieties such as "Nubi, Sango, and Kituba have been structurally and communicatively so vastly restructured that they are probably no more (but also perhaps no less) like their lexical donor language than Haitian Creole is like French" (p. 118). My argument is simply that the term *creole* is not necessary to capture similarities in these adaptive evolutions.

10 For an informative discussion of *linguistic evolution* parallel to, but more elaborate than, what is presented in this paragraph, see McMahon (1994, chapter 12). McMahon highlights the different ways in which evolutionary biological metaphors have been used in linguistics since the nineteenth century and why they have been shunned in most of the twentieth century. She also observes that "these unsuccessful experiments with [the biological] metaphor need not deter us, but should warn us to lay out the basis of comparison carefully, and that we need not equate to compare" (p. 334). This book is written in this spirit.

11 For an elaborate discussion of this notion, see Labov (1994, chapter 3). In this approach, evolution is inferred from comparisons of data collected from speakers of different coexistent generations. However, one must beware of age-grading phenomena (Rickford 1992), and such evidence must be corroborated by real-time data, as in Labov (1966) about /r/-constriction in New York City, Trudgill (1974) about the labialization of /θ, r/ in Norwich, and more recently Bailey and Thomas (1998) who argue that AAVE and American White Southern English are diverging from each other.

12 The analogy can be traced as far back as the early nineteenth century, in Bopp (1833) and Becker (1833). For informative discussions, see Koerner (1983) and Yngve (1996).

13 In the case of Copper Island Aleut (CIA), Anderson (1999) shows that layers of contact can affect the structure of language in curious ways. CIA's mixed system from the nineteenth-century contact of Aleut and Russian has undergone more influence from Russian since the 1960s. Its speakers were relocated to nearby Bering Island and its ethnographic status was eroded, which made allowance for its verb-complex and interclausal syntax to borrow more Russian patterns.

14 Justifiably, DeGraff (p.c., September 1999) takes issue with this position, arguing that the identification of creoles as offspring of only their lexifiers ignores the role of language contact and the contribution of the **substrate** languages to their structures. He is partly supported by Nettle (1999:7) who observes: "Thus our classification of Fyem as Niger-Congo is really a simplification that hides the true, mixed nature of its parentage. The fact that individual grammatical items can pass between languages that are unrelated in the conventional sense means that there are many linguistic patterns in the world that are

not explicable in the conventional family-tree framework." I am not sure that the question can be answered to anybody's full satisfaction, unless the **Stammbaum** model itself is rejected or modified to represent multiple parents (chapter 5). The only justification I can offer for my statement is ideological, assuming that those who developed creoles did actually target their lexifiers and the latter were restructured during their appropriation by these new speakers.

15 In the case of nonlinguistic gestures, I have in mind here studies such as McNeill (1992) which show indirectly that in face-to-face interactions the mixing of codes is hardly constrained by the modalities (e.g., speech organs vs. hands) used by the different codes. Gestures can complement the spoken utterances in some communicative acts.

2 THE FOUNDER PRINCIPLE IN THE DEVELOPMENT OF CREOLES

1 I am grateful to Jacques Arends, Philip Baker, John McWhorter, Matthew Roy, Elisa Steinberg, Sali Tagliamonte, and *Diachronica*'s anonymous reviewers for useful feedback on earlier versions of this essay. I am solely responsible for all the remaining shortcomings.

2 Montgomery (1995, 1996) argues that this probably did not happen in spoken English in North America, at least not by the eighteenth century. According to him, settlement patterns favored the preservation of diversity. What he does not explain is why North America has not preserved English varieties which reflect the origins of those seventeenth- and eighteenth-century colonists. It is possible for koinéization to have taken place regionally, on smaller scales.

3 Tagliamonte (1999) shows that a partial model for this exists in British nonstandard English. This fact may explain why no comparable construction is attested in French creoles. I argue that substrate influence applies the most when some partial model can be identified in the lexifier. Similarly, most English creoles have a complementizer "say," patterned partially on abundant quotative uses of the verb *say* in English, whereas no French creole to my knowledge has grammaticized the verb *dire* "say" for the same function (Frajzyngier 1984; Mufwene 1996a).

4 A related idea to this is presented by Sankoff (1980:146) regarding the choice of lingua franca in interactions between European colonists and Native Americans. She proposes a "first past the post" principle, "according to which a contact vernacular that already has a toehold is, by virtue of its existence, likely to remain for a while as a target for subsequent entrants to the fray. Non-European contact vernaculars were not replaced overnight by newly pidginized European languages." Thus the linguistic choices that were made by those engaged in the initial trade contacts were likely to be inherited by those who followed them.

5 Creoles are not exceptional in modifying features that they have selected from one of their sources (Boretzky 1993).

6 It is quite possible that *does* + Verb occurred earlier in colonial Barbadian English speech to denote habits, especially with nonstative verbs, but the ethnographic contact ecology did not then favor its selection as a HABITUAL marker into the vernacular that would evolve from it. The same may be true of Jamaica and Suriname. Historical documentation shows that the indentured servants for

the different colonies came from more or less the same parts of the metropole and Europe. The early preponderance of Africans in Jamaica and Suriname may have also disfavored these particular selections, in favor of the ways their creoles mark habits today, although many sub-Saharan African languages have specific markers for HABIT. There is simply much more that must be investigated in closer detail about feature selection.

7   I assume that creoles developed **not** because the people brought together on plantations and similar settings wanted "to *create* a medium for interethnic communication" (Baker 1994:65, PB's emphasis). Rather, as argued in chapter 1, they *emerged by accident*, as the populations in contact attempted to communicate in languages that a large proportion of them apparently did not command well.

8   The term *vernacularization* is translated here from Chaudenson (1989), in the sense of "usage as a vernacular" or "becoming a vernacular." I too consider this process, rather than nativization, the primary factor that helps the new vernacular develop its own norm, autonomous from, though related to, the lexifier. This process, which Chaudenson calls *normalization* (i.e., "development of a norm"), may be equated with "stabilization" in much of the creolistic literature. It does not entail elimination of variation, since this may be stable.

9   Hazaël-Massieux (1993, 1996†), who espouses the same position, argues that exclusive substrate influence may be primarily lexical, which is minimal compared to the large proportion of lexical items from the lexifier, and it is confined to certain cognitive domains of which the substrate populations had more knowledge.

10 The complementary hypothesis has also been associated with such creolists as Baker and Corne (1986), Baker (1993), and Hancock (1986a, 1993). However, the authors do not articulate their positions in quite the same way, especially regarding the function of the bioprogram. For instance, both Baker and Hancock saw the bioprogram in competition with substrate and superstrate influences, whereas I do not. Baker then believed greatly in the role of children, but he no longer does (Baker 1994).

11 Charleston in table 6 represents the arrival and distribution point of the nonindigenous populations almost throughout the first half of the eighteenth century.

12 The generalization in terms of homestead and plantation phases is an oversimplification. The kind of labor used on the plantations was also an important factor. For instance, in a way partly reminiscent of Barbados, Virginia, colonized in 1607, switched early to the tobacco plantation system, within twenty years of its foundation. However, most of the planters used primarily indentured servants up to about 1680 (Kulikoff 1986; Perkins 1988). They accepted more African labor only after indentured servants became reluctant and expensive. The first Africans were introduced in Virginia in 1619 but they remained a small minority, hardly exceeding 15 percent of the total population by the late seventeenth century, and most of them worked on small farms or as domestics in urban centers like Williamsburg (Tate 1965). By 1770, Africans numbered 38 percent of the population in Virginia, Maryland, and North Carolina combined, whereas in South Carolina "they [then] outnumbered whites by roughly 50 percent" (Perkins 1988:98–9).

13 This stipulation is hardly ever met in colonies such as South Carolina and Georgia. Discussing Gullah and the like as creoles is contingent on focusing on the plantations alone as a special contact ecology and on interpreting language communities as metapopulations consisting of "habitat patches" connected by dispersing individuals (chapters 1 and 6). The 80%:20% population disproportion – more typical of the Caribbean plantations – is perhaps not a necessary condition for a creole to have developed (Mufwene 1997a). While it is significant that creoles developed mostly on sugar cane plantations and rice fields but not on tobacco and cotton plantations, it is equally noteworthy that some sugar cane plantations in Iberian America, for instance in Cuba and Brazil, did not produce creoles. The explanation of such differences lies in the specific ways in which particular colonial communities developed and in the kinds of interethnic interactions that their members had.

14 The tradition of determining what features or varieties of creoles are basilectal by comparing them to standard varieties of their lexifiers is sadly ironic, because the lexifiers were the nonstandard vernaculars spoken by the proletarian colonists with whom the non-Europeans interacted. As we learn more about the origins of basilectal features, it becomes more and more obvious that even those basilectal features which some may want to attribute exclusively to substrate influence (up to phonological features such as the pronunciation of /θ/ as /t/, of the word *pear* as /pyɛ/ or of *carry* as/kyari/, or of the word *very* as /βɛri/) can be traced back to the lexifier itself. This is not to deny deterministic substrate influence, which is clearly acknowledged by those who have been mischaracterized as (extreme) superstratists, such as Chaudenson (1989, 1992). Interestingly, Sylvain (1936) would qualify as a superstratist if we ignored the last sentence of her book, because she provides several connections between features of Haitian Creole with those of several nonstandard French dialects, aside from the much appreciated connections proposed with African languages.

15 Current research on the development of AAVE suggests the kind of conclusion proposed here. Especially relevant to it is the fact that African Nova Scotian English and the system inferable from the Ex-Slave Recordings are closer to White nonstandard speech than they are to creoles (Poplack and Tagliamonte 1989 and later works; Schneider 1989; Poplack 1999). Note that where AAVE developed, segregation was institutionalized later than in creole-speaking territories. Where there was continual massive importation of labor from Africa and Asia, the ensuing basilectalization process produced varieties more and more divergent from the lexifier. Where AAVE developed, race segregation (following the passage of the Jim Crow laws in 1877) was institutionalized after importation of labor from Africa had already stopped. The divergence of White and Black vernaculars is due largely to changes in the White population's speech (Bailey 1997 and later works).

On the other hand, Chaudenson (1992) argues that the Indian indentured laborers contributed very little, except lexically, to the structure of Mauritian Creole. This observation does not contradict Rickford's (1987:65–9) position that East Indian indentured laborers must have continued to restructure Guyanese Creole further away from its lexifier. He cites from Devonish (1978) only a couple of features that are identifiable as particularly East Indian and recognizes that the influence is minimal. One may assume that by the time of the abolition of slavery, most of the current structures of creoles were in place. Those who came later learned them in the same way that immigrants acquire the local vernaculars, with the adults taking their accents with them when they die and their children acquiring it natively and transmitting it with typically minor changes to the next generation or newcomers. Once more, leaving alone age-graded jargons, children contribute more to stabilizing the local vernaculars than to changing them. At least they do not restructure them any faster than other fluent speakers do, by the simple accident of imperfect replication in their communicative acts.

16 I maintain that in the vast majority of cases the role of the substrate languages was often, though not exclusively, to help select among competing options in the lexifier. Several of the features selected into creoles' structures were shared by their lexifiers and several substrate languages. Corne (1999) corroborates this observation in the context of New Caledonian French and Tayo with compelling evidence. In the case of Atlantic creoles, the Kwa languages are often singled out because they present the highest combinations of matches with features of these new vernaculars, not necessarily because they were the only driving force behind the selection of those particular features. However, a close examination of creoles such as Mauritian, in whose development Kwa speakers do not seem to have played a central role, also suggests that the lexifier remains an important critical factor in the selection of features (see below). Demographics are only one of several factors bearing on feature selection. Being the target language is a central factor that should never be downplayed. Learners do their best in acquiring it, even if imperfectly.

17 I am ignoring here initial-stage population movements which may have contributed elements from already-formed creoles to new ones, which Chaudenson (1979, 1992) identifies as "**second-generation**" creoles. He had in mind the contribution of varieties then emerging on Réunion to the development of Mauritian Creole. The same applies to the role putatively played by English varieties spoken in Barbados in the development of Gullah (Cassidy 1980, 1986a; Hancock 1980), of AAVE (Winford 1992, 1993), and of Jamaican and Guyanese Creoles (Le Page and Tabouret-Keller 1985). The position is less disputable as presented in Le Page and Tabouret-Keller in terms of no new creole really starting from scratch. The debate is recast in Baker and Bruyn (1999), regarding the significance of Kittitian in the development of Atlantic creoles.

18 Tagliamonte (1996) is particularly informative on models of PERFECT available in the lexifier that were likely to gain selective advantage with very little adaptation, including the omission of the auxiliary *have*.

19 The "Cafeteria Principle" was originally invoked by Dillard (1970) to argue, against dialectologists, that African-American English (including Gullah) could not have developed from a mixture of features taken from different British and/or colonial English dialects. Bickerton (1981:49) used it to promote his language bioprogram hypothesis by arguing that "if it is absurd to suppose that a creole could mix fragments of Irish, Wessex, Norfolk, and Yorkshire dialects, it is at least as absurd to suppose that a creole could mix fragments of Yoruba, Akan, Igbo, Mandinka, and Wolof." The two linguists share the incorrect assumption that grammatical principles from different languages do not mix

into a new grammar. All one had to do was to look at the evidence provided by historical linguistics and factor in language contact to disprove this.

20 Jacques Arends (p.c., March 1995) reminded me that European languages other than Dutch were spoken in Suriname after the British left. As noted above, European societal multilingualism obtained in almost all colonies. This makes more interesting the fact that the language of the colony's political rulers typically prevailed as the lexifier of European creoles, unless the rulers made ethnographic concessions as in Suriname and in the Netherlands Antilles.

21 Much of the historical information about the origins of Portuguese in Suriname has recently been questioned by Arends (1999) and Ladhams (1999). They argue that the proportion of Jews and slaves who came from Brazil was smaller than previously estimated. It is not clear yet from where else Portuguese was brought to Suriname nor how it came to play such an important role in the development of Saramaccan.

22 The abbreviations stand for the following: AGReement, Tense-Aspect, CONNective.

23 We also know now that no Atlantic creole ever actually selected an exclusively SVC subsystem over prepositional alternatives. Byrne (1987) shows that in Saramaccan, "dative and instrumental SVCs" alternate with prepositionless dative and prepositional instrumental constructions, respectively, just like in Kituba (Mufwene 1991a).

24 The terms INDIVIDUATED and NONINDIVIDUATED are Mufwene's. Bickerton and Dijkhoff discuss basically the same thing using Stewart's (1974) SPECIFIC/NONSPECIFIC distinction. Dijkhoff (1987) rejects the Bickerton–Stewart model, arguing that Mufwene's distinction accounts more adequately for complex nominals and compound nouns in Papiamentu.

25 There were of course several concurrent changes that would have produced the would-be homophones, including the merger of front rounded and unrounded vowels and of the alveolar and palatal fricatives during the restructuring of French into Mauritian.

3 THE DEVELOPMENT OF AMERICAN ENGLISHES: FACTORING CONTACT IN AND THE SOCIAL BIAS OUT

1 Highlighting diversity does not of course entail denying that several of these varieties, for instance African-American and White nonstandard English, or New England and Southern varieties, share features which justify identifying them all with the name *English*. Below I argue that we should indeed pay attention to both diversity and shared features synchronically and diachronically, so we can adequately address the question of how American varieties of English developed.

2 This question applies to AAVE especially when one assumes that it originally had a Gullah-like structure. I argue against the Gullah-like creole origin of AAVE in Mufwene (1992c, 1997c). For my views against the "decreolization" hypothesis, especially as applied to Gullah, see Mufwene (1991d, 1992d, 1994a, 1999c).

3 As pointed out in section 1.1, the above practice is an old one, according to

which languages are identified by the same name as their speakers. Creole vernaculars were thus largely the varieties spoken by creole people, with the social
twist that excludes creoles of European descent.

4 Rickford represents a weaker position now, according to which the contribution
   of Caribbean creoles to the development of AAE must still be recognized, along
   with other influences identified in the literature that disputes the creole origins
   of AAVE (Rickford 1998). Winford has moved closer and closer to the dialectologist position (1993, 1997b, 1998).

5 This position has typically been attributed to Turner (1949). However, his own
   conclusion was that "Gullah is indebted to African sources" (p. 254), which
   does not make African linguistic influence exclusive of others.

6 Schneider (1993) has weakened his position, making allowance for substrate
   influence.

7 Assuming the debasilectalization scenario, Brasch assumes that the original
   variation is due in part to inaccurate misrepresentations of AAE. Because of
   the then-natural tendency to disfranchise the speech of Africans, I would have
   expected exaggerations of non-English features rather than the other way
   around. It is especially significant that in the reported classified ads on runaway
   slaves, almost half the runaways are reported to speak (very) good English relative to the prevailing colonial speech. It is equally significant that an important
   proportion of those slaves described as speaking poor or no English had just
   arrived or were imported as adults. One of those reported to speak "very good
   English" was "imported very young" (Brasch 1981:7).

8 Interestingly Turner suggests by the title of his book that Gullah is a dialect of
   English, contrary to the strong stance of several creolists who treat it as a separate language.

9 Some of these followers, such as Holloway and Vass (1993), have narrowed even
   further the scope of Turner's work by capitalizing exclusively on proper names
   and seeking no further proof than phonetic similarities between toponyms in
   the United States and words in African languages. See more comments on this
   in Mufwene (1994d). Others, such as Wade-Lewis (1988), do not clearly
   differentiate between lexical contributions which African languages have made
   to the English language in general and the specific contributions made directly
   to AAE varieties which make them distinct from WAEVs.

10 There is room for entertaining Morgan's (1993) hypothesis that a counterlanguage may have been developed deliberately to conceal meanings from outsid-
   ers, who would interpret the relevant utterances only literally. However, this is a
   discourse strategy, based on the more basic structural features on which it
   depends for the literal interpretation.

11 The date for South Carolina seems to be 1720 (Wood 1974), i.e., when it became
   a crown colony, fifty years after it was founded. A segregated *modus vivendi* was
   not adopted in Virginia until the late seventeenth century or perhaps early eighteenth century, when the proportion of slaves started to exceed 15 percent of the
   overall population, thus much later than the first slaves were acquired in 1619.
   (Recall from chapter 2 the hightest proportion of Africans was only close to 40
   percent by the end of the eighteenth century.)

12 On a visit to Louisiana in November 1994, I noticed that African Americans

from the bayou area sounded different, at least prosodically, in a way somewhat reminiscent of coastal South Carolina or the Bahamas. Even in the choice of some lexical items their speech differs from varieties typically identified as AAVE, although I could not quite identify their speech as Gullah-like. John McWhorter (p.c., December 1994) and Charles DeBose (p.c., January 1995) confirmed this observation. Troike (1973) had already recommended that scholars look into regional differences. Also noteworthy is the fact that African Americans can identify AAE-speakers regionally based on linguistic features.

13 To be sure, Kurath (1928) notes phonetic similarities between some British varieties and WAEVs. However, this approach is limited to pinpointing specific features and not demonstrating similarities between the systems in which the features are integrated. The differences I claim are at the level of systems.

14 I am not suggesting that there is no German influence at all. This has been shown convincingly for some varieties, e.g., the construction *Bring it with* < *Bringe es mit* (Goodman 1993). The question is how extensive such structural influence is and whether it marks some WAEVs as distinctively as African languages have marked AAE, according to the reinterpretation of substrate influence proposed above.

15 The basic position underlying this argument is that the extent of divergence of a particular vernacular from other geographically related varieties is in part inversely related to the degree of integration within the community of model speakers. Part of the evidence for this lies in the ecological explanation provided above for differences between AAVE and Gullah.

16 Montgomery disputes a notion of "koiné" that is associated with leveling and simplification (which was criticized in section 2.2.1). Under the interpretation that a koiné is a new language variety that has developed by competition and selection of features from the contact of related dialects of the same language, he would probably agree that colonial American English was a koiné, or consisted of many of them (as he suggests on p. 230).

17 I cannot now answer the question of why English pidgins developed on the West Coast of Africa under similar conditions of sporadic contact. A better understanding of the West African and New World trade ecologies should shed light on this question.

4 THE LEGITIMATE AND ILLEGITIMATE OFFSPRING OF ENGLISH

1 I am grateful to Victor Friedman and Anthea Gupta for kind feedback on an earlier version of this essay. I am alone responsible for all the remaining shortcomings.

2 Crystal (1995) also equivocates on the genetic status of English pidgins and creoles, stating that scholars do not agree on the subject matter (pp. 106, 108, 344), but suggesting in his discussion and his count of speakers of English around the world that they are varieties of English. Even Turner (1949), who pioneered the African Substrate Hypothesis, identifies this vernacular as a "dialect," presumably of English. Creolists are perhaps the greatest culprits in the trend that has disfranchised pidgins and creoles as separate languages from their lexifiers.

3 Interestingly, terms such as *indigenized English* are also intended not only to claim legitimacy, which such varieties have been denied (cf., e.g., Kachru 1992), but also to distinguish them, as having non-European educated norms, from the pidgin varieties, which are typically associated with little or no education (Mufwene 1994c).

4 Aside from Trudgill (1986), there are some interesting studies of dialect contact today which highlight the development of new varieties in England (e.g., Kerswill and Williams 1994; Britain 1997). There is yet little literature on the fact that pervasive dialect contact was taking place in England during the colonization of the New World and other territories, which must have affected the shape of English in England itself. This is separate from the contact with Welsh and Gaelic around the same time, which has also produced new "native" varieties, such as Welsh and Irish Englishes. Other interesting contact perspectives on the development of North American English include Kahane (1992) and Heath (1992).

5 The Germanic colonization of England is in several ways reminiscent of that European colonization of North America. In the early stages, the indigenous populations were driven to the frontiers, where their numbers decreased because of changing ecologies and through wars with the invaders, and they were not integrated in the development of the colonies. Under such circumstances, the Celtic languages exerted little substrate structural influence on the development of English in England, at least during the formation of Old English. One would have to wait until the period when the Celts started adopting English as a vernacular to see such influence, as made evident by varieties such as Welsh and Irish English. Scots English is an earlier manifestation of the same kind evolution. Native American influence on North American Englishes is admittedly minimal, limited to the lexicon.

6 Because there is no language shift involved in these evolutions – only mutual influence of the linguistic systems on each other – there is no particular reason for confusing these evolutions with those identified as "creolizations."

7 In a way this characterization is not accurate, because scholarship on Irish English suggests that it was then developing as a vernacular, to be distinguished in form and ethnographic status from the second-language variety spoken mostly by the elite up to the seventeenth century. The development of Irish vernacular English seems to have been concurrent with those of North American English varieties (Harris 1991; Hickey 1995). It is very likely that some of the Irish immigrants to North America did not develop proficiency in it until after they had left the British Isles, especially those who did not live for some time in one of the major British port cities before crossing the Atlantic. Thus in at least some cases, rather than (Scots-)Irish English, Gaelic must have been the actual source of some of the peculiarities discussed in the literature.

8 French in England seems to have maintained the same position as English in most former British exploitation colonies, where it is typically spoken as a second-language and only by a small proportion of the population.

9 From an ecological point of view, scholars must still explain why, contrary to the Celts in England, a significant proportion of those on the mainland shifted from their languages, contributing to the development of Old French. It is not evident that the Celtic languages contributed to the development of Old

English, nor did England's Celts shift to Latin before the Germanic colonization. No Romance language developed in England as a consequence of Roman colonization. These disparities suggest differences either in colonization styles and dynamics of interaction in a contact setting or in continuity of the colonial tradition. The fact that Germanic colonization replaced Roman colonization for good in England is a significant ecological factor. I discuss aspects of these ecological factors below and in chapter 8.

10 Gupta (1991) shows that in the particular case of Singapore, teachers who served as models did not all come from the United Kingdom. A large proportion of them were Eurasians from other British colonies; some others came from other European countries and did not have full command of English either.

11 Some dialectologists will argue that the linguistic differences between AAVE and some nonstandard English dialects are more statistical than structural (see below) and perhaps more manifest prosodically. They may be right and one may maintain that the proportion of features shared by these varieties is inversely related to the time of the onset of racial segregation (different from discrimination!), which apparently was not as rigidly instituted on the tobacco and cotton plantations as on the rice fields of the American Southeast. However, dialectal differences need not be numerous or clearcut. What may matter the most is how they are construed socially, and this social interpretation has influenced, if not determined, the direction of dialectological research in North America. Such observations by dialectologists do not of course question the basic aim of this chapter, which is to highlight similarities in the processes of restructuring which produced new English varieties, even commonalities in the sources of the features, despite variation in the ethnographic ecologies which determined their selection.

12 However, this plausible scenario also raises the interesting question of why New England English is still very much an American phenomenon and not a conservative British dialect. Research on the patterns of later immigrations, and their socioeconomic relations to the founder population, whose linguistic influence they apparently reduced, should shed light on how English was restructured in this part of the world.

13 Rickford (1998) is equally informative in highlighting patterns of the copula distribution which support what I interpret as typological similarity to the basic pattern in Gullah and Caribbean creoles. However, all these new vernaculars developed more or less concurrently (Mufwene 1999b). Ultimately the so-called "creole features" can be traced to other (nonpidgin) sources which also influenced the development of AAVE. Creole ancestry is not needed to account for their presence in AAVE.

14 I have used conventional eye dialect, making sure not to exaggerate differences between Gullah and English. *Ga* is pronounced [gə] and is so represented to keep it distinct as a marker of FUTURE from its cognate *go* [go:]. *Da* and *duh* are homophones, pronounced [də], but are represented differently so that the former may be mechanically recognized as the definite article and the second as the DURATIVE/PROGRESSIVE marker.

15 This text is in its original phonetic-spelling transcription commonly used by Caribbean scholars.

16 Despite what the title of Gupta's book suggests, I have selected only constructions from adult speakers.

17 This is not to claim that such processes have not occurred in language change.
For instance, the word *apron* developed by a similar mis-segmentation from
Middle English *napron* (Victor Friedman, p.c., March 1997). The difference lies
in where such restructuring would be so pervasive as to produce an apparently
new language variety, like Arumbaya.

5 WHAT RESEARCH ON DEVELOPMENT OF CREOLES CAN CONTRIBUTE TO
GENETIC LINGUISTICS

1 According to Hjelmslev (not cited by Thomason and Kaufman), it is not so
much shared typology in grammatical structures that has militated for grouping
the Indo-European languages together, but mostly their vocabularies. Posner
(1996) argues that even for Romance, "the only extended 'family' with a well-
attested 'mother' (*Ursprache* or **proto-language**)" (p. 11) , the lexicon remains the
most common thread of the languages (p. 35). Grammatical similarities hardly
distinguish them from other European languages, at least at the level of their
standard varieties (which reduce differences among them all), and also could
lead one to exclude some maverick Romance languages such as French from the
inner "Romance Club," as opposed to the "extended family" which includes
varieties spoken outside Europe. Once things are put in perspective, there is little
doubt that contact plays a role in this situation (see also Martin Harris 1988).

2 This generalization applies even to Melanesian pidgins. According to Keesing
(1988), the ancestor of these varieties developed aboard whaling ships and was
brought from them to plantations, where it evolved into Tok Pisin, Bislama, and
the like.

3 It is tempting to speak of *creolization* on the pattern of *Gallicization* or
Germanicization, in the sense of acquiring features that are creoles' peculiarities,
just as a language variety would acquire French or Germanic peculiarities.
However, this is not the sense in which some scholars have interpreted the emergence of Middle/Modern English or of the Romance languages when they
describe the processes as creolization. They have used the term inadequately to
refer mostly to the evolution from their inflectional strategies to analytical/peri-
phrastic ones, as if these processes were peculiar to creoles alone. They are
attested also in Chinese, Thai, and the Kwa languages, among others, whose
creole status is dubious. The strategies are often more regular and better integrated in these other languages (Mufwene 1986b). Besides, putting history back
in the right perspective, creoles selected these features largely from their
European lexifiers, of course not without the helping hand of the substrate languages. Characterizing their developments in the European languages as creolization is anachronistic.

4 This distinction made by Chaudenson (1979 and later works) highlights the fact
that, being at home, the Celts were not under the same kinds of pressure as the
Africans in the New World or Indian Ocean to shift to a new vernacular. Thus,
shifts proceeded naturally at different speeds, with more likelihood for greater
substrate influence where the substrate populations were linguistically more
homogeneous.

5   These observations concern the more obvious grammatical phenomena that
    can be identified today. Celtic influence can apparently be traced back to the
    Middle-English period (Tristram 1997, 2000; Haspelmath 1998; Vennemann
    2000). Still, it is remarkable that the development of Old English does not reflect
    significant Celtic influence.
6   One may argue that those changes are often so minimal that they bear very little
    on the evolution of a language. Actually, if changes did not proceed this way,
    there would be little continuity in a communal language. Overlaps in innovative
    and conservative patterns guarantee continuity. At the same time, when changes
    catch on in a community, they are similar to effects of attractors in chaos theory,
    being amplified as they are reproduced by the same and more and more speak-
    ers, until a stochastic event stops, stabilizes, reduces, or reverses the process.
    Keller (1994) is quite informative on this in his discussion of the "invisible
    hand" that effects change in a language.

6 LANGUAGE CONTACT, EVOLUTION, AND DEATH: HOW ECOLOGY ROLLS
THE DICE

1   This position does not entail that all variation leads to change toward unifor-
    mity. Most variation remains stable if the ecology of a species does not change.
    Some variation is actually not affected by changes in the ecology, at least not
    drastically. For instance, the variable relativization strategies in English have not
    been seriously affected by patterns of relativization in French, and not all
    dialects bear French influence for that matter. Most nonstandard English
    dialects make no use of *who* and *which* as relative pronouns, and some of them
    do not even use *whose*. Thus, when changes occur or fail to occur under chang-
    ing ecologies, it is rewarding to learn what in the ecological changes favored or
    disfavored a particular pattern of variation.
2   There are also cases where, regardless of whether it is truly a change, a phenom-
    enon is contained within one particular segment of the population, without
    (seriously) affecting other members of the community. Such appears to be the
    case with usage of *like* as a discourse marker to introduce what may be inter-
    preted as a quotation (albeit an unfaithful one) but especially to signal change
    of speakers or of points of view in a narrative. It seems to be associated with a
    particular generation (the young), and speakers outgrow it, consistent with age-
    grading. The language-qua-organism metaphor fails to capture this, especially
    because speakers do not graduate from age-groups all at the same time nor at
    the same rate, making it difficult even to use the notion of "generation" usefully.
    Members of a community are not all born the same day, month, or year. The life
    of a community depends on an uneven and quite variable staggering of several
    individual lives.
3   The reason why I capitalize here on the notion of "species" rather than "popula-
    tion" is that no justification need be provided for lumping several individuals
    together as a population. A justification is needed for grouping them as a species,
    for example, if the individuals descend from the same ancestor and/or share
    genes (O'Hara 1994). Such is also the case for people who claim, or are said, to
    speak the same language. They need not understand each other, as long as one
    can show some genetic and/or structural connection among their idiolects or

dialects. Things are more complicated with language, since native speakers may claim or deny such a connection on ideological grounds, such as in the Balkans, where language boundaries have often been redefined (Friedman 1996). For the purposes of academic classifications, however, the above explanation stands. This is the reason why I have not resorted to the usual biologist position that membership in a species is determined by the potential of its members to inter-breed and reproduce like members. In the case of language, speakers who com-municate successfully with each other sometimes deny that they speak the same language.

4 The assumption of variation among idiolects as the default state of affairs in a language is dictated by how language is acquired in naturalistic settings, includ-ing child language. Learners work out their idiolectal systems individually, on their own. The overall system that emerges and the order in which it develops vary from one speaker to another, just as do individual knowledges of cultural systems. Mutual accommodation is what reduces differences among idiolects.

5 Consistent with variation theory in linguistics, one may assume such variability in a speech community to be the counterpart of the distribution of advanta-geous and disadvantageous genes among the members of a changing species. The only difference is that in a species where the selective advantage of some genes depends primarily on their vertical transmission, it takes many genera-tions before the disadvantageous genes become latent and the change at the level of the species conspicuous.

6 Robert Perlman observes that "the 'family resemblance' model is problematic in biology because, beyond the ability to interbreed (and a common evolutionary history), there are no immutable, essential characters that define membership in a species" (p.c., November 1999). In fact, aside from unrewarding attempts in creolistics to define creoles by structural features, languages are not defined by features either. Family resemblance is invoked here simply to highlight the kinds of relations that obtain among idiolects of a dialect or language in terms of both similarities and differences, which vary with every pair one decides to compare.

7 The counterpart of this process in population genetics is *stabilizing selection*, "in which the mean value of a phenotype has greater fitness than deviations from this mean" (Robert Perlman, p.c., November 1999). By this process, some variants are selected out by ecology. For instance, the typical human birth weight has stabilized around seven pounds, because infant mortality is higher at weights below or above this average and the statistical probability of babies with such deviant weights to survive and procreate similar babies keeps decreasing. The overall effect of this in a population is "a narrowly focused distribution of birth weights in the range of lowest infant mortality."

8 There are of course several situations in which no particular competing feature prevails over others, due to the fact that in the linguistic species competing fea-tures may coexist in the same speaker. Such is the case when, for instance, a speaker pronounces the verb *direct* as either [dayrɛkt] or [dɪrɛkt], or alternates among the following relative clause strategies: *the person to whom you spoke* vs. *the person who you spoke to* vs. *the person (that) you spoke to*.

9 Robert Perlman (p.c., November 1999) also observes the following in biology:

Colonization of an individual host by two strains of the same parasite, or even by different parasitic species, creates the opportunity for genetic recombination or gene flow between these parasites. This process is thought to be important in the spread of bacterial antibiotic resistance. Many people carry normal, nonpathogenic, bacterial flora that are resistant to antibiotics. These parasites provide a reservoir of antibiotic-resistant genes that can be transferred to new, antibiotic-sensitive organisms that invade and colonize the same individual.

10 Dixon (1997) and Mazrui and Mazrui (1998) may be interpreted in this light too, although they hardly use the term *ecology*. Manheim (1991:31) also invokes ecology, characterizing it as "the ways in which linguistic differences are organized and set into a social landscape," including, among other things, "the ways in which language and dialect differences are institutionally channeled and used." I focus in this essay mostly on the variation aspect of ecology, which bears directly on competition and selection.

11 Space constraints prevent me from discussing all these factors, some of which are dealt with in chapter 2 and in much of the literature on the development of creoles. I focus here on a subset that bears on the few language evolution topics that I discuss.

12 This is a development observable even today in African urban centers, where the majority of children express more interest, or find it more practical, to speak only the city's lingua franca, which becomes their native vernacular. This is part of the trend that endangers some indigenous languages in Africa (chapter 7).

13 Part of the attrition process followed from the intervention of European colonists in promoting some Native American languages, such as Quechua, as lingua francas (Calvet 1987, 1998). Mühlhäusler (1996) discusses consequences of similar European interventions in Melanesia.

14 Also inspired by evolutionary biology, especially by the views of Steven Jay Gould (1993), Dixon (1997:73–84, 139–41) invokes punctuated equilibrium to account for language change, arguing that significant changes happen in shorter periods of time than historical linguistics has led us to believe. This suggests, contrary to his own position, that creoles are normal instances of punctuation of the equilibrium in a particular language qua species in a new ecology.

15 The deaths of Old Norse and Norman French in England illustrate again those situations in which part of a species is disfavored by one particular ecology, while the remainder is well sustained by another. Old Norse developed into Norwegian and Danish, and continental varieties of medieval French have developed into today's varieties of French in and outside France. Power may not be an important component of the explanation, because Old Norse and Norman French were associated with the powerful in England, unlike the African languages that died in the Americas and the Indian Ocean. Integration into the demographically dominant population in the case of England may be a more plausible explanation.

16 Regarding integration, there is apparently much more that deserves explanation. In the same way that American White Southerners speak varieties akin to AAVE, Caribbean Whites speak like Caribbean Blacks, and class for class there are probably more similarities within the Caribbean than may be evidenced in

the United States. The social colonial ecologies were obviously not identical and it will help to articulate more adequately how different they were. Could segregation not have been institutionalized in identical ways in the Caribbean as in North America? Or did integration and segregation proceed in reverse orders, as suggested by Berlin (1998) for some colonies (e.g., French Louisiana versus English North America)? Or could social integration be more real in the Caribbean than in North America, even if it was implemented around the same time? Note that in the Caribbean, neighborhoods are segregated more on economic grounds than on ethnic ones, although color lines are still very much detectable through the prevalence of some complexions in different socioeconomic classes.

17 Integration and segregation in North America have always been relative. There has always been some segregation even among the original European settlers, with communities that were almost exclusively German, for instance. This accounts for the development of (Old) Amish vernacular English, aside from Pennsylvania Dutch, aside from other vernaculars cited earlier. The main difference is that segregation has decreased among populations of European descent. Where such populations have been integrated, the stigmatized varieties have been disappearing. Such is the case in the endangerment of Ocracoke English (Wolfram and Schilling Estes 1995), in contrast with Gullah (Mufwene 1994a). On Ocracoke, the White islanders are being integrated with the more affluent White in-migrants. Such is not Gullah speakers' experience on their South Carolina islands.

7 PAST AND RECENT POPULATION MOVEMENTS IN AFRICA: THEIR IMPACT ON ITS LINGUISTIC LANDSCAPE

1 Apparently some of these islands, such as Mauritius, São Tomé, and Principe, were uninhabited. In this case, part of the change itself lies in peopling them and transforming them into arenas where imported languages would compete with each other for prevalence.

2 Krio is a more complex case. Its birth place in the way it is known today is undoubtedly Sierra Leone. However, other than the ultimate origin of its English lexifier, the sources of the other contributing elements are not exclusively African. Some of them came with the freed slaves who were brought back from England in the late eighteenth century and from Jamaica and the United States in the early nineteenth century. They spoke Creole or other restructured English varieties. Other contributing influences came from the languages formerly spoken by "**recaptives**" from slave ships, who were also relocated partly in Sierra Leone. By the eighteenth century some form of restructured English (pidgin, creole, or otherwise) was also spoken along the "Guinea Coast" (Hancock 1986a), but Huber (1999) doubts its importance next to pidgin Portuguese as a trade language. The ensuing complex contacts account for the restructuring that produced present-day Krio (Corcoran 1998).

3 I return below to new, nonpidgin-creole varieties of European languages appropriated by descendants of non-Europeans. The term *South African English* can perhaps be extended to similar varieties of English spoken by White settlers in Zimbabwe and Namibia.

4 Perhaps a more apt comparison here should be with foreign workers in Europe, who, though surrounded geographically, and to some extent socially, by the majority of native speakers, are still not integrated enough to acquire the target without extensive restructuring.

5 There were apparently problems in recruiting labor locally, because the local populations often feared being enslaved (Samarin 1989).

6 This was apparently slavery of a different kind than in the Americas, more like a system of unpaid domestics and concubines.

7 This makes more intriguing the case of the Cushitic–Bantu mixed language Ma'a in the region (Thomason 1997), especially how it is related to Newman's Maa. Are they the same, or different languages which happen to have related names?

8 Vansina (1990) conjectures that the rainforest may have been inhabited not only by hunter-gatherers, the Pygmies, but also by fisherfolks who were absorbed or replaced faster by the Bantu populations.

8 CONCLUSIONS: THE BIG PICTURE

1 I use *heredity* loosely here, in the sense that the linguistic features attested in every group of speakers have their (partial) sources in the group from which they learned their language, regardless of whether the features were in the same language they still (claim to) speak or in a different one. The epidemiology model is consistent with the polyploidic model of blending inheritance presented in chapter 1.

References

Adam, Lucien. 1882. *Les classifications, l'objet, la méthode, les conclusions de la linguistique.* Paris VII.

1883. *Les idiomes négro-aryens et malayo aryens: essai d'hybridologie linguistique.* Paris: Maisonneuve.

Algeo, John. 1991. Language. In Foner and Garraty, 637–40.

Alleyne, Mervyn C. 1971. Acculturation and the cultural matrix of creolization. In Hymes, 169–86.

1980. *Comparative Afro-American.* Ann Arbor: Karoma.

1986. Substratum influences: guilty until proven innocent. In Muysten and Smith, 301–15.

1993. Continuity versus creativity in Afro-American language and culture. In Mufwene 1993a, 167–81.

1996. *Syntaxe historique créole.* Paris: Karthala.

Allsopp, Richard. 1977. Africanisms in the idioms of Caribbean English. In *Language and linguistic problems in Africa*, ed. Paul F. Kotey and Haig Der-Houssitkian, 429–41. Columbia, SC: Hornbeam.

Andersen, Roger W. 1983. Transfer to somewhere. In *Language transfer in language learning*, ed. by Susan M. Gass and Larry Selinker, 177–201. Rowley, MA: Newbury House.

Anderson, Gregory D.S. 1999. Language mixing in a mixed language: on Russian–Copper Island Aleut codemixing. Ms.

Arends, Jacques. 1986. Genesis and development of the equative copula in Sranan. In Muysken and Smith, 57–70.

1989. *Syntactic developments in Sranan.* Doctoral thesis, University of Nijmegen.

1995. *The early stages of creolization.* Amsterdam: John Benjamins.

1999. The origin of the Portuguese element in the Suriname Creoles. In Huber and Parkvall, 195–208.

Arends, Jacques, Pieter Muysken, and Norval Smith, eds. 1995. *Pidgins and creoles: an introduction.* Amsterdam: John Benjamins.

Bailey, Beryl. 1965. Toward a new perspective in Negro English dialectology. *American Speech* 40.171–7.

Bailey, Guy. 1997. When did Southern American English begin? In *Englishes around the world I: General studies, British Isles, North America: studies in honor of Manfred Görlach*, ed. by Edgar W. Schneider, 255–75. Amsterdam: John Benjamins.

Bailey, Guy and Natalie Maynor. 1987. Decreolization? *Language in Society* 16.449–73.

1989. The divergence controversy. *American Speech* 64.12–39.

Bailey, Guy, Natalie Maynor, and Patricia Cukor-Avila, eds. 1991. *The emergence of Black English: text and commentary*. Amsterdam: John Benjamins.

Bailey, Guy and Garry Ross. 1988. The shape of the superstrate: morphosyntactic features of ship English. *English World-Wide* 9.193–212.

Bailey, Guy and Erik Thomas. 1998. Some aspects of African-American English phonology. In Mufwene et al., 85–109.

Bailyn, Bernard. 1986. *The peopling of British North America: an introduction*. New York: Random House.

Baissac, Charles 1880. Etude sur le patois créole mauricien. Nancy: Imprimerie Berger-Levrault.

Baker, Philip. 1984. Agglutinated French articles in creole French: their evolutionary significance. *Te Reo* 27.89–129.

1990. Off target? Column, *Journal of Pidgin and Creole Languages* 5.107–19.

1993. Assessing the African contribution to French-based creoles. In Mufwene, 1993a, 123–55.

1994. Creativity in creole genesis. In *Creolization and language change*, ed. by Dany Adone and Ingo Plag, 65–84. Tübingen: Niemeyer.

1995a. Some developmental inferences from the historical studies of pidgins and creoles. In Arends 1995, 1–24.

1995b. Motivation in creole genesis. In *From contact to creole and beyond*, ed. by Philip Baker, 3–15. London: University of Westminster Press.

1996. Pidginization, creolization and *français approximatif*. Review article on Chaudenson 1992. *Journal of Pidgin and Creole Languages* 11.95–120.

1997. Directionality in pidginization and creolization. In Spears and Winford, 91–109.

Baker, Philip and Adrienne Bruyn, eds. 1999. *St. Kitts and the Atlantic creoles: the texts of Samuel Augustus Matthews in perspective*. London: University of Westminster Press.

Baker, Philip and Chris Corne. 1986. Universals, substrata and the Indian Ocean creoles. Muysken and Smith, 163–83.

Baker, Philip and Peter Mühlhäusler. 1990. From business to pidgin. *Journal of Asian Pacific Communication* 1.87–115.

Baker, Philip and Anand Syea, eds. 1996. *Changing meanings, changing functions: papers relating to grammaticalization in language contact*. London: University of Westminster Press.

Bakker, Peter. 1997. *A language of our own: the genesis of Michif, the mixed Cree–French language of the Canadian Métis*. Oxford: Oxford University Press.

Bambgose, Ayo et al., eds. 1995. *New Englishes: a West African perspective*. Ibadan: Mosuro.

Baugh, John. 1980. A reexamination of the Black English copula. In *Locating language in time and space*, ed. by William Labov, 83–106. New York: Academic Press.

Becker, Karl Ferdinand. 1833. *Das Wort in seine organischen Verwandlung*. Frankfurt am Main: Joh. Christ. Harmannsche Buchhandlung.

Beckles, Hilary. 1990. *A history of Barbados: From Amerindian settlement to nation-state*. Cambridge: Cambridge University Press.

Bennett, John. 1908 & 1909. Gullah: a Negro patois. *South Atlantic Quarterly* 7.332–47 & 8.39–52.

Berlin, Ira. 1998. *Many thousands gone: the first two centuries of slavery in North America*. Cambridge, MA: Harvard University Press.

Bickerton, Derek. 1975. *Dynamics of a creole system*. Cambridge: Cambridge University Press.

1981. *Roots of language*. Ann Arbor: Karoma.

1984. The Language Bioprogram Hypothesis. *Behavioral and Brain Sciences* 7.173–221.

1992. The creole key to the black box of language. In *Thirty years of linguistic evolution: studies in honor of René Dirven on the occasion of his sixtieth birthday*, ed. by Martin Pütz, 97–108. Amsterdam: John Benjamins.

1999. How to acquire language without positive evidence: what acquisitionists can learn from creoles. In DeGraff 1996b, 49–74.

Blackmore, Susan. 1999. *The meme machine*. Oxford: Oxford University Press.

Bopp, Franz. 1833. *Vergleichende Grammatik des Sanskrit, Zend, Griechischen, Lateinischen, Gothischen und Deutchen*. Berlin.

Boretzky, Norbert. 1993. The concept of rule, rule borrowing, and substrate influence in creole languages. In Mufwene 1993a, 74–92.

Brasch, Walter M. 1981. *Black English and the mass media*. New York: University Press of America.

Britain, David. 1997. Dialect contact and phonological reallocation: Canadian raising in the English fens. *Language in Society* 26.15–46.

Brown, James H. 1995. *Macroecology*. Chicago: University of Chicago Press.

Bruyn, Adrienne. 1996. On identifying instances of grammaticalization in creole languages. In Baker and Syea, 29–46.

Buccini, Anthony F. 1995. The dialectal origins of New Netherland Dutch. In *The Berkeley conference on Dutch linguistics 1993*, ed. by Thomas F. Shannon and John Snapper, 211–63. Lanham, MD: University Press of America.

1999. Dutch, Swedish and English elements in the development of Pidgin Delaware. *American Journal of Germanic Linguistics & Literatures* 11.63–87.

Byrne, Francis X. 1987. *Grammatical relations in a radical creole: verb complementation in Saramaccan*. Amsterdam: John Benjamins.

Byrne, Francis and Thomas Huebner, eds. 1991. *Development and structures of creole languages: essays in honor of Derek Bickerton*. Amsterdam: John Benjamins.

Byrne, Francis and Donald Winford, eds. 1993. *Focus and grammatical relations in creole languages*. Amsterdam: John Benjamins.

Calvet, Louis-Jean. 1987. *La guerre des langues et politiques linguistiques*. Paris: Payot.

ed. 1992. *Les langues des marchés en Afrique*. Aix-en-Provence: Institut d'Etudes Créoles et Francophones.

1998. *Language wars and linguistic politics*. Oxford: Oxford University Press.

1999. *Pour une écologie des langues du monde*. Paris: Plon.

Carrington, Lawrence D., ed. 1983. *Studies in Caribbean language*. St. Augustine, Trinidad: Society for Caribbean Linguistics.

Cassidy, Frederic G. 1980. The place of Gullah. *American Speech* 55.3–16.

1986a. Barbadian Creole: possibility and probability. *American Speech* 61.195–205.

1986b. Some similarities between Gullah and Caribbean creoles. In *Language varieties in the South: perspectives in black and white*, ed. by Michael Montgomery and Guy Bailey, 30–7. University: University of Alabama Press.

Chambers, J.K. 1991. Canada. In Cheshire 1991b, 89–107.

Chaudenson, Robert. 1979. *Les créoles français*. Paris: Fernand Nathan.

1981. *Textes créoles anciens (La Réunion et Ile Maurice): comparaison et essai d'analyse*. Hamburg: Helmut Buske Verlag.

1989. *Créoles et enseignement du français*. Paris: L'Harmattan.

1992. *Des îles, des hommes, des langues: essais sur la créolisation linguistique et culturelle*. Paris: L'Harmattan.

1993. Francophonie, "français zéro" et français régional. In *Le français dans l'espace francophone*, ed. by Didier de Robillard and Michel Beniamino, 385–405. Paris: Champion.

Cheshire, Jenny. 1991a. Variation in the use of *ain't* in an urban British English Dialect. In Trudgill and Chambers 1991, 54–73.

ed. 1991b. *English around the world: sociolinguistic perspectives*. Cambridge: Cambridge University Press.

Childs, Tucker. 1997. The status of Isicamtho, a Nguni-based urban variety of Soweto. In Spears and Winford, 341–67.

Christian, Donna, Walt Wolfram, and Nanjo Bube. 1988. *Variation and change in geographically isolated communities: Appalachian English and Ozark English*. Publication of the American Dialect Society 74. Tuscaloosa: University of Alabama Press.

Clarke, Sandra. 1997a. On establishing historical relationships between New and Old World varieties: habitual aspect and Newfoundland vernacular English. In *Englishes around the world* I: *General studies, British Isles, North America: Studies in honor of Manfred Görlach*, ed. by Edgar W. Schneider, 277–93. Amsterdam: John Benjamins.

1997b. English verbal *-s* revisited: the evidence from Newfoundland. *American Speech* 72.227–59.

Coelho, F. Adolpho. 1880–86. Os dialectos romanicos ou neo-latinos na Africa, Asia, e América. *Lisboa* 2.129–96 (1880–81); 3.451–478 (1882); 6.705–755 (1886). Reprinted in *Estudos linguisticos crioulos*, ed. by Jorge Morais-Barbosa, 1967. Lisbon: Academica Internacional de Cultura Portuguesa.

Coleman, Kenneth. 1978. *Georgia history in outline*. Revised edition. Athens: University of Georgia Press.

Corcoran, Chris. 1998. The place of Guinea Coast Creole English and Sierra Leone Krio in the Afrogenesis debate. Paper presented at Annual Meeting of the Society for Pidgin and Creole Linguistics, New York.

Corcoran, Chris and Salikoko S. Mufwene. 1999. Sam Matthews' Kittitian: what is it evidence of? In Baker and Bruyn, 75–102.

Corne, Chris. 1999. *From French to Creole: the development of new vernaculars in the French colonial world*. London: University of Westminster Press.

Croft, William. 2000. *Explaining language change: an evolutionary approach*. London: Longman.

Crosby, Afred W. 1986. *Ecological imperialism: the biological expansion of Europe, 900–1900*. Cambridge: Cambridge University Press.

1992. Ills. In *Atlantic American societies: from Columbus through abolition*

1492–1888, ed. by Alan L. Karras and J.R. McNeill, 19–39. London: Routledge.

Crum, Mason. 1940. *Gullah: Negro life in the Carolina Sea Islands*. Durham, NC: Duke University Press.

Crystal, David. 1995. *The Cambridge encyclopedia of the English language*. Cambridge: Cambridge University Press.

Curtin, Philip D. 1969. *The Atlantic slave trade: a census*. Madison: University of Wisconsin Press.

1990. *The rise and fall of the plantation complex: essays in Atlantic history*. Cambridge: Cambridge University Press.

Daelman, Jan, S.I. 1972. Kongo elements in Saramacca Tongo. *Journal of African Languages* 11.1–44.

Deacon, Terrence W. 1997. *The symbolic species: the co-evolution of language and the brain*. New York: Norton.

DeBose, Charles and Nicholas Faraclas. 1993. An approach to the linguistic study of Black English: getting to the roots of Tense–Aspect–Modality and copula systems in Afro-American. In Mufwene 1993a, 364–87.

DeCamp, David. 1971. Toward a generative analysis of a post-creole speech continuum. In Hymes, 349–70.

DeGraff, Michel. 1993. A riddle on negation in Haitian. *Probus* 5.63–93.

1999a. Creolization, language change, and language acquisition: a prolegomenon. In DeGraff 1999b, 1–46.

ed. 1999b. *Language creation and language change: creolization, diachrony, and development*. Cambridge, MA: MIT Press.

D'Eloia, Sarah. 1973. Issues in the analysis of Negro Nonstandard English: a review of Dillard (1972). *Journal of English Linguistics* 7.87–106.

Devonish, Hubert St. Laurent. 1978. *The selection and codification of a widely understood and publicly useable language variety in Guyana, to be used as a vehicle of national development*. Doctoral thesis, University of York.

Dillard, J.L. 1970. Principles in the history of American English: paradox, virginity, and cafeteria. *Florida FL Reporter* 8.32–3.

1972. *Black English: Its history and usage in the United States*. New York: Random House Vintage.

1985. *Toward a social history of American English*. New York: Mouton.

1992. *A history of American English*. London: Longman.

Dijkhoff, Marta. 1983. The process of pluralization in Papiamentu. In Carrington, 217–29.

1987. Complex nominals and composite nouns in Papiamentu. In Maurer and Stolz, 1–10.

Dixon, R.M.W. 1997. *The rise and fall of languages*. Cambridge: Cambridge University Press.

Domínguez, Virginia R. 1986. *White by definition: social classification in creole Louisiana*. New Brunswick, NJ: Rutgers University Press.

Dyde, Brian. 1993. *St. Kitts: cradle of the Caribbean*. Second edition. London: Macmillan.

Edwards, Walter F. 1975. Sociolinguistic behavior in urban and rural circumstances in Guyana. Doctoral thesis, University of York.

Eliason, Norman E. 1956. *Tarheel talk: an historical study of the English language in North Carolina to 1860*. New York: Octagon.

Escure, Geneviève. 1994. The acquisition of creole by urban rural Black Caribs in Belize. *York Papers in Linguistics* 11.95–106. (Special issue edited by Mark Sebba and Loreto Todd.)

Faine, Jules. 1937. *Philologie créole: études historiques et étymologiques sur la langue créole d'Haïti.* Port-au-Prince: Imprimerie de l'Etat.

Faraclas, Nicholas. 1987. Creolization and the tense-aspect-modality system of Nigerian Pidgin. *Journal of African Languages and Linguistics* 9.45–59.

    1988a. Nigerian Pidgin and the languages of southern Nigeria. *Journal of Pidgin and Creole Languages* 3.177–97.

    1988b. Rumors of the demise of Descartes are premature. Review of Mühlhäusler 1986. *Journal of Pidgin and Creole Languages* 3.119–35.

Fasold, Ralph. 1976. One hundred years from syntax to phonology. In *Papers from the parasession on diachronic syntax*, ed. by Sanford B. Steever, Carol A. Walker, and Salikoko Mufwene, 779–87. Chicago Linguistic Society.

    1981. The relationship between black and white speech in the South. *American Speech* 56.163–89.

Féral, Carole de. 1989. *Pidgin-English du Cameroun.* Paris: Peters/SELAF.

Ferraz, Luis Ivens. 1979. *The creole of São Tomé.* Johannesburg: Witwatersrand University Press.

Fields, Linda. 1995. Early Bajan: creole or non-creole? In Arends, 89–112.

Filppula, Markku. 1991. Urban and rural varieties of Hiberno-English. In Cheshire 1991b, 51–60.

Fischer, David Hackett. 1989. *Albion's seed: four British folkways in America.* Oxford: Oxford University Press.

Fisiak, Jacek, ed. 1995. *Language change under contact conditions.* Berlin: Mouton de Gruyter.

Foner, Eric and John A. Garraty, eds. 1991. *The reader's companion to American history.* Boston: Houghton Mifflin.

Fracchia, Joseph and R.C. Lewontin. 1999. Does culture evolve? *History and Theory: Studies in the Philosophy of History* 38 (4). 52–78.

Frajzyngier, Zygmunt. 1984. On the origin of *say* and *se* as complementizers in Black English and English-based creoles. *American Speech* 59.207–10.

Friedman, Victor A. 1996. Observing the observers: language, ethnicity, and power in the 1994 Macedonian census and beyond. In *Toward comprehensive peace in Southeastern Europe: conflict prevention in the South Balkans*, ed. by Barnett R. Rubin, 81–105. New York: Twentieth Century Fund Press.

Giles, Howard and Philip Smith. 1979. Accommodation theory: optimal levels of convergence. In *Language and social psychology*, ed. by Howard Giles and Robert St. Clair, 45–65. Oxford: Basil Blackwell.

Gilman, Charles. 1986. African areal characteristics: Sprachbund, not substrate? *Journal of Pidgin and Creole Languages* 1.33–50.

    1993. Black identity, homeostasis, and survival: African and metropolitan speech varieties in the New World. In Mufwene 1993a, 388–402.

Giner, Maria F. Garcia-Bermejo and Michael Montgomery. 1999. Yorkshire English two hundred years ago. Paper presented at the 10th Conference on Methods in Dialectology, Memorial University of Newfoundland.

Givón, T. 1986. Prototypes: between Plato and Wittgenstein. In *Noun classes and categorization*, ed. by Collette Craig, 77–102. Amsterdam: John Benjamins.

Goddard, Ives. 1997. Pidgin Delaware. In Thomason 1997b, 43–98.

Golovko, Eugeni V. and Nikolai Vakhtin. 1990. Aleut in contact: the CIA enigma. *Acta Linguistica Hafniensia* 22.97–125.

Goodman, Morris. 1982. The Portuguese element in New World creoles. In *Papers from the parasession on nondeclaratives*, ed. by Robinson Schneider, Kevin Tuite, and Robert Chametzky, 54–62. Chicago: Chicago Linguistic Society.

1993. African substratum: some cautionary words. In Mufwene 1993a, 64–73.

Gould, Stephen Jay. 1993. *Eight little piggies: reflections in natural history*. New York: Norton.

Green, John N. 1988. Romance creoles. In Harris and Vincent, 420–73.

Gumperz, John J. and Robert Wilson. 1971. Convergence and creolization: a case from the Indo-Aryan/Dravidian border. In Hymes, 151–67.

Gupta, Anthea Fraser. 1991. Almost a creole: Singapore colloquial English. *California Linguistic Notes* 23.9–21.

1994. *The step-tongue: children's English in Singapore*. Clevedon: Multilingual Matters.

Hagège, Claude. 1993. *The language builder: an essay on the human signature in linguistic morphogenesis*. Amsterdam: John Benjamins.

Hall, Robert, Jr. 1966. *Pidgin and creole languages*. Ithaca: Cornell University Press.

Hancock, Ian F. 1969. The English-derived Atlantic creoles: a provisional comparison. *African Language Review* 8.7–72.

1980. Gullah and Barbadian: origins and relationships. *American Speech* 55.17–35.

1986a. The domestic hypothesis, diffusion and componentiality: an account of Atlantic anglophone creole origins. In Muysken and Smith 1986, 71–102.

1986b. On the classification of Afro-Seminole Creole. In Montgomery and Bailey 1986, 85–101.

1993. Creole language provenance and the African component. In Mufwene 1993a, 182–91.

Hanski, Ilkka. 1996. Metapopulation ecology. In *Population dynamics in ecological space and time*, ed. by Olin E. Rhodes, Jr., Ronald K. Chesser, and Michael H. Smith, 13–43. Chicago: University of Chicago Press.

Harris, Alice C. and Lyle Campbell. 1995. *Historical syntax in cross-linguistic perspective*. Cambridge: Cambridge University Press.

Harris, John. 1991. Ireland. In Cheshire 1991b, 37–50.

Harris, Martin. 1988. The Romance languages. In Harris and Vincent, 1–25.

Harris, Martin and Nigel Vincent, eds. 1988. *The Romance languages*, London: Routledge.

Harrison, G.A., J.M. Tanner, D.R. Pillbeam, and P.T. Baker. 1988. *Human biology: an introduction to human evolution, variation, growth, and adaptability*. Oxford: Oxford University Press.

Haspelmath, Martin. 1998. How young is standard average European? *Language Sciences* 20.271–87.

Haugen, Einar. 1971. The ecology of language. *The Linguistic Reporter*, Supplement 25. 19–26. Reprinted as Haugen (1972), 324–39.

1972. *The ecology of language*, ed. by Anuar Dil. Stanford: Stanford University Press.

Hazaël-Massieux, Guy. 1993. The African filter in the genesis of Guadeloupean Creole: at the confluence of genesis and typology. In Mufwene 1993a, 109–22.

1996† *Les créoles: problèmes de genèse et de description*. Aix-en-Provence: Publications de l'Université de Provence.

Heath, Brice Shirley. 1992. American English: quest for a model. In Kachru, 220–32.

Hergé. 1975. *The adventures of Tintin: the broken ear*. Translated by Leslie Lonsdale-Cooper and Michael Turner. London: Methuen (Boston: Little, Brown 1978).

Herskovits, Melville. 1941. *The myth of the Negro past*. New York: Herper.

Hickey, Raymond. 1995. An assessment of language contact in the development of Irish English. In Fisiak, 109–30.

Hill, Kenneth C., ed. 1979. *The genesis of language*. Ann Arbor: Karoma.

Hjelmslev, Louis. 1938. Etudes sur la notion de parenté linguistique. *Revue des Etudes Indo- Européennes* 1.271–86.

Hock, Hans Henrich and Brian D. Joseph. 1996. *Language history, language change, and language relationship*. Berlin: Mouton de Gruyter.

Hoeningswald, Henry M. 1989. Language obsolescence and language history: matters of linearity, leveling, loss, and the like. In *Investigating obsolescence: studies in language contraction and death*, ed. by Nancy C. Dorian, 347–54. Cambridge: Cambridge University Press.

Hogg, Richard M., ed. 1992. *The Cambridge history of the English language* I: *The beginnings to 1066*. Cambridge: Cambridge University Press.

Holloway, Joseph E. and Winifred K. Vass. 1993. *The African heritage of American English*. Bloomington: Indiana University Press.

Holm, John. 1976. Variability of the copula in Black English and its creole kin. Paper presented at First Biennial Conference of the Society for Caribbean Linguistics, Georgetown, Guyana.

1984. Variability of the copula in Black English and its creole kin. (Updated and expanded version of Holm 1976.) *American Speech* 59.291–309.

1988. *Pidgins and creoles* I: *Theory and structure*. Cambridge: Cambridge University Press.

1989. *Pidgins and Creoles* II: *Reference survey*. Cambridge: Cambridge University Press.

1991. The Atlantic creoles and the language of the ex-slave recordings. In *The emergence of Black English: text and commentary*, ed. by Guy Bailey, Natalie Maynor, and Patricia Cukor-Avila, 231–48. Amsterdam: John Benjamins.

1993. Phonological features common to some West-African and Atlantic creole languages. In Mufwene 1993a, 317–27.

Hopper, Paul J. 1991. On some principles of grammaticalization. In Traugott and Heine, 17–35.

Huber, Magnus. 1999. Atlantic creoles and the Lower Guinea Coast: a case against Afrogenesis. In Huber and Parkvall, 81–110.

Huber, Magnus and Mikael Parkvall, eds. 1999. *Spreading the word: the issue of diffusion among the Atlantic creoles*. London: University of Westminster Press.

Hymes, Dell, ed. 1971. *Pidginization and creolization of languages*. Cambridge: Cambridge University Press.

1974. *Foundations in sociolinguistics: an ethnographical approach*. Philadelphia: University of Pennsylvania Press.

Ihalainen, Ossi. 1991. Periphrastic *do* in affirmative sentences in the dialect of East Somerset. In Trudgill and Chambers, 145–7.

Jespersen, Otto. 1931. *A modern English grammar on historical principles.* Part IV: *Syntax* III: *Time and tense.* Heidelberg: Carl Winters Universitätsbuchhandlung.

Johnson, Guy. 1930. *Folk culture on St. Helena Island, South Carolina.* Chapel Hill: University of North Carolina Press.

Jones, Hugh. 1724. *The present state of Virginia, from whence is inferred a short view of Maryland and North Carolina.* 1956 edition by Richard L. Morton. Chapel Hill: North Carolina University Press.

Joseph, Brian D. and Arnold Zwicky, eds. 1990. *When verbs collide: papers from the 1990 Ohio State Mini-Conference on Serial Verbs,* Columbus, Ohio: Department of Linguistics.

Joyner, Charles. 1984. *Down by the riverside: a South Carolina slave community.* Chicago: University of Illinois Press.

Kachru, Braj. 1983. South Asian English. In *English as a world language,* ed. by Richard W. Bailey and Manfred Görlach, 353–83. Ann Abor: University of Michigan Press.

ed. 1992. *The other tongue: English across cultures.* Second edition. Urbana: University of Illinois Press.

Kahane, Henry. 1992. American English: from a colonial substandard to a prestige language. In Kachru, 211–19.

Kallen, Jeffrey. 1997. Irish English: contexts and contacts. In *Focus on Ireland.* Varieties of English Around the World G21, ed. by Jeff Kallen, 1–33. Amsterdam: John Benjamins.

Kapanga, Mwamba Tshishiku. 1991. Language variation and change: a case study of Shaba Swahili. Ph.D. dissertation, University of Illinois, Urbana.

Katzman, David M. 1991. Black migration. In Foner and Garaty, 114–16.

Keesing, Roger M. 1988. *Melanesian Pidgin and the Oceanic substrate.* Stanford: Stanford University Press.

Keller, Rudi. 1994. *On language change: the invisible hand in language.* London: Routledge.

Kerswill, Paul and Ann Williams. 1994. A new dialect in a new city: children's and adults' speech in Milton Keynes. Final Report on a project funded by the Economic and Social Research Council.

Kibbee, Douglas A. 1999. French language policy timeline. Ms., University of Illinois, Urbana-Champaign.

Klerk, Vivian de, ed. 1996. *Focus on Africa.* Varieties of English Around the World 15. Amsterdam: John Benjamins.

Koerner, Konrad, ed. 1983. *Linguistics and evolutionary theory: three essays by August Schleicher, Ernst Haeckel, and Wilhelm Bleek.* Amsterdam: John Benjamins.

Kouwenberg, Silvia. 1994. *A grammar of Berbice Dutch Creole.* Berlin: Mouton De Gruyter.

Krapp, George Philip. 1924. The English of the Negro. *The American Mercury* 2.190–5.

Krapp, George Philip. 1925. *The English language in America.* New York: Century.

Kroch, Anthony, Ann Taylor, and Donald Ringe. 2000. The Middle-English verb-second constraint: a case study in language contact and language change. In *Textual parameters in older language*, ed. by Susan Herring, Lene Schoesler, and Pieter van Reenen, 353–91. Amsterdam: John Benjamins.

Kulikoff, Allan. 1986. *Tobacco and slaves: the development of southern cultures in the Chesapeake, 1680–1800*. Chapel Hill: University of North Carolina Press.

1991a. Colonial Culture. In Foner and Garraty, 197–201.

1991b. Colonial Economy. In Foner and Garraty, 201–3.

Kurath, Hans. 1928. The origin of dialectal differences in spoken American English. *Modern Philology* 25.385–95.

Labov, William. 1963. The social motivation of sound change. *Word* 19.273–309. Reprinted in Labov 1972b, 1–42.

1966. *The social stratification of English in New York City*. Washington, DC: Center for Applied Linguistics.

1972a. *Language in the inner city*. Philadelphia: University of Pennsylvania Press.

1972b. *Sociolinguistic patterns*. Philadelphia: University of Pennsylvania Press.

1982. Objectivity and commitment in linguistic science: the case of the Black English trial in Ann Arbor. *Language in Society* 11.165–201.

1994. *Principles of linguistic change: internal factors*. Oxford: Blackwell.

1998. Co-existent systems in African–American vernacular English. In Mufwene et al., 110–53.

Labov, William and Wendell Harris. 1986. De facto segregation of black and white vernaculars. In *Diversity and diachrony*, ed. by David Sankoff, 1–24. Amsterdam: John Benjamins.

Ladhams, John. 1999. The Pernambuco connection? An examination of the nature and origin of the Portuguese elements in the Suriname Creoles. In Huber and Parkvall, 209–40.

Lalla, Barbara and Jean D'Costa. 1990. *Language in exile: three hundred years of Jamaican Creole*. Tuscaloosa: University of Alabama Press.

Lass, Roger. 1997. *Historical linguistics and language change*. Cambridge: Cambridge University Press.

Lefebvre, Claire. 1986. Relexification in creole genesis revisited. In Muysken and Smith, 279–300.

1989. Instrumental *take*-serial constructions in Haitian and Fon. In Lefebvre and Lumsden, 319–37.

1993. The role of relexification and syntactic reanalysis in Haitian Creole: methodological aspects of a research program. In Mufwene 1993a, 254–79.

1998. *Creole genesis and the acquisition of grammar: the case of Haitian Creole*. Cambridge: Cambridge University Press.

Lefebvre, Claire and John Lumsden, eds. 1989. La créolisation. *Revue Canadienne de Linguistique* 34, 3.

Lemann, Nicholas. 1991. *The promised land: the Great Black Migration and how it changed America*. New York: Knopf.

Le Page, R.B. 1960. An historical introduction to Jamaican Creole. In *Jamaican Creole*, by R. B. Le Page and David De Camp, 1–124. Cambridge: Cambridge University Press.

Le Page, R.B. and Andrée Tabouret-Keller. 1985. *Acts of identity: creole-based approaches to language and identity*. Cambridge: Cambridge University Press.

Lewontin, Richard C. 1970. The units of selection. *Annual Review of Ecology and Systematics* 1.1–18.

Lichtenberk, Frantisek. 1991. On the gradualness of grammaticalization. In Traugott and Heine, 37–80.

Lightfoot, David. 1999. *The development of language: acquisition, change, and evolution*. Oxford: Blackwell.

Lord, Carol. 1993. *Historical change in serial verb constructions*. Amsterdam: John Benjamins.

Lovejoy, Paul E. 1982. The volume of the Atlantic slave trade: a synthesis. *Journal of African History* 23.473–501.

    1989. The impact of the Atlantic slave trade on Africa: a review of the literature. *Journal of African History* 30.365–94.

Lüdtke, Helmut. 1995. On the origin of Modern and Middle English. In Fisiak, 51–3.

Lumsden, John. 1999. Language acquisition and creolization. In DeGraff 1999b, 129–57.

McCawley, James D. 1976. Some ideas not to live by. *Die neueren Sprachen* 75.151–65.

McDavid, Raven, Jr. 1950. Review of Lorenzo Dow Turner 1949. *Language* 26.323–33.

McDavid, Raven, Jr. and Virginia McDavid. 1951. The relationship of the speech of the American Negroes to the speech of whites. *American Speech* 26.3–17.

McEvedy, Colin. 1980. *The Penguin atlas of African history*. London: Penguin.

McMahon, April. 1994. *Understanding language change*. Cambridge: Cambridge University Press.

McNeill, David. 1992. *Hand and mind: what gestures reveal about thought*. Chicago: University of Chicago Press.

McWhorter, John H. 1995. Sisters under the skin: a case of genetic relationship between the Atlantic English-based creoles. *Journal of Pidgin and Creole Languages* 10.289–333.

    1997. It happened at Cormantin: locating the origin of Atlantic English-based creoles. *Journal of Pidgin and Creole Languages* 12.59–102.

    1998. Identifying the creole prototype: vindicating a typological class. *Language* 74.788–818.

Magens, Jochum. 1770. Grammatica over e det Creolske Sprog. Copenhagen.

Manheim, Bruce. 1991. *The language of the Inka since the European invasion*. Austin: University of Texas Press.

Martin, Danielle and Sali Tagliamonte. 1999. *Oh, it beautiful!* Copula variability in Britain. Paper presented at NWAV 28, Toronto.

Maurer, Philippe. 1987. La comparaison des morphèmes temporels du papiamento et du palenquero: arguments contre la théorie monogénétique de la genèse des langues créoles. In Maurer and Stolz, 27–70.

    1988. *Les modifications temporelles et modales du verbe dans le papiamento de Curaçao (Antilles Néerlandaises)*. Hamburg: Helmut Buske Verlag.

Maurer, Philippe and Thomas Stolz, eds. 1987. *Varia creolica*. Bochum: Brockmeyer.

Mayr, Ernst. 1997. *This is biology: the science of the living world*. Cambridge, MA: Harvard University Press.

Mazrui, Ali and Alamin Mazrui. 1998. *The power of Babel: language in the African experience*. Oxford: James Currey/Chicago: University of Chicago Press.

Meillet, Antoine. 1929. Le développement des langues. In *Continu et discontinu*, 119ff. Paris: Bloud and Gay. Reprinted in Meillet 1951, 71–83.

1951. *Linguistique historique et linguistique générale* II. Paris: Klincksieck.

Menard, Russell R. 1991. Indentured Servitude. In Foner and Garraty, 542–3.

Mesthrie, Rajend. 1992a. *English in language shift: the history, structure and sociolinguistics of South African Indian English*. Cambridge: Cambridge University Press.

1992b. Fanakalo in colonial Natal. In *Language and society in South Africa*, ed. by Robert K. Herbert, 305–24. Johannesburg: Witwatersrand University Press.

Migge, Bettina M. 1993. *Substrate influence in creole language formation: the case of serial verb constructions in Sranan*. MA thesis, Ohio State University.

1999. *Substrate influence in the formation of Surinamese plantation Creole: a consideration of sociohistorical data and linguistic data from Ndyuka and Gbe*. Ph.D. dissertation, Ohio State University.

Mille, Katherine. 1990. *A historical analysis of tense-mood-aspect in Gullah Creole: a case of stable variation*. PhD dissertation, University of South Carolina.

Miller, Catherine. 1985. Un exemple d'évolution linguistique: le cas de la particule *ge* en Juba Arabic. *Matériaux Arabes et Sudarabiques-GELLAS* 3,156–66. Paris: Paul Geuthner.

Milroy, James. 1992. *Linguistic variation and change: on the historical sociolinguistics of English*. Oxford: Blackwell.

1997. Internal vs. external motivations for linguistic change. *Multilingua* 16.311–23.

Milroy, James and Lesley Milroy. 1985. Linguistic change, social network and speaker innovation. *Journal of Linguistics* 21.339–84.

Mithun, Marianne. 1992. The substratum in grammar and discourse. In *Language contact: theoretical and empirical studies*, ed. by Ernst Håkon Jahr, 103–15. Berlin: Mouton de Gruyter.

Montgomery, Michael. 1989. Exploring the roots of Appalachian English. *English World-Wide* 10.227–78.

1995. The koinéization of colonial American English. In *Sociolinguistic studies and language planning: proceedings of the XVIth Annual Meeting of the Atlantic Provinces Linguistic Association*, ed. by Catherine Phliponneau, 309–31. Moncton, NB: Center de Recherche en Linguistique Appliquée.

1996. Was colonial American English a koiné? In *Speech past and present: studies in English dialectology in memory of Ossi Ihalainen*, ed. by Juhani Klemola, Merja Kyto, and Matti Rissanen, 213–35. University of Bamberg Studies in English Linguistics 38. Frankfurt am Main: Peter Lang.

Montgomery, Michael and Guy Bailey, eds. 1986. *Language variety in the South: perspectives in black and white*. University: University of Alabama Press.

Montgomery, Michael, Janet M. Fuller, and Sharon Paparone. 1994. "The black men has wives and Sweet harts [and third person plural -*s*] Jest like the white men": evidence from verbal -*s* from written documents on 19th-century African American speech. *Language Variation and Change* 5.335–57.

Morgan, Marcyliena. 1993. The Africanness of counterlanguage among Afro-Americans. In Mufwene 1993a, 423–35.

Mufwene, Salikoko S. 1981. Non-individuation and the count/mass distinction. In *Papers from the Seventeenth Regional Meeting of the Chicago Linguistic Society*, ed. by Roberta A. Hendrick, Carries S. Masek, and Mary Frances Miller, 221–38. CLS, University of Chicago

1983. *Some observations on the verb in Black English Vernacular.* African and Afro-American Studies and Research Center, University of Texas, Austin.

1984. The language bioprogram hypothesis, creole studies, and linguistic theory. Commentary on Derek Bickerton's "The language bioprogram hypothesis." *Behavioral and Brain Sciences* 7.202–3.

1986a. Les langues créoles peuvent-elles être définies sans allusion à leur histoire? *Etudes Créoles* 9.135–50.

1986b. The universalist and substrate hypotheses complement one another. In Muysken and Smith, 129–62.

1986c. Number delimitation in Gullah. *American Speech* 61.33–60.

1988a. Formal evidence of pidginization/creolization in Kituba. *Journal of African Languages and Linguistics* 10.33–51.

1988b. Why study pidgins and creoles. Column. *Journal of Pidgin and Creole Languages* 3.265–76.

1989a. Equivocal structures in some Gullah complex sentences. *American Speech* 64.304–26.

1989c. Some explanations that strike me as incomplete. Column. *Journal of Pidgin and Creole Languages* 4.117–28.

1989b. La créolisation en bantou: les cas du kituba, du lingala urbain, et du swahili du Shaba. *Etudes Créoles* 12.74–106.

1990a. Creoles and universal grammar. In *Issues in creole linguistics*, ed. by Pieter Seuren and Salikoko Mufwene, 783–807. *Linguistics* 28.

1990b. Time reference in Kituba. In *Tense-modality-aspect systems in pidgins and creoles*, ed. by John V. Singler, 97–117. Amsterdam: John Benjamins.

1991a. Pidgins, creoles, typology, and markedness. In Byrne and Huebner 1991, 123–43.

1991b. Review of Holm (1988, 1989). *Language* 67.380–7.

1991c. Review of Chaudenson (1989). *Journal of Pidgin and Creole Languages* 6.148–55.

1991d. Is Gullah decreolizing? A comparison of a speech sample of the 1930's with a speech sample of the 1980's. In Bailey, Maynor, and Cukor-Avila 1991, 213–30.

1992a. Why grammars are not monolithic. In *The joy of grammar: a festschrift in honor of James D. McCawley*, ed. by Diane Brentari, Gary N. Larson, and Lynn A. Macleod, 225–50. Amsterdam: John Benjamins.

1992b. Africanisms in Gullah: a re-examination of the issues. In *Old English and new: studies in language and linguistics in honor of Frederic G. Cassidy*, ed. by Joan H. Hall, Dick Doane, and Dick Ringler, 156–82. New York: Garland.

1992c. Ideology and facts on African-American English. *Pragmatics* 2.141–66.

1992d. Some reasons why Gullah is not dying yet. *English World-Wide* 12.215–43.

ed. 1993a. *Africanisms in Afro-American language varieties.* Athens: University of Georgia Press.

1993b. African substratum: possibility and evidence. Discussion of Alleyne's and Hancock's papers. In Mufwene 1993a, 192–208.

1994a. On decreolization: the case of Gullah. In *Language and the social construction of identity in creole situations*, ed. by Marcyliena Morgan, 63–99. Los Angeles: Center for Afro-American Studies.

1994b. Restructuring, feature selection, and markedness: from Kimanyanga to Kituba. In *Historical issues in African linguistics*, ed. by Kevin Moore, David Peterson, and Comfort Wentum, 67–90. Berkeley Linguistics Society.

1994c. New Englishes and criteria for naming them. *World Englishes* 13.21–31.

1994d. Review of Holloway and Vass. *American Anthropologist* 96.477–8.

1994e. Review of Mesthrie 1992. *World Englishes* 13.425–30.

1996a. Creolization and grammaticization: what creolistics could contribute to research on grammaticization. In Baker and Syea 1996, 5–28.

1996b. Creole genesis: a population genetics perspective. In *Caribbean language issues: old and new*, ed. by Pauline Christie, 168–209. Kingston, Jamaica: University of the West Indies Press.

1997a. Jargons, pidgins, creoles, and koinés: what are they? In Spears and Winford, 35–70.

1997b. Native speaker, proficient speaker, and norm. In *Native speaker: Multilingual perspectives*, ed. by Rajendra Singh, 111–23. New Dehli: Sage.

1997c. Gullah's development: myths and sociohistorical evidence. In *Language variety in the South revisited*, ed. by Cynthia Bernstein, Robin Sabino, and Tom Nunally, 113–22. Tuscaloosa: University of Alabama Press.

1997d. Kituba. In Thomason 1997b, 173–208.

1997e. Métissages des peuples et métissages des langues. In *Contacts de langues, contacts de cultures, créolisation*, ed. by Marie-Christine Hazaël-Massieux and Didier de Robillard, 51–70. Paris: L'Harmattan.

1999a. The language bioprogram hypothesis: hints from Tazie. In DeGraff 1999b, 95–127.

1999b. Some sociohistorical inferences about the development of African-American English. In *The English history of African-American English*, ed. by Shana Poplack, 233–63. Oxford: Blackwell.

1999c. Accountability in descriptions of creoles. In *Creole genesis, attitudes, and discourse: studies celebrating Charlene J. Sato*, ed. by John Rickford and Suzanne Romaine, 157–85. Amsterdam: John Benjamins.

1999d. North American varieties of English as byproducts of population contacts. In *The workings of language: from prescriptions to perspectives*, ed. by Rebecca Wheeler, 15–37. Westport, MA: Greenwood.

2000a. Creolization is a social, not a structural, process. In *Degress of restructuring in creole languages*, ed. by Edgar Schneider and Ingrid Neumann-Holzschuh, 65–84. Amsterdam: John Benjamins.

2000b. African-American English. In *The Cambridge history of the English language* VI: *History of American English*, ed. by John Algeo. ____ Cambridge: Cambridge University Press.

forthcoming. Contact and speciation in English: some dialects of English are creole. In *English globalized* I: *Perspectives and prospects*, ed. by Anne Pakir, Vincent Ooi, and Ismail Talib. Amsterdam: John Benjamins.

Mufwene, Salikoko S., John R. Rickford, Guy Bailey, and John Baugh, eds. 1998. *African- American English: structure, history, and use*. London: Routledge.

Mühlhäusler, Peter. 1985. The number of pidgin Englishes in the Pacific. *Papers in Pidgin and Creole Linguistics* 1. *Pacific Linguistics* A-72.25–51.

1986. *Pidgin and creole linguistics*. Oxford: Blackwell. Revised edition 1997. London: University of Westminster Press.

1996. *Linguistic ecology: language change and linguistic imperialism in the Pacific region*. London: Routledge.

Muysken, Pieter, ed. 1981. *Generative studies on creole languages*. Dordrecht: Foris.

1983. Review of Bickerton 1981. *Language* 59.884–901.

Muysken, Pieter and Norval Smith, eds. 1986. *Universals versus substrata in creole genesis*. Amsterdam: John Benjamins.

Nagle, Stephen. 1995. The English double modals: internal or external change? In Fisiak, 207–15.

Nettle, Daniel. 1999. *Linguistic diversity*. Oxford: Oxford University Press.

Newman, James L. 1995. *The peopling of Africa: a geographic interpretation*. New Haven, CN/London: Yale University Press.

Nichols, Johanna. 1994. *Linguistic diversity in space and time*: Chicago: University of Chicago Press.

Nichols, Patricia C. 1993. Language contact and shift in early South Carolina. Paper present ed at the annual meeting of the Linguistic Society of America, Los Angeles, California.

Nurse, Derek. 1997. Prior pidginization and creolization in Swahili? In Thomason 1997b, 271–363.

Nurse, Derek and Thomas J. Hinnebusch. 1993. *Swahili and Sabaki: a linguistic history*. Berkeley/Los Angeles/London: University of California Press.

Nurse, Derek and Thomas Spear. 1985. *The Swahili: reconstructing the history of an African society 800–1500*. Philadelphia: University of Pennsylvania Press.

Odlin, Terence. 1989. *Language transfer: cross-linguistic influence in language learning*. Cambridge: Cambridge University Press.

1992. Transferability and linguistic substrates. *Second Language Research* 8.171–202.

1997. Hiberno-English: pidgin, creole, or neither? Occasional Paper 49, Center for Language and Communication Studies, Trinity College, Dublin.

forthcoming. Language ecology and the Columbian exchange. In *Language conflict/Language competition*, ed. by Brian Joseph, Neil Jacobs, Ilse Lehiste, and Johanna De Stefano. Columbus: Ohio State University Press.

O'Hara, Robert J. 1994. Evolutionary history and the species problem. *American Zoology* 34:12–22.

Ohly, Rajmund. 1982. *Swahili: the diagram of crises*. Vienna: Afro-Pub.

Owens, Jonathan. 1997. Arabic-based pidgins and creoles. In Thomason 1997b, 125–72.

1998. Representativeness in the data base: polemical update for the twenty-first century. *Language Sciences* 20.113–35.

Papen, Robert A. 1987. Le métif: le nec plus ultra des grammaires en contact. *Revue Québecoise de Linguistique Théorique et Appliquée* 6.57–70.

Pasch, Helma. 1997. Language contact. In *Encyclopedia of Africa south of the Sahara*, ed. by John Middleton et al., 515–17. New York: Charles Scribner's Sons.

Perkins, Edwin J. 1988. *The economy of colonial America*. Second edition. New York: Columbia University Press.

Plag, Ingo. 1993. *Sentential complementation in Sranan: on the formation of an English- based creole language*. Tübingen: Niemeyer.

1999. Review of Baker and Syea 1996. *Journal of Pidgin and Creole Languages* 14.202–8.

Polomé, Edgar. 1971. The Katanga (Lubumbashi) Swahili Creole. In Hymes, 57–61. Cambridge: Cambridge University Press.

1983. Creolization and language change. In *The social context of creolization*, ed. by Ellen Woolford and William Washabaugh, 126–36. Ann Arbor: Karoma.

1985. Swahili in the Shaba region of Zaire. In *Swahili language and society*, ed. by Joan Maw and David Parkin, 47–65. Vienna: Afro-Pub.

Poplack, Shana, ed. 1999. *The English history of African-American English*. Oxford: Blackwell.

Poplack, Shana and Sali Tagliamonte. 1989. There's no tense like the present: verbal *-s* inflection in early Black English. *Language Variation and Change* 1.47–84.

1991. African American English in the diaspora: evidence from old line Nova Scotians. *Language Variation and Change* 3.301–39.

1994. *-S* or nothing: marking the plural in the African American diaspora. *American Speech* 69.227–59.

1996. Nothing in context: variation, grammaticization and past time marking in Nigerian Pidgin English. In *Changing meanings, changing functions: papers relating to grammaticalization in contact languages*, ed. by Philip Baker and Anand Syea, 71–94. London: University of Westminster Press.

Posner, Rebecca. 1985. Creolization as typological change: some examples from Romance syntax. *Diachronica* 2.167–88.

1996. *The Romance languages*. Cambridge: Cambridge University Press.

Price, Richard. 1976. *The Guiana maroons: a historical and bibliographical introduction*. Baltimore, MD: Johns Hopkins University Press.

Pullum, Geoffrey K. 1990. Constraints on intransitive quasi-serial verb constructions in Modern Colloquial English. In Joseph and Zwicky, 218–39.

Rawley, James A. 1981. *The transatlantic slave trade*. New York: Norton.

1991. Slave trade. In Foner and Garraty, 994–5.

Rickford, John R. 1977. The question of prior creolization of Black English. In *Pidgin and creole linguistics*, ed. by Albert Valdman, 190–221. Bloomington: Indiana University Press.

1985. Ethnicity as a sociolinguistic boundary. *American Speech* 60.99–125.

1986. Social contact and linguistic diffusion. *Language* 62.245–90.

1987. *Dimensions of a creole continuum: history, text, and linguistic analysis of Guyanese Creole*. Stanford: Stanford University Press.

1992. Grammatical variation and divergence in Vernacular Black English. In *Internal and external factors in syntactic change*, ed. by Marinel Gerritsen and Dieter Stein, 175–200. Berlin: Mouton de Gruyter.

1998. The creole origins of African-American vernacular English: evidence from copula absence. In Mufwene et al., 154–200.

Rickford, John R. and Jerome S. Handler. 1994. Textual Evidence of the Nature of Early Barbadian Speech. *Journal of Pidgin and Creole Languages* 9.221–55.

Roberge, Paul. 1994. *The formation of Afrikaans*. Stellenbosch Papers in Linguistics Plus 24. Department of Linguistics, University of Stellenbosch, South Africa.

Robertson, Ian. 1993. The Ijo element in Berbice Dutch and the pidginization/creolization process. In Mufwene 1993a, 296–316.

Romaine, Suzanne. 1982. *Socio-historical linguistics: its status and methodology*. Cambridge: Cambridge University Press.

1988. *Pidgin and creole languages*. London: Longman.

Samarin, William. 1982. Colonization and pidginization on the Ubangi River. *Journal of African Languages and Linguistics* 4.1–42.

1989. *The black man's burden: African colonial labor on the Congo and Ubangi Rivers, 1880–1900*. Boulder, CO: Westview.

1990. The origins of Kituba and Lingala. *Journal of African Languages and Linguistics* 12.47–77.

Sankoff, Gillian. 1979. The genesis of a language. In Hill, 23–47.

1980. Variation, pidgins and creoles. In Valdman and Highfield, 139–64.

1984. Substrate and universals in the Tok Pisin verb phrase. In *Meaning, form, and use in context: linguistic applications*, ed. by Deborah Schiffrin, 104–19. Washington, DC: Georgetown University Press.

1993. Focus in Tok Pisin. In Byrne and Winford, 117–40.

Sankoff, Gillian and Penelope Brown. 1976. The origins of syntax in discourse: a case study of Tok Pisin relatives. *Language* 52.631–66.

Schmied, Josef. 1991. *English in Africa: an introduction*. London: Longman.

Schneider, Edgar W. 1982. On the history of Black English in the USA: some new evidence. *English World-Wide* 3.18–46.

1983. The diachronic development of the Black English in the USA: some new evidence. *Journal of English Linguistics* 16.55–64.

1989. *American earlier Black English: morphological and syntactic variables*. Tuscaloosa: University of Alabama Press.

1990. The cline of creoleness in English-oriented creoles and semi-creoles of the Caribbean. *English World-Wide* 11.79–113.

1993. Africanisms in the grammar of Afro-American English: the significance of African substratum. In Mufwene 1993a, 209–21.

Schuchardt, Hugo. 1884. *Slavo-deutsches und Slavo-italienisches*. Graz: Leuschner and Lubensky.

1909. Die Lingua Franca. *Zeitschrift fur Romanische Philologie* 33.441–61.

Seuren, Pieter. 1990. Serial verb constructions. In Joseph and Zwicky, 14–33.

Siegel, Jeff. 1998. Substrate reinforcement and dialectal differences in Melanesian Pidgin. *Journal of Sociolinguistics* 2.347–73.

Simms, William Gilmore. 1839. The lazy crow. Reprinted in *The wigwam and the cabin*, 333–60. Chicago: Donohue.

Singler, John V. 1988. The homogeneity of the substrate as a factor in pidgin creole genesis. *Language* 64.27–51.

1991a. Liberian Settler English and the ex-slave recordings: a comparative study. In *The emergence of Black English: text and commentary*, ed. by Guy Bailey, Natalie Maynor, and Patricia Cukor-Avila, 249–74. Amsterdam: John Benjamins.

1991b. Social and linguistic constraints on plural marking in Liberian English. In Cheshire 1991b, 544–62.

1992. Nativization and pidgin/creole genesis: a reply to Bickerton. *Journal of Pidgin and Creole Languages* 7.319–33.

1993. The African influence upon Afro-American varieties. In Mufwene 1993a, 235–53.

1995. The demographics of creole genesis in the Caribbean: a comparison of Martinique and Haiti. In Arends, 203–32.

1997. The configuration of Liberia's Englishes. *World Englishes* 16.205–31.

Smith, Larry E. 1992. The spread of English and issues of intelligibility. In Kachru, 75–90.

Smith, Neil. 1999. *Chomsky: ideas and ideals*. Cambridge: Cambridge University Press.

Spears, Arthur K. 1993. Where did Haitian Creole come from? A discussion of Hazaël-Massieux's and Baker's papers. In Mufwene 1993a, 156–66.

Spears, Arthur K. and Donald Winford, eds. 1997. *The structure and status of pidgins and creoles*. Amsterdam: John Benjamins.

Spitulnik, Debra. 1999. The language of the city: Town Bemba as urban hybridity. *Journal of Linguistic Anthropology* 8.30–59.

Stewart, William A. 1967. Sociolinguistic factors in the history of American Negro dialects. *Florida Foreign Language Reporter* 5.11, 22, 24, 26, 30.

1968. Continuity and change in American Negro dialects. *Florida Foreign Language Reporter* 6.3–4, 14–16, 18.

1969. Historical and structural bases for the recognition of Negro dialect. In *Report of the Twentieth Annual Round Table Meeting on Linguistics and Language Studies*, ed. by James E. Alatis, 239–47. Washington, DC: Georgetown University Press.

1974. Acculturative processes in the language of the American Negro. In *Language in its social setting*, ed. by William W. Gage, 1–46. Washington, DC: Anthropological Society of Washington

Sutcliffe, David, with John Figueroa. 1992. *System in Black language*. Clevedon, OH: Multilingual Matters.

Sylvain, Suzanne. 1936. *Le créole haitien: morphologie et syntaxe*. Wettern, Belgium: Imprimerie De Meester.

Tagliamonte, Sali. 1996. Has it ever been "perfect": Uncovering the grammar of Early Black English. *York Papers in Linguistics* 17.351–96.

1999. Back to the roots: what British dialects reveal about North American English. Paper presented at the Methods in Dialectology meeting, University of Newfoundland.

Tagliamonte, Sali and Shana Poplack. 1988. Tense and aspect in Samaná English. *Language in Society* 17.513–33.

1993. The zero-marked verb: testing the creole hypothesis. *Journal of Pidgin and Creole Languages* 8.171–206.

Tate, Thad W. 1965. *The Negro in eighteenth-century Williamsburg*. Williamsburg, VA: Colonial Williamsburg Foundation.

Tay, Mary. 1981. The uses, users, and features of English in Singapore. In *New Englishes*, ed. by John B. Pride, 51–70. Rowley, MA: Newbury House.

Thomas, Hugh. 1998. *The slave trade*. New York: Simon and Schuster.

Thomason, Sarah G. 1980. On Interpreting "The Indian Interpreter." *Language and Society* 9.167–93.

1997a. Ma'a (Mbugu). In Thomason 1997b, 467–87.

1997b. *Contact languages: a wider perspective*. Amsterdam: John Benjamins.

1983. Chinook jargon in areal and historical context. *Language* 59.820–70.

Thomason, Sarah G. and Terrence Kaufman. 1988. *Language contact, creolization, and genetic linguistics*. Berkeley: University of California Press.

Thompson, John N. 1994. *The coevolutionary process*. Chicago: University of Chicago Press.

Todd, Loreto. 1984. *Modern Englishes: pidgins and creoles*. London: Blackwell.

Traugott, Elizabeth Closs. 1972. *The history of English syntax*. New York: Holt, Rinehart, and Winston.

Traugott, Elizabeth Closs and Bernd Heine, eds. 1991. *Approaches to grammaticalization*. I: *Focus on theoretical and methodological issues*; II: *Focus on types of grammatical markers*. Amsterdam/Philadelphia: John Benjamins.

Tristram, Hildegard L.C., ed. 1997. *The Celtic Englishes* I. Heidelberg: Winter.

ed. 2000. *The Celtic Englishes* II. Heidelberg: Winter.

Troike, Rudolph C. 1973. On social, regional, and age variation in Black English. *The Florida Foreign Language Reporter*, 8–9.

Trubetzkoy, Nikolai S. 1939. Gedanken über das Indogermanenproblem. *Acta Linguistica* 1.81–9.

Trudgill, Peter. 1974. *The social differentiation of English in Norwich*. Cambridge: Cambridge University Press.

1986. *Dialects in contact*. Oxford: Blackwell.

Trudgill, Peter and J.K. Chambers, eds. 1997. *Dialects of English: studies in grammatical variation*. London: Longman.

Turner, Lorenzo Dow. 1949. *Africanisms in the Gullah dialect*. Chicago: University of Chicago Press.

Valdman, Albert and Arnold Highfield, eds. 1980. *Theoretical orientations in creole studies*. New York: Academic Press.

Valkhoff, Marius. 1966. *Studies in Portuguese and Creole – with special reference to South Africa*. Johannesburg: Witwatersrand University Press.

Valli, André. 1994. A propos de l'emploi productif de la détermination zéro en moyen français et en créole réunionnais. In *Créolisation et acquisition des langues*, ed. by Daniel Véronique, 89–103. Aix-en-Provence: Publications de l'Université de Provence.

Vansina, Jan. 1990. *Paths in the rainforest: toward a history of political tradition in Equatorial Africa*. Madison: University of Wisconsin Press.

Vennemann, Theo. 2000. Semitic → Celtic → English: transitivity in language contact. Lecture at the Max Planck Institute, Leipzig.

Vinson, Julien. 1882. Créole. In *Dictionnaire des sciences anthropologiques et ethnologiques*. Paris.

1888. La linguistique. *La grande encyclopédie* 22.286–96. Paris.

Voegelin, C.F. and F.M. Voegelin, and Noel W. Schutz, Jr. 1967. The language situation in Arizona as part of the Southwest culture area. *Studies in Southwestern ethnolinguistics: meaning and history in the languages of the American Southwest*, ed. by Dell Hymes and William E. Bittle, 403–51. The Hague: Mouton.

Voorhoeve, Jan. 1964. "Creole Languages and Communication" *Symposium on Multilingualism (Brazzaville, 1962)*, 233–42. (CSA/CCTA Publication 87). London: Commission de Coopération Technique en Afrique.

Wade-Lewis, Margaret. 1988. The African substratum in American English. Ph.D. dissertation, New York University.

Warner-Lewis, Maureen. 1996. *Trinidad Yoruba: from mother tongue to memory.* Tuscaloosa: University of Alabama Press.

Weinreich, Uriel. 1953. *Languages in contact: findings and problems.* New York: Linguistic Circle of New York.

Whinnom, Keith. 1971. Linguistic hybridization and the "special case" of pidgins and creoles. In Hymes, 91–115.

Williams, Jeffrey P. 1983. Dutch and English Creole on the Windward Netherlands Antilles: an historical perspective. *Amsterdam Creole Studies* 5.93–112.

1985. Preliminaries to the study of the dialects of White West Indian English. *Nieuwe West-Indische Gids* 59.27–44.

Williams, Selase. 1993. Substantive Africanisms at the end of the African linguistic diaspora. In Mufwene 1993a, 406–22.

Wimsatt, William C. 2000. Generativity, entrenchment, evolution, and innateness. In *Biology meets psychology: constraints, connections, conjectures*, ed. by V. Hardcastle, 139–79. Cambridge, MA: MIT Press.

1999. Genes, memes and cultural heredity. *Biology and Philosophy* 14.279–310.

Winford, Donald. 1992. Another look at the copula in Black English and Caribbean creoles. *American Speech* 67.21–60.

1993. Back to the past: the BEV/creole connection revisited. *Language Variation and Change* 4.311–57.

1997a. Re-examining Caribbean English creole continua. *World Englishes* 16.233–79.

1997b. Re-examining the Caribbean English creole continua. *World Englishes* 16.233–79.

1998. On the origins of African-American vernacular English: a creolist perspective. Part II: Linguistic features. *Diachronica* 15.99–154.

Wolfram, Walt. 1974. The relationship of white Southern speech to vernacular Black English. *Language* 50.498–527. Reprinted in *Verb phrase patterns in Black English and creole*, ed. by Walter Edwards and Donald Winford, 60–100. Detroit: Wayne State University Press, 1991.

1980. *a*-Prefixing in Appalachian English. In *Locating language in time and space*, ed. by William Labov, 107–42. New York: Academic Press.

Wolfram, Walt and Natalie Schilling Estes. 1995. Moribund dialects and the endangerment canon: the case of the Ocracoke Brogue. *Language* 71.696–721.

Wood, Peter H. 1974. *Black majority: negroes in colonial South Carolina from 1670 through the Stono rebellion.* New York: Knopf.

1989. The changing population of the colonial South: an overview by race and region, 1685–1790. In *Powhatan's Mantle: Indians in the colonial Southeast*, ed. by Peter H. Wood, Gregory A. Waselkov, and M. Thomas Hatley, 35–103. Lincoln, NB/London: University of Nebraska Press.

Wright, Laura. 1995. Middle English {-ende} and {-ing}: a possible route of grammaticalization. In Fisiak, 365–82.

Yngve, Victor H. 1996. *From grammar to science.* Amsterdam: John Benjamins.

Zelinksy, Wilbur. 1992 (original 1973). *The cultural geography of the United States, a revised edition.* Englewood Cliffs, NJ: Prentice Hall.

Author index

Subject index